World-Class Universities

Global Perspectives on
Higher Education

World-Class Universities

Global Trends and Institutional Models

Edited by

Nian Cai Liu, Yan Wu and Qi Wang

BRILL

SENSE

LEIDEN | BOSTON

Cover illustration: The Old Library at Shanghai Jiao Tong University, Xuhui Campus, photograph by Shu Chen

All chapters in this book have undergone peer review.

Library of Congress Cataloging-in-Publication Data

Names: Liu, Niancai, 1965- editor. | Wu, Yan, 1978- editor. | Wang, Qi,
   1979- editor. | International Conference on World-Class Universities
   (8th : 2019 : Shanghai, China)
Title: World-class universities : global trends and institutional models /
   edited by Nian Cai Liu, Yan Wu and Qi Wang.
Description: Leiden ; Boston : Brill | Sense, 2021. | Series: Global
   perspectives on higher education, 2214-0859 ; volume 51 | Includes
   bibliographical references.
Identifiers: LCCN 2021017466 | ISBN 9789004463141 (paperback) | ISBN
   9789004463158 (hardback) | ISBN 9789004463165 (ebook)
Subjects: LCSH: Universities and colleges--Ratings and
   rankings--Congresses. | Education, Higher--Aims and
   objectives--Congresses. | Education and globalization--Congresses.
Classification: LCC LB2331.62 .W66 2021 | DDC 378--dc23
LC record available at https://lccn.loc.gov/2021017466

Typeface for the Latin, Greek, and Cyrillic scripts: "Brill". See and download: brill.com/brill-typeface.

ISSN 2214-0859
ISBN 978-90-04-46314-1 (paperback)
ISBN 978-90-04-46315-8 (hardback)
ISBN 978-90-04-46316-5 (e-book)

This book is printed on acid-free paper and produced in a sustainable manner.

Printed by Printforce, the Netherlands

Contents

PART 1
Global Trends

PART 2
Institutional Models

Acknowledgements

The editors wish to thank Mr John Bennett, Brill | Sense, for his support in the publication of this volume; Professor Philip G. Altbach, research professor and founding director of the Centre for International Higher Education at Boston College; Dr Jan Sadlak, former President of IREG – International Observatory on Ranking and Academic Excellence; and Dr Paul Deacon for the linguistic editing of the manuscript.

Figures and Tables

Figures

Tables

Notes on Contributors

Jean Chambaz

was elected First President of Sorbonne University on 11th December 2017. He was President of Pierre and Marie Curie University between 2012 and 2017. He was previously Vice President for Research and then Vice President for Resources. Professor of Cell Biology at the Pierre et Marie Curie Faculty of Medicine, Jean Chambaz was Head of the Endocrine Biochemistry Department at the Pitié-Salpêtrière Hospital. In 1999, he created a joint Inserm-UPMC research unit in the field of intestinal metabolism and differentiation, which in 2007 was merged into the Cordeliers Research Centre, of which he was then deputy director. In 2005, he created the UPMC Doctoral Training Institute. From 2008 to 2011 he chaired the Council for Doctoral Education of the European University Association (EUA). He has been a member of the EUA board since 2015. He was president of the Coordination of French Research-Intensive Universities (CURIF) from 2014 to 2018. He was elected head of the League of European Research Universities (LERU) in 2018.

Christine Clerici

was elected First President of the University of Paris on the 21st of June 2019. She was President of Paris Diderot University between 2014 and 2019. She is also President of CURIF, the Coordination of French Research-Intensive Universities and a member of the College of Ethics of the Ministry of Higher Education, Research and Innovation. She defended her doctoral thesis in Medicine in 1984 and in Science in 1990. After specializing in pneumology, she became a hospital practitioner in functional explorations. She was appointed Professor of Physiology in 1995 and joined the Faculty of Medicine of Paris Diderot University in 2002. From 2005, Christine Clerici led the Department of Physiology-Functional Explorations for Adults and Children at Bichat and Louis-Mourier Hospitals. As a member of the Inserm unit "Pathophysiology and Epidemiology of Respiratory Failure", her research focuses on the mechanisms involved in the reduction of pulmonary edema lesions, including in vitro and in vivo models of acute respiratory distress syndrome.

Luiz Cláudio Costa

is Full Professor and Former Rector of the University Federal of Viçosa, Brazil. He was previously Member of the Brazilian National Council for Education (2011–2012), Vice President of the Pisa Board (Programme for International Student Assessment) of OECD, from 2012 to 2016; Brazilian Secretary of Higher Education (2011–2012); President of the National Institute of Educational

Studies and Research Anísio Teixeira (INEP) from 2012 to 2014, Vice-Minister of Education from 2014–2016; Minister of Education between March and April 2015. He has been President of IESB University since March 2021, and President of IREG Observatory on Academic Ranking and Excellence since May 2018.

Futao Huang

is Professor at the Research Institute for Higher Education, Hiroshima University, Japan. Before he going to Japan in 1999, he taught and conducted research in several Chinese universities. His research interests include the internationalization of higher education, the academic profession, and higher education in East Asia. He has published widely in the Chinese, English, and Japanese languages. He is the editor of *Higher Education Forum*, which is included in Scopus, and a member of Advisory Editorial Boards of *Higher Education*, the *Journal of Studies in International Education*, the *International Journal of Educational Development*, and the *Policy Review in Higher Education*, etc. Currently, he is also guest professor at Shanghai Jiao Tong University and adjunct professor at Zhejiang University, China.

Eric W. Kaler

served as the 16th President of the University of Minnesota from 2011 to 2019. He became President Emeritus and Professor in 2019. Prior to returning to the University of Minnesota, Dr. Kaler was the Provost and Senior Vice President for Academic Affairs at Stony Brook University. Dr. Kaler received his bachelor's in Chemical Engineering from the California Institute of Technology in 1978 and his PhD from the University of Minnesota in 1982. He taught at the University of Washington and the University of Delaware, where he was the Dean of the College of Engineering. Dr. Kaler is a world-renowned scholar in the field of surfactant and colloid science and engineering. He was elected to the U.S. National Academy of Engineering in 2010. In 2014 he was named a Fellow of the American Academy of Arts and Sciences for his work as both an engineer and an educational leader. He is a Charter Fellow of the National Academy of Inventors.

Zhongqin Lin

is President of Shanghai Jiao Tong University (SJTU) and Academician of the Chinese Academy of Engineering. Professor Lin is on the editorial board of many international and national journals including *ASME Trans.*, *JSME*, and the *International Journal of Sustainable Design*. He plays a major role in numerous professional organizations such as the Chinese Academy of Engineering and the Chinese Mechanical Engineering Society. He is a member of the Academic Degree Committee of the State Council of China, and also serves as a member of the International Advisory Committee of College of Engineering, the University of Michigan.

Nian Cai Liu

is currently the Director of the Centre for World-Class Universities and Dean of the Graduate School of Education at Shanghai Jiao Tong University. He is a member of the Executive Committee of the IREG Observatory on Academic Ranking and Excellence. His research interests include world-class universities and research universities, university evaluation and academic ranking, research evaluation and science policy, and the globalization and internationalization of higher education. He moved to the field of educational research in 1999, before which he was a professor in polymer science and engineering. He did his undergraduate study in chemistry at Lanzhou University of China and obtained his doctoral degree in polymer science and engineering from Queen's University at Kingston, Canada. He is on the editorial/advisory boards of several international and national journals.

Simon Marginson

is Professor of Higher Education at the University of Oxford, Director of the ESRC/OFSRE Centre for Global Higher Education (CGHE), Joint Editor-in-Chief of *Higher Education,* Professorial Associate of the Melbourne Centre for Study of Higher Education at the University of Melbourne, and Lead Researcher with Higher School of Economics in Moscow. CGHE is a funded 2015–2023 research partnership of six U.K. and nine international universities conducting project research on global, national and local aspects of higher education. Simon's research is focused primarily on global and international higher education, higher education in East Asia, global science, and higher education and social inequality. Recent books are *Changing Higher Education for a Changing World,* edited with Claire Callender and William Locke (Bloomsbury, 2020) and *High Participation Systems of Higher Education,* edited with Brendan Cantwell and Anna Smolentseva (Oxford University Press, 2018).

Brajesh Panth

is Chief, Education Sector Group of the Asian Development Bank. He has over 25 years of experience in the education sector covering all levels. He was a senior education specialist for the World Bank.

Gerard A. Postiglione

is Emeritus Professor, Honorary Professor, and former Chair Professor in Higher Education in the Faculty of Education, the University of Hong Kong, and coordinator of the Consortium for Research on Higher Education in Asia. His scholarship includes 20 books and over 150 articles and chapters. His books include *Mass Higher Education in East Asia, Crossing Borders in East Asian Higher Education, Asian Higher Education*, and *Society, Culture, Education and Globalization in Asia*. He has been a consultant to the Asian Development Bank, Department for International Development (U.K.), Institute of International Education (U.S.), International Development Research Centre (CA), Organization of Economic Cooperation and Development (OECD), United Nations Development Programme (UNDP), United Nations Educational, Scientific and Cultural Organization (UNESCO), World Bank, and other international agencies. He has advised major international foundations, including the Carnegie Foundation for the Advancement of Teaching and the Ford Foundation.

Jamil Salmi

is a global tertiary education expert providing policy advice to governments, universities, professional associations, multilateral development banks, and bilateral cooperation agencies. Until January 2012, he was the World Bank's tertiary education coordinator. Over the last twenty-five years, he has provided advice on tertiary education development, financing reforms, and strategic planning to governments and university leaders in more than 100 countries all over the world. He is Emeritus Professor of higher education policy at Diego Portales University in Chile and Research Fellow at Boston College's Centre for Higher Education. He is also a member of the International Quality Assurance Advisory Group, Emeritus Advisor on the President's Council at Olin College of Engineering, and chair of the Board of the Chilean EdTech startup u-planner. His 2009 book is *The Challenge of Establishing World-Class Universities*. His 2011 book, co-edited with Professor Phil Altbach, was entitled *The Road to Academic Excellence: the Making of World-Class Research Universities*. His latest book, *Tertiary Education and the Sustainable Development Goals*, was published in August 2017. He holds a Master in Public and International Affairs from the University of Pittsburgh and a PhD in development studies from the University of Sussex.

Sebastian Stride

is a founding partner of SIRIS Academic, a hybrid research centre and consulting company based in Barcelona. Before this he worked for 15 years as an archaeologist in Uzbekistan, at the heart of the Silk Road, at the time of the collapse of the Soviet system of higher education and research. During this period, he helped set up and coordinate international partnerships between the Uzbek Academy of Sciences and research teams from the rest of the world in order to save and systematize Soviet knowledge on Central Asia. SIRIS Academic was born out of this experience to help institutions question their models, redefine their vision and mission and rethink their strategy. Currently SIRIS Academic works with over 100 universities, research institutions, public administrations, government agencies and charities in 25 countries, as well as being a scientific partner in various Horizon 2020 research projects.

Lin Tian

is a PhD candidate in the Centre for World-Class Universities (CWCU) at Shanghai Jiao Tong University. She is also a Research Associate on CGHE's global higher education engagement research programme. After graduating from the University of Edinburgh, she worked in Shanghai Jiao Tong University as a research assistant (2014–2015) and began to pursue her doctoral degree there from 2016. Currently, her research interests include the functions of world-class universities and the internationalization of higher education.

Christine A. Victorino

serves as Associate Chancellor at the University of California, Riverside (UCR). Dr. Victorino serves as a principal advisor to university leadership and plays a key role in developing and executing UCR's strategic vision and goals. Dr. Victorino completed her PhD in Education at UC Santa Barbara and holds an adjunct faculty appointment in UCR's Graduate School of Education.

Qi Wang

is an Assistant Professor at the Graduate School of Education (GSE), Shanghai Jiao Tong University (SJTU), and a Research Fellow at the Centre for International Higher Education, Boston College. She completed her MA and PhD studies at the Department of Education, University of Bath, U.K., from September 2002 to November 2008. She joined SJTU in May 2009 and works at the Centre for World-Class Universities. Her research interests include building world-class universities, employability management and skill training, and globalization and education development. Her current research focuses on building world-class research universities from a theoretical and comparative perspective, and in particular how different governments and universities in East Asia and Europe adopt policies to implement this global aspiration.

Kim A. Wilcox

was appointed University of California Riverside's (UCR) ninth chancellor in August 2013. During his tenure, UCR has seen transformative growth including the establishment of new schools of medicine and public policy. Over the last four years, UCR has grown its faculty by over 200, including two Nobel Laureates, while increasing the racial, ethnic, and gender diversity among incoming faculty members. Under Professor Wilcox's leadership, UCR has become the nation's fastest-rising university and a model for achieving student success. UCR is one of few institutions nationwide to eliminate graduation-rate gaps across income levels and ethnicity. A first-generation college graduate, Professor Wilcox received his B.A. in audiology and speech sciences from Michigan State University, and master's and doctoral degrees in speech and hearing science from Purdue University. He was formerly Provost at Michigan State and Dean of the College of Liberal Arts and Sciences at the University of Kansas.

Mark S. Wrighton

is Chancellor Emeritus and the first holder of the James and Mary Wertsch Distinguished University Professorship at Washington University in St. Louis. He served as the 14th Chancellor for 24 years, 1995–2019. From 1972 until 1995, he was on the faculty of chemistry at the Massachusetts Institute of Technology and served as Provost 1990–1995. During his tenure as Chancellor, Washington University made significant progress in the quality of the undergraduate student body, campus improvement, resource development, and international engagement. New programmes developed during Wrighton's chancellorship include the McDonnell International Scholars Academy, the Alvin J. Siteman Cancer Centre, the International Centre for Energy, Environment and Sustainability, the Living Earth Collaborative, the Gephardt Institute for Civic and Community Engagement, and the Institute for Public Health.

Yan Wu

is an Assistant Professor at the Centre for World-Class Universities (CWCU) of Shanghai Jiao Tong University (SJTU). She has been in the ranking team at CWCU since 2005. She obtained her bachelor (2000) and master degree (2003) both in Philosophy from East China Normal University. Her primary research interests include the ranking and evaluation of universities. She had been responsible for the Global Research University Profiles (GRUP) project, which started in 2011 and has been developing a database on the facts and figures of around 1200 research universities in the world. The database has been used to produce much more comprehensive and customized comparisons of research universities at a global level. Since 2016, She has been responsible for organizing the biennial International Conference on World-Class Universities.

Akiyoshi Yonezawa

is Professor and Vice-Director, International Strategy Office, Tohoku University. With a background in sociology, he mainly conducts research on comparative higher education policy – especially focusing on world-class universities, internationalization and public-private relationships in higher education. He established his expertise in higher education policy and management through working experience at Nagoya University, OECD, and the University of Tokyo, etc. He is a board member at Japan Association for Higher Education Research and at Japan Comparative Education Society. His recent co-edited book *Researching Higher Education in Asia* (Springer, 2018) was granted the "Best Book Award 2019" from the Comparative and International Education Society (SIG Higher Education).

CHAPTER 1

World-Class Universities

Global Trends and Institutional Models

Nian Cai Liu, Yan Wu and Qi Wang

Abstract

This volume sheds light on the challenges that world-class universities face, their opportunities, and the roles and strategies they have, in response to the changing landscape of higher education and our society as a whole. It is composed of two parts: "Global Trends" and "Institutional Models". The collected essays originated from papers presented at the 8th International Conference on World-Class Universities (WCU-8), held in October 2019 in Shanghai, China.

Keywords

world-class universities – global trends – institutional models

1   Introduction

World-class universities (WCUs), often used interchangeably with global research universities or flagship universities, are regarded as cornerstone institutions of any academic system and imperative for developing a nation's competitiveness in the global knowledge economy. It is widely agreed that world-class universities are committed to creating and disseminating knowledge in a range of disciplines and fields; delivering elite education at all levels; and serving as a global common good at local, national, and global levels (Altbach, 2009; Liu, 2009; van der Wende, 2009; Marginson, 2018; Tian, 2018). Their roles and contributions to economic, social, and cultural development respectively are indispensable. Thus, to promote academic excellence is high on the policy agenda of various stakeholders across the globe in the past two decades. Such a "world-class" movement has been further intensified and manifested by the proliferation of university rankings (Salmi, 2009; Hazelkorn, 2011).

© KONINKLIJKE BRILL NV, LEIDEN, 2021 | DOI: 10.1163/9789004463165_001

It was in this context that the Graduate School of Education at Shanghai Jiao Tong University initiated the biennial International Conference on World-Class Universities in 2005. The conferences gather university administrators, government officials, leading scholars and policy researchers from around the world to discuss the various issues and topics related to world-class universities. These timely topics include: world-class universities' influences on affecting global higher education; strategies and the challenges of developing academic excellence from global, national and institutional perspectives; issues on balancing and integrating visibility and performance; and the contributions of these leading universities to the global common good.

The Eighth International Conference on World-Class Universities was held in October 2019. The conference theme was "World-Class Universities: Global Trends and Institutional Models". To continue our previous topics and discussion, this volume focuses on how world-class universities respond to the rapidly changing landscape of higher education at global, national and institutional levels.

2　　World-Class Universities in a Changing World: Recent Trends

The theme of this volume is embedded in the context of an ever-evolving and complex world. Change is continuous and disruptive in the social, economic, cultural, and political spheres. While the past two decades have witnessed momentous technological transformation and an increasingly connected world, we also have seen a backlash against globalization and the emerging forces of nationalism in various parts of the world, as well as growing inequality and disparity of wealth, economic, and social opportunities. During the time we were compiling this volume, the world was battling against the tragic coronavirus pandemic. These challenges impact higher education practices and induce mounting pressure on world-class universities to respond effectively to the ferocity of social change. A few common trends can be identified from the recent discussions and research on developing WCUs.

2.1　　*Increasing Emphasis on WCUs Serving as a Global Common Good*
While research on WCUs continues to discuss the definition, features and attributes, and strategies and approaches to building academic excellence, recent literature increasingly points to the dual roles of WCUs in relation to global common good(s): these leading universities serve as a global common good in their emphasis of global development and the well-being of global communities on the one hand, and contributing to global common goods by conducting

global science and emphasizing human development, global interconnectedness and well-being, on the other (Marginson, 2018; Tian, 2018).

This increasingly important discussion stems from two reasons. First, the long uncontested view that higher education as a public good has been questioned. The simplistic dichotomy between public and private higher education has been contested by a range of factors, including increasing marketization and privatization, calls to cut public funding, greater diversification of stakeholders and engagement from non-state actors, and emerging forms of global governance (United Nations Educational, Social and Cultural Organization [UNESCO], 2015; Marginson, 2018). Internationalization – the growing collaboration and interaction between or among universities, faculties, and students across the globe – has also weakened the concept of the nation-state and thus makes the concept of public good(s) "in which human well-being is framed by individualistic socio-economic theory" (UNESCO, 2015, p. 78) difficult to apply to higher education. Second, universities' civic roles and social responsibilities are facing challenges in the current context of global higher education. Researchers have raised concerns that higher education is becoming a marketplace "with customers and stakeholders". World-class universities are no exception to this. The quest for academic excellence has spread across the globe. Governments of both developed and developing countries have been actively seeking excellence. However, problems and issues are raised. These leading universities are driven by market forces, constantly searching for additional funds (due to severely reduced public funding in recent years), trapped by the proliferation of ranking games (Chapters 4 and 5). The battle for excellence and global status has been criticized for reinforcing pre-existing hierarchies (Rhoads, Li and Ilano, 2014). Further, world-class universities are considered to have kept themselves away from the broader post-secondary environment and are thus questioned for compromising their social responsibilities, their roles, and their contributions to the local communities.

Taking the above-mentioned into consideration, the notion of a global common good takes a participatory view in defining the nature of higher education and places emphasis on the collective and inclusive dimension of education as a shared social action, responsibility, and commitment to solidarity; it values "the diversity of contexts, worldviews and knowledge systems, while respecting fundamental rights" for all people (ibid.). Nevertheless, world-class universities are considered to be in a unique position as "the open global space" and to serve as a global common good (Chapters 2 and 3). With a concentration of talent, abundant resources, and favourable governance, these leading universities are believed to be able to embrace opportunities, confront challenges, and enhance sustainable development for the benefit of the whole world; should nurture world-class education and research, and serve both local society and global imperatives.

2.2   *Continuing Effort to Promote Excellence Initiatives*

In pursuit of academic excellence, both governments and higher education institutions world-wide have adopted various strategies and approaches. There has been a great deal of research and literature analysing and comparing these initiatives and incentives.

At the government level, an increasing number of strategic funding schemes have been implemented to promote excellence by an increasing number of countries and regions around the world. The very first group of special funding schemes took place mostly between the 1990s and the early 21st century in Asian and European countries, including China's 985 Project (1998), Japan's Centres of Excellence and World Premier International Research Centres (2002), the Republic of Korea's Brain Korea 21 (1996), as well as research excellence projects in Germany, Denmark, Finland, Ireland, Norway, and Canada (Salmi, 2018). This group of countries has continued to invest in these initiatives and initiate new projects, such as Japan's Top Global Universities Project (2014). Some have replaced these initiatives with new initiatives, such as China's Double World-Class Universities (2015) (Chapter 7). Meanwhile, other governments in the last decade have adopted "concentration and selection" policies, such as Russia's National Research University Programme (2012), Saudi Arabic's University and Education City projects (2012), and the United Kingdom's Knowledge Exchange Framework (2017).

Selected universities and research centres in these countries and regions have had extra and concentrated funding provided to develop excellence in teaching and research. Despite different organizational and management approaches, these initiatives all propose clear aims for excellence, providing adequate funding to "cherry-picked" institutions and research centres, and ensuring essential policy support from governments. Furthermore, these competitive funding schemes are proposed, agreed on and legislated by governments and associated organizations. The legislative processes turn these educational initiatives into regulations and laws, which strengthen the authoritative and compulsory nature of the policies. Also, these funding programmes have further raised awareness of international competition among institutions. Nevertheless, there have been concerns as to how governments can sustain their investments, and how to ensure such excellence initiatives do not interrupt and overshadow healthy and meaningful reform of the whole higher education system.

Realizing that excellence initiatives cannot act on their own and that appropriate governance is one of the key elements to determine university performance, higher education systems as well as their institutions have increasingly implemented structural reforms to nurture favourable governance in order to develop academic excellence. These reforms focus on leadership, strategic planning (Chapter 8), access and equity (Chapter 9), institutional interaction with industries in terms of research and innovation (Chapter 10), global partnership (Chapter 11), and enhancing competitive environments and organizational cultures (Chapter 12).

2.3   *Sustaining an Ecosystem in Seeking Academic Excellence*

Recent literature on world-class universities shows an increasing emphasis on the importance of developing a world-class university system. This point is reflected throughout the current volume. Higher education expansion involves all post-secondary institutions from all missions – research, teaching, social services – but with different foci.

Altbach and Salmi (2011) also remind us that education reform and changes do not happen in a vacuum, and a complete analysis of operating a world-class university needs to take into consideration the ecosystem within which institutions evolve. That ecosystem includes elements of the macro environment, leadership at the national level, governance and regulatory frameworks, quality assurance frameworks, financial resources and incentives, articulation mechanisms, access to information, location, and digital and telecommunications infrastructure. Some of these factors might be absolute requisites and others might not be entirely indispensable, due to each country's cultural, socio-economic, and political context. However, all these factors are certainly significant (ibid.). Countries and those overseeing their higher education systems need to carefully assess their needs, resources, and long-term interests, and to design their strategies based on their national and institutional models. There is no universal model or recipe for academic excellence (Salmi, 2009).

3   Contributions to This Volume

To continue and further deepen our previous conferences' discussions on building a world-class higher education system and the roles of world-class universities in teaching, research, service, and particularly in contributing to the global common good, this volume will shed light on world-class universities' challenges, opportunities, roles, and strategies in response to the changing landscape of higher education and our society as a whole. The volume is composed of two sections: "Global Trends" and "Institutional Models".

3.1   *Global Trends*

The first section focuses on global trends in developing academic excellence. It analyses the opportunities and challenges facing global higher education, particularly the world-class university sector. It provides in-depth discussions on the functions and roles of world-class universities, and the employment and impact of university rankings in building excellence, and it compares relevant policies and strategies adopted by different countries.

Tian and Liu (Chapter 2) explore world-class universities' unique functions and unique mission that are different from other research universities. Taking a structural functionalism perspective and through an explanatory mixed-method research design (document analysis, semi-structured interviews and survey), the authors summarize the unique mission of world-class universities as Globalizing. That is to say, these leading universities' function have a dual role: serving the global common good and acting as a global role model for other research universities; and continuously improving their global-oriented functions – global positioning, global contribution, global influence, and global cooperation.

Marginson (Chapter 3) explores the relationship between global and national science systems. A few trends can be witnessed since the 1990s: the rapid growth in scientific capacity worldwide in terms of research and development and publications; the increasing number and diversification of leading research countries and regions; and growth in terms of the number and proportion of cross-border collaborations between scientists. Marginson proposes that the global science system is featured as a flat, open, and inclusive network, with autonomous and bottom-up collaboration between researchers; while the national science system is heteronomous, bounded, and governed in nature. These two systems overlap and have two-way effects, but also have different dynamics.

The next two chapters both focus on university rankings, higher education quality, and excellence. Salmi (Chapter 4) and Costa (Chapter 5) share viewpoints: university rankings have impacted higher education exponentially, have influenced and guided institutional strategic plans, and have affected universities' and their stakeholders' behaviour. However, rankings have limitations in terms of methodologies, and cannot measure every aspect of university development. The excellence culture promoted by the rankings may "side-tracking universities from contributing to progress in several critical dimensions of human life, such as the inclusion of minorities, scientific truth, social justice, and sustainability" (Chapter 4). Costa (Chapter 5) argues that, if adopting and using rankings correctly in universities' daily work, a university can have a more objective idea of their performance from a local and global perspective. Rankings and related indicators can guide and provide details to improve the quality of their learning environment. Salmi reiterates the significance of the Shanghai Principles in emphasizing the social responsibilities of world-class universities. This set of principles were proposed in 2017 and emphasize social inclusion, scientific truth, ethical values, responsible research, and global solidarity as moral pillars for world-class universities.

Postiglione and Panth's chapter (Chapter 6) focuses its analysis on Asia's higher education systems. The authors argue that higher education in Asia has undergone great changes; however, to further develop the region and place it as a global economic hub, research universities will play an indispensable role to enhance academic and research quality, diversity, and governance of higher education institutions. This chapter reviews distinct forces reshaping universities and the challenges they faced in Asia, and it highlights the importance of inter-regional academic partnerships among Asian countries.

From a comparative perspective, Yonezawa and Huang (Chapter 7) examines Mainland China's and Japan's approach and practice of developing academic excellence. Both countries have adopted clear top-down excellence initiatives and policies to support selected universities; however, differences exist. China currently implements the Double World-Class Universities which focuses on disciplines instead of the whole institution; Japan adopts an institution-wide, cross-disciplinary approach to stimulate innovation through university-industry partnerships. The authors suggest the implications respectively for each country to further their world-class movement.

3.2 *Institutional Models*

The second section on "Institutional Models" reviews key issues in enhancing universities' competitiveness, including strategic planning, equity and access, partnership with industries, etc. The discussion may provide implications for both national governments and higher education institutions around the world.

Lin (Chapter 8) shares Shanghai Jiao Tong University's experience. The university has devised three-step strategies to achieve academic excellence and carries out planning every five years accordingly. Its strategic planning exercise and enactment process is combined with both strong leadership and faculty input, and unifies different ideas. Its three-step strategy shows a clear purpose and a planned sequence, but allows great flexibility to changes. The university's current plan aims to promote university development through talent, facilitating innovation through interdisciplinary cooperation, achieving development through opening-up and integration, and guiding development through culture.

The next three chapters set the analysis in the context of American higher education. Wilcox and Victorino (Chapter 9) argues that one important dimension, which might be missing from defining world-class universities, is the diversity of student and faculty body. This chapter shares the practice of the University of California, Rivierside (UCR), in terms of growing faculty excellence and improving student success. UCR's success is driven by three factors: creating "a student-focused culture", attracting a diverse group of "people", and offering "programmes" aimed at increasing the participation and educational success of low-income students and of an under-represented faculty, staff, and students. Kaler (Chapter 10) uses the case of the University of Minnesota, Twin Cities, to illustrate how a large land-grant public university plays its role in innovation, the creation of new start-up business, and knowledge application to tackle societal challenges. Also, Wrighton (Chapter 11) shared the story of the McDonnell International Scholars Academy at Washington University at St. Louis. This programme builds global partnership with world-leading institutions to develop graduate and professional education. This partnership programme manages to attract elite students and prepare them to be global leaders in various fields; and to develop research to address major global problems.

Clerici, Chambaz, and Stride's chapter (Chapter 12) shares the experience of French higher education institutions' recreating excellence. French higher education was challenged by the world-class movement to rethink its research performance and quality. French students and academic staff also increasingly see their education and career at a global level. These factors led to a series of reforms and the emergence of four leading universities. These universities are built through integrating and merging existing institutions.

This book not only represents a contribution to ongoing discussions on the topic of building world-class universities, but it is also a continuation of the previous seven volumes on this topic: *World-Class Universities and Ranking: Aiming beyond Status*; *The World-Class University as Part of a New Higher Education Paradigm: From Institutional Qualities to Systemic Excellence*; *Paths to a World-Class University*; *Building World-Class Universities: Different Approaches to a Shared Goal*; *Global Influences and Responses: How World-Class Universities Affect Higher Education Systems*; *Matching Visibility and Performance: A Standing Challenge for World-Class Universities*; and *World-Class Universities: Towards a Global Common Good and Seeking National and Institutional Contributions*.

References

Altbach, P. G. (2009). Peripheries and centres: Research universities in developing countries. *Asia Pacific Education Review, 10*, 15–27.
Hazelkorn, E. (2011). *Rankings and the reshaping of higher education: The battle for world-class excellence*. Palgrave.

Liu, N. C. (2009, February). *Building up world-class universities: A comparison.* Presentation at 2008–2009, Research Institute for Higher Education, Hiroshima University.

Marginson, S. (2018). Public/private in higher education: A synthesis of economic and political approaches. *Studies in Higher Education, 43*(2), 322–337.

Rhoads, R. A., Li, S., & Ilano, L. (2014). The global quest to build world-class universities: Toward a social justice agenda. *New Directions for Higher Education, 2014*(168), 27–39.

Salmi, J. (2009). *The challenge of establishing world-class universities.* The World Bank.

Tian, L. (2018). World-class universities: A dual identity related to global common good(s). In Y. Wu, Q. Wang, & N. C. Liu (Eds.), *World-class universities: Towards a global common good and seeking national and institutional contributions.* Brill Sense.

United Nations Educational, Social and Cultural Organization. (2015). *Rethinking education: Towards a global common good.* UNESCO. Retrieved June 1, 2020, from http://unesdoc.unesco.org/images/0023/002325/232555e.pdf

van der Wende, M. C. (2009). *European responses to global competitiveness in higher education.* Research and Occasional Paper Series, No. 7. Centre for Studies in higher Education, University of California.

PART 1

Global Trends

∵

CHAPTER 2

Globalizing as World-Class Universities' Special Function or Unique Mission

Lin Tian and Nian Cai Liu

Abstract

World-class universities (WCUs), which are generally regarded as global research universities, are important constituents of the global higher education system. There are agreed-upon features of WCUs when compared with other research universities (RUs). However, there has been an absence of attempts to explore the special features of WCUs from a functional perspective that emphasizes a function which is unique to WCUs, apart from the widely-acknowledged three basic functions of education, research and service. Using a mixed research method, including the document analysis of 83 research universities, 74 semi-structured interviews with university leaders, academics and experts worldwide as well as an online survey for WCUs' leaders and international academic experts (N = 118), this study examines the differences between WCUs and RUs in the three basic functions (that is, education, research and service), while at the same time investigating the special function or unique mission that is possessed exclusively by WCUs. This study identifies two core dimensions of WCUs' special function or unique mission: to serve the global common good and to act as a global role model for research universities, with four main features: global positioning, global contribution, global influence and global cooperation. It then summarizes WCUs' special function or unique mission in a word: *Globalizing*.

Keywords

world-class universities – research universities – special function – unique mission – globalizing

1　Introduction

1.1　*Phenomenon of WCU*

In the past two decades, the term world-class university (WCU) has become a catchphrase to describe research universities at the pinnacle of the tertiary education hierarchy (Salmi, 2011). It is commonly agreed that WCUS are academic institutions committed to creating and disseminating knowledge in a range of disciplines and fields, delivering elite education at all levels, serving national needs and furthering the international public good (Altbach, 2009; Liu, 2009). In general, there are some agreed-upon features of WCUS, including: (1) talent concentration; (2) abundant resources; (3) global engagement; (4) international reputation; (5) favorable governance (Salmi, 2009; Marginson, 2011a; Wang, Cheng and Liu, 2013).

The deepening of globalization has witnessed the increasing importance of WCUS, as they produce the intellectual capital required by the worldwide knowledge society (Mohrman et al., 2008). Van der Wende (2018) proposes that globalization brings both opportunities and challenges for WCUS, which means that WCUS not only need to respond to the profitable side of globalization (that is, the global flow of talents), but also to address the challenges of globalization (for example, migration and social exclusion); to be more open and inclusive; and to become truly international and intercultural learning space. In this sense, WCUS are both agents of globalization and instruments of its influence, as well as entities influenced by it. As a result, WCUS are more globalized or global than other research universities (RUS). This is also partly explained why WCUS are often regarded as global research universities with academic excellence (Cheng, Wang and Liu, 2014).

From the very beginning, in the domain of higher education, the terms *globalized* and *global* do not in fact denote excellence or quality but refer more directly to the competition in a free market economy, indicating that most higher education institutions (HEIS), which label them as globalized and global, are in a competition with their counterparts for limited resources. As choices widen with the increased accessibility that comes with globalization, HEIS competing in the finite space thus feel the need to position themselves as global institutions to compete for prospective students, faculty, business partners, and investors. In this aspect, the higher education market is similar to other market domains, as consumers nowadays hope to be associated with such brands that connote, among others, being globally connected, being globally recognized, and having a global standing (Xavier and Alsagoff, 2013). However, when the concept of being *world-class* emerged in the field of higher education, the terms *globalized* and *global* often appeared congruently, highlighting more the competition for excellence rather than resources, implying that the main global feature of WCUS is the pursuit of excellence at a global level (ibid.). This is supported by Liu and Gu's (2011) study, as they consider the pursuit of global excellence to be an important symbol of WCUS, and it is also the fundamental difference distinguishes them from other universities.

1.2   *Functions of WCU*

WCUs' pursuit of excellence is closely related to their multiple functions (that is, in education, research, service, etc.), implying that excellence and world-class status, or identity, of universities are often achieved through performing their functions. For example, Ouda and Ahmed (2015) mention that WCU is a complex term and associated with the notions of academic excellence or appraising university quality, and in fact excellence in the same function is considered – excellence in education, research and service. This accords with the framework of structural functionalism, which emphasizes that universities form a relatively stable and small-scale social structure and their positioning in the society hinges on their functions (Parsons and Platt, 1973). In other words, functions can be used to define universities' identity, categories and levels, by which their different positioning in the social system can be realized. Structural functionalism focuses on not only a specific function of universities, but also the combination of universities' different functions, so as to define and understand universities rationally (Ren, 2012).

Most scholars consider that excellence in research is a major symbol determining the world-class status or identity. For example, Jiang and Sun (2000) note that WCUs' significant research contributions create their world-renowned academic reputation; universities cannot be world-class without leading research outputs, and they are also unable to foster top talents without excellent research as a foundation. Also, Zhang (2011) believes that research excellence is a vital sign that distinguishes WCUs from RUs. WCUs are the birthplace of new knowledge, ground-breaking research and technological breakthroughs for both their own countries and the whole world, leading the direction of new ideas and global research. Similarly, Reichert (2009) finds that in five European countries (Slovakia, the United Kingdom, France, Norway and Switzerland), the quality, level and type of research are used to define whether a university is a top-tier research university or a non-elite research university. Consequently, various projects concerning the building and development of WCUs in the past decades highlighted the investment in research that is considered to be the most important constituent of WCUs, including Brain Korea 21 in the Republic of Korea (1996), 21st Century and Global COE Programme in Japan (2002), Exzellenzinitiative in Germany (2004), Double World-Class in the People's Republic of China (2015), and the Knowledge Exchange Framework (2017) in the United Kingdom. This indicates a fact that, for most countries, research capability and output are the major differences between WCUs and RUs.

However, based on the development of higher education, WCUs' influences on global higher education are not only brought by their research function, but also by their leadership of educational ideas and the corresponding innovations in the education system, reflecting their roles in leading the global education trends (Wu, 2018). Additionally, in the process of development, WCUs also make efforts to respond to external demands, such as providing excellence in education and high-quality services (Lee, 2013; Song, 2003). Therefore, the world-class status or identity of universities does not merely depend on their research contributions, but also on their advanced educational ideas, innovative educational models and extensive social engagement, reflecting the importance of WCUs' education and service functions.

In terms of education, Zhang (2005) believes that WCUs are the cradle of world-class talents, and the cultivation of top talents has become an important indicator of the social reputation and academic status of WCUs. He also suggests that education in WCUs should adhere to the development principle of pursuing excellence and also focus on cultural aspects. In the same vein, Song (2003) assumes that almost all WCUs emphasize the training of excellent, outstanding and high-achieving talents, as well as global leaders, which fully reflects the high positioning and requirements of WCUs in education. This is supported by Shin's (2013) idea that WCUs educate global leaders and emphasizes more on creativity than knowledge transmission, with abundant public funds and resources.

As for service, Gu and Liu (2011) mention that serving society is the ultimate goal of WCUs and they are oriented towards wider or global society (that is, both the country and the world) when compared with other universities. This service function is enhanced through WCUs' excellent education and research. Shin (2013) also suggests that WCUs prioritize their services at global and national levels, mainly focusing on addressing global and national problems, highlighting nonprofit generating service activities. However, Douglass (2016) thinks that WCUs may ignore or neglect local concerns and challenges, being "footloose from local society", because they often give more weight to the international community. In fact, some scholars have begun to explore how WCUs should balance their local and global roles (van der Wende, 2018; Cheng et al., 2014).

Apart from this, against the background of globalization, Chen (2004) and Zhao (2007) point out that WCUs have the function of international communication and exchanges, which is partly based on WCUs' abundant resources and global engagement. Specifically, the function of international communication and exchanges emphasizes WCUs' role in the following two aspects: First, through extensive international and comparative research on other countries, nations, and cultures, WCUs provide information and decision-making suggestions for society, the government, and the public; second, WCUs implement cross-cultural and multicultural education to promote mutual understanding among different nations and countries. This comes close to Scott's (2006) idea that universities have an internationalization function, which means that the universities internationalize their three functions of education, research, and service in the global information age, serving the body of nation-states. Hence, the function of international communication and exchanges can be viewed as part of the internationalization function and may not be exclusively possessed by WCUs.

1.3 *Purpose of This Study*

By and large, it is possible to glean from the available studies that WCUs' functions underpin models of WCUs, which are also partly based on their distinctive features, such as abundant resources, global engagement, favorable governance, etc. Meanwhile, their positioning as global and international institutions as well as their pursuit of excellence are important symbols that represent fundamental differences between WCUs and RUs. However, little empirical research makes systematic comparison between WCUs and RUs from a functional perspective, in terms of education, research, and service; also, few empirical studies examine whether WCUs have different functions that are exclusively possessed by them in this globalized and ever-changing world. Based on this, what intrigues us most are: What do WCUs do differently with their distinctive features when compared with RUs? Do WCUs have a "special function" that RUs do not have? Given there is little research on this topic, and in order to fill the research gap, this paper aims to investigate: (1) the differences in the three basic functions (education, research, and service) between WCUs and RUs; (2) the special function that is possessed exclusively by WCUs when compared with RUs, with an international comparative perspective among different countries and regions (China, the United States, and Europe).

This paper began with the broad literature on the phenomenon and functions of WCUs. What follows is the research method, procedures, and empirical data. The paper concludes by linking the findings to the previous literature, to deepen and extend the understanding of this topic.

2 Research Method

This research follows the exploratory design framework: the qualitative methods (documentary method and semi-structured interview) help develop and inform the quantitative method (online survey). The full use of triangulation enhances the validity of the results (Creswell and Clark, 2011).

2.1 *Documentary Method (Qualitative)*

Four kinds of official documents (president's message, mission statement, vision statement and strategic plan) on the university websites were collected, classified, and analysed, in order to compare WCUs and RUs (see Table 2.1) on the functional orientation (education, research, and service) stated by the universities themselves.

TABLE 2.1   Case universities for data analysis

Groups	Number	Details
World-class universities (WCUs)	$N = 43$	Public research universities that are ranked among the top 100 list in ARWU, QS and THE; they have declared themselves to be "world-class".
Other research universities (RUs)	$N = 40$	Public research universities that are not ranked among the top 200 list in ARWU, QS and THE; they have never declared themselves to be "world-class".

1. This classification is based on major global rankings (ARWU, QS and THE) in 2018;
2. The 43 top-100 universities in the major rankings are in the intersection of the top-100 universities of the three major rankings. In order for comparison, originally, 43 RUs are chosen; however, 3 RUs have no relevant documents, thus a total of 40 RUs are listed here.
3. For the purpose of making a generalization based on the comparison, this study mainly focuses on public research universities;
4. "Other research universities" can also be called general research universities.

MAXQDA 2018 qualitative software and qualitative content analysis were used to analyse the document data (Mayring, 2014). Documents were coded and analysed according to their relevance to the universities' three basic functions, that is, education, research, and service.

2.2 *Semi-Structured Interviews (Qualitative)*

This study adopted purposive sampling to identify participants, and potential participants were invited by the researchers through email. From December 2016 to May 2019, a total of 74 in-depth interviews were conducted (see Table 2.2 for details). For comparative purposes, only public research universities were chosen.

TABLE 2.2   Basic information of the interviewees

Groups	Country/Region	University	Interviewees
WCUS	China	3 WCUs in China	$N = 14$ University leaders = 2 Deans and directors = 9 Professors = 3
	U.S.	3 WCUs in the U.S.	$N = 10$ University leaders = 2 Deans and directors = 4 Professors = 4
	Europe	3 WCUs in Europe	$N = 12$ University leaders = 2 Deans and directors = 6 Professors = 4
RUS	China	3 RUs in China	$N = 7$ University leaders = 2 Deans and directors = 3 Professors = 2
	U.S.	3 RUs in the U.S.	$N = 5$ University leaders = 2 Deans and directors = 1 Professors = 2
	Europe	3 RUs in Europe	$N = 12$ University leaders = 4 Deans and directors = 4 Professors = 4
International Experts	Global	International (academic) experts in relevant fields	$N = 14$ Including experts from China, the U.S., Europe, Japan, Australia, etc.

1. WCUs refer to the top 100 institutions in the major global rankings (ARWU, QS and THE), which also declare themselves to be WCUs; RUs refer to institutions that are not ranked among the top 200 list in the three rankings as mentioned above, which never declared themselves to be WCUs. All based on major global rankings in 2018.
2. University leaders include the (vice) president/chancellor/rector, (vice) provosts, etc.
3. European universities were located in the Netherlands, theUnited Kingdom, Switzerland and Portugal.

Interview data were also coded and analysed using MAXQDA 2018 based on qualitative content analysis. Transcripts were coded and analysed according to participants' responses to each question and to the most salient categories emerging across the set of interviews.

Participants in the interviews are referred to by different code names, for the purposes of both ensuring anonymity and facilitating tracing references from the data. W = WCUs; R = RUs; C = China; U = the U.S.; E = Europe; L = Leader; D = Dean or director; P = Professor; EXP = Expert. For example, WCL1 means the first participant in a Chinese WCU, who is a university leader.

2.3 *Survey (Quantitative)*

The survey was designed based on the results from the documents and interviews, to confirm and verify the qualitative findings; thus, the survey questions were more general. The survey was computer-delivered, with respondents directed to a website (SurveyMonkey). This survey was bilingual (English and Chinese) to make sure that all participants had a better understanding of each statement.

From May to July 2019, the researchers invited 552 public WCUs leaders from the top 100 universities in three major global rankings and 51 international (academic) experts to participate in this survey. A total of 118 people participated in this survey, including 100 university leaders from 77 WCUs and 18 international academic experts, with a response rate of 19.6%. Details of survey respondents are shown in Table 2.3.

The quantitative data (survey) were analysed using the statistical package SPSS22.0. As the survey mainly included multiple-choice questions and multiple response questions, descriptive statistics analysis and multiple response analysis were adopted. After analysing data from the interviews and survey separately, steps were taken for data triangulation.

TABLE 2.3   General profile of survey respondents

Location group	China	U.S.	Europe	Other	Total
University leaders	9	19	49	23	100
International academic experts	11	2	4	1	18
Total	20	21	53	24	118

Note: In the Europe group, the number of respondents from British universities ranks the first; in the "other place" group, the number of respondents from Australian universities ranks the first.

3 Findings

3.1 *Differences in Three Basic Functions between WCUS and RUS*

3.1.1 Differences in Education between WCUS and RUS

After coding and analysing the qualitative data (official documents and interviews), WCUS and RUS were compared in terms of education (summarized in Table 2.4). Though WCUS have better resources and conditions than RUS in terms of education, in the interviews, some participants pointed out that the quality of education (especially undergraduate education) is difficult to compare between WCUS and RUS, as it may depend on various factors. Also, some interviewees (N = 5) believed that undergraduate education at RUS is better than that of WCUS in some cases, because RUS invest more energy in undergraduate education and their faculty have more time to participate in teaching activities.

In the questionnaire, the top three differences between WCU and RUS in education chosen by respondents are: (1) the idea and the cultural or academic atmosphere of education (61.9%); (2) the resources of education (participants, funding, etc.) (59.3%); and (3) the aim or purpose of education (more related to the types and levels of talents cultivated by universities) (52.5%) (see Figure 2.1).

Although respondents' choices are consistent to some extent, after comparing the choices of respondents from different countries and regions, it is found that most Chinese respondents believed that the idea and atmosphere (80%) as well as the aim or purpose (70%) of education, in WCUS and RUS were significantly different. For respondents from the United States, Europe and other countries and regions, they believed that obvious differences exist in the resources of education (participants, funding, etc.); the idea and atmosphere of education; and the aim or purpose of education (see Figure 2.2).

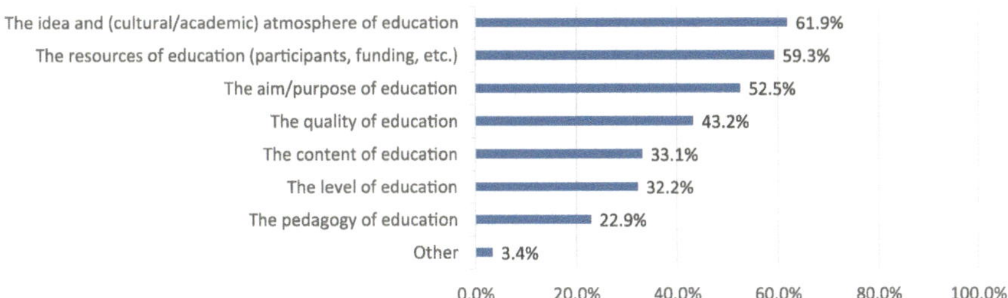

FIGURE 2.1   Responses of "the differences between WCUS and RUS in education" (multiple answers). Note: Multiple response questions have additional answer choices as "other" that can be freely filled out

TABLE 2.4   A comparison of education between WCUS and RUS based on AGIL scheme

AGIL scheme[a]	WCUS	RUS
A: Adaption	– Responding to the needs of the global labour market and future society. – Focusing on opportunities and challenges brought by globalization and internationalization.	– Responding to the needs of the local and national labour markets. – Meeting national and local needs first and then focusing on global needs.
G: Goal Attainment	– Providing a world-class learning experience and educational programmes with the highest quality. – Focusing on graduate (especially doctoral) education. – Fostering global citizens and leaders. – Educating top and future-oriented talents with digital literacy.	– Providing a high-quality learning experience. – Focusing on improving the employability of students. – Educating students to become leaders in a certain field (e.g., business). – Educating socially responsible citizens.
I: Integration	*Resources and conditions:* – Best faculty members and students sourced from across the globe. – Advanced teaching facilities. – Abundant resources. – Outstanding international reputation.	*Resources and conditions:* – Highly qualified faculty members (RUS often recruit graduates from WCUS as their faculty). – More students come from local areas.

(*cont.*)

TABLE 2.4   A comparison of education between WCUS and RUS based on AGIL scheme (*cont.*)

AGIL scheme[a]	WCUS	RUS
	Approaches and pathways: – Actively innovating talent training models and setting up more flexible degree programmes. – Providing comprehensive and diverse academic programmes. – Applying interdisciplinary and research-led training method. – A higher degree of internationalization.	*Approaches and pathways:* – Some RUs still maintain the traditional large-scale class teaching model. – The academic programmes are not as comprehensive as those of WCUS, and differ in breadth and depth from WCUS. – Emphasizing close connections with local communities and industry. – Their global cooperation networks are not as extensive as that of WCUS.
L: Latent Pattern Maintenance	– Maintaining an atmosphere that encourages free inquiry and discussion. – Providing an open and inclusive learning environment. – Creating a campus culture with creativity and innovation.	– Creating a diverse, inclusive, fair, open, and free academic environment.

a   The AGIL scheme developed by Parsons and Smelser (1956) was used to analyse the above-listed documents from the 83 universities. This is often used to analyse the operation of a system or an organization based on structural functionalism, and it is helpful in this study to understand how universities function differently. The explanation of the elements in the AGIL model used in this study is: Adaptation, or the capacity of a system to interact with the environment. This means the response to the outside world (sometimes about obtaining the required resources from the external environment); Goal Attainment, or the capability to set goals for the future and make decisions accordingly (for example, goals of a sub-functional system, such as the type, level, and quality of research); Integration, or the harmonization of the entire system is a demand that the resources and approaches for achieving the goals are applicable and sufficiently convergent; Latent Pattern Maintenance highlights the value, idea, culture, and relevant policies in a system to sustain its operation.

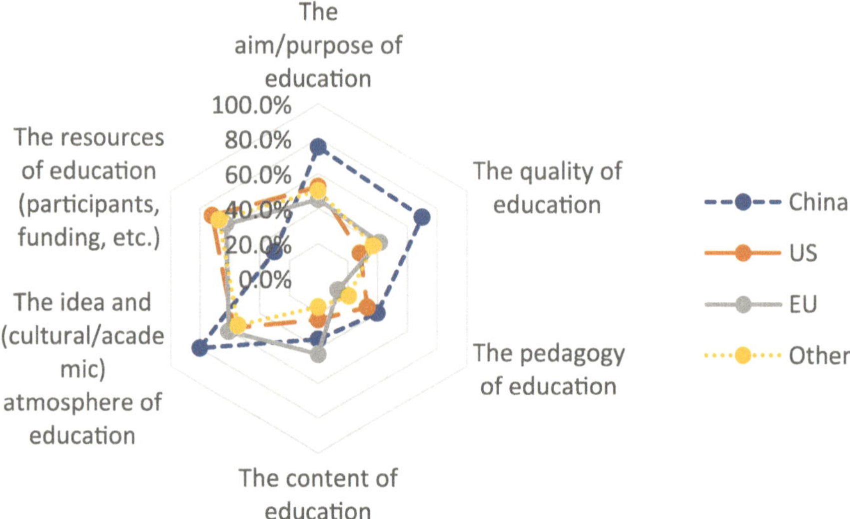

FIGURE 2.2   Choices of respondents from different countries/regions on the differences between WCUs and RUs in education

3.1.2   Differences in Research between WCUs and RUs

Table 2.5 summarizes the comparison between WCUs and RUs in terms of research. At the same time, in the interviews, most participants believed that WCUs and RUs are significantly different in their research function when compared with education and service functions.

In the questionnaire, the top three differences between WCU and RUs in research chosen by respondents are: (1) The quality of research (72.9%); (2) the size and level of research (66.1%); (3) the idea and (cultural or academic) atmosphere of research (61.9%) (see Figure 2.3).

Though most participants in the survey considered that "the quality of research" differed most between WCUs and RUs, there were also different opinions. For instance, apart from "the quality of research", most Chinese respondents believed that in terms of ideas and atmosphere (95%) as well as resources (75%) of research, WCUs and RUs are significantly different, while the majority of American respondents suggested that the size and level (81%) as well as resources (71.4%) of research are significantly different in WCUs and RUs (Figure 2.4).

3.1.3   Differences in Service between WCUs and RUs

Table 2.6 summarizes the comparison between WCUs and RUs in terms of service.

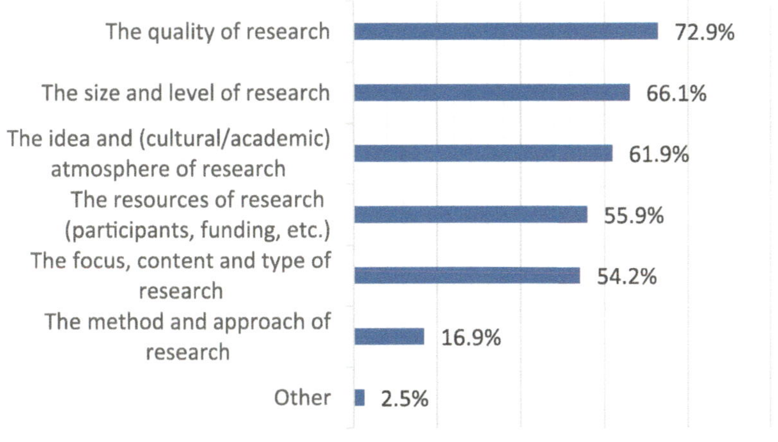

FIGURE 2.3 Responses of "the differences between WCUS and RUS in research" (multiple answers)

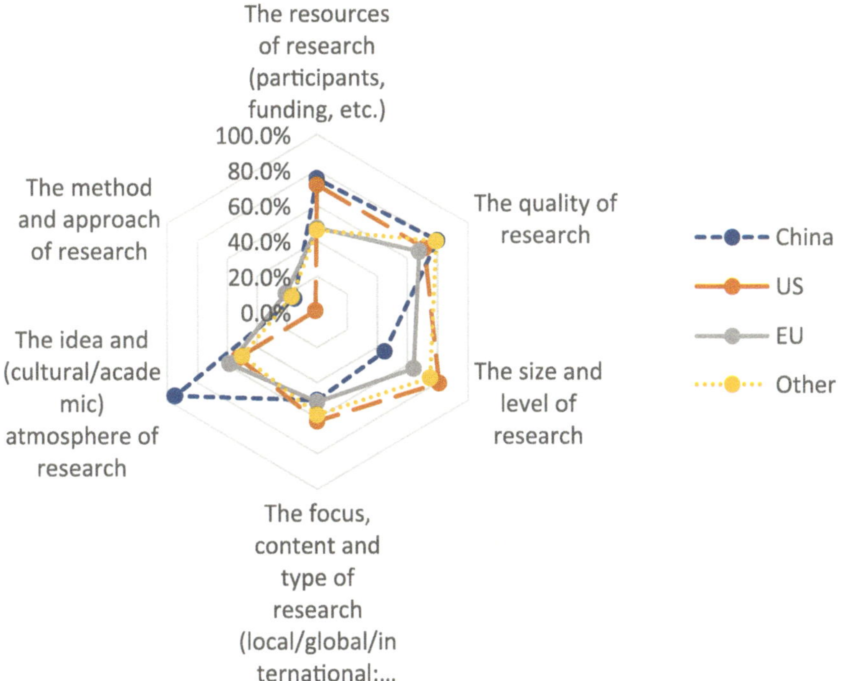

FIGURE 2.4 Choices of respondents from different countries/regions on the differences between WCUS and RUS in research

TABLE 2.5   A comparison of research between WCUs and RUs based on AGIL scheme

AGIL scheme	WCUs	RUs
A: Adaption	– Providing solutions to major global issues of common concern. – Meeting the social development needs of countries and regions.	– Paying more attention to social issues and focusing on major (global) issues in certain areas.
G: Goal Attainment	– Acting as the most important scientific research centre in the world. – Carrying out leading research projects of the highest quality. – Discovering and disseminating cutting-edge knowledge. – Carrying out basic research of innovative discovery and high-level applied research. – Providing timely solutions to the most complex problems of global concern. – Pursuing global excellence and scientific breakthroughs.	– Becoming top national research universities and striving to become world-class research universities. – Some RUs carry out small-scale basic research and conduct research of high level and quality in certain fields. – Being committed to becoming leaders in applied research and innovation. – Emphasizing the commercial value of applied research. – Paying more attention to local and national issues, as well as problems of local enterprises. – Regarding WCUs as role models in research.

(cont.)

TABLE 2.5   A comparison of research between WCUS and RUS based on AGIL scheme (*cont.*)

AGIL scheme	WCUS	RUS
I: Integration	*Resources and conditions:* – Obtaining generous national funding and having multi-channel funding sources. – Investing heavily in research activities. – Having strong international scientific cooperation networks. – Having the most outstanding scientific research teams. – Having advanced scientific research facilities. *Approaches and pathways:* – Highlighting graduate education and interdisciplinary research methods. – Applying the latest scientific knowledge and technology to conduct cutting-edge research.	*Resources and conditions:* – Diversifying funding sources through cooperation with external societies (especially enterprises); guiding and attracting funds into some key research areas. – Cooperation networks are more established at the regional and national levels. – Some RUS have also joined the global research networks. *Approaches and pathways:* – The research activities of RUS take root in local society and are closely connected with the local community.
L: Latent Pattern Maintenance	– Promoting and maintaining a free and inclusive academic culture and tradition. – Creating an open, transparent and efficient research environment. – Most WCUS have specific financial policies for research activities. – Most WCUS have specific research strategic plans and research excellence initiatives (for example, the Strategic Research Plan in McGill University).	– Striving to build a supportive and cooperative research environment. – A few RUS have specific research support frameworks.

TABLE 2.6   A comparison of service between WCUS and RUS based on AGIL scheme

AGIL scheme	WCUS	RUS
A: Adaption	– Focusing on global challenges and the future development of society. – Making efforts to meet regional, national, and global needs through research and education.	– Giving priority to local, national, and regional needs; focusing on regional economic issues in a globalized context. – Focusing on social issues and global issues in certain areas.
G: Goal Attainment	– Taking root in the local society, serving the country, and benefiting the world. – Promoting the development and progress of the world in a transformative way. – Contributing to the sustainable, stable, and peaceful development of the world. – Promoting national economic development, preserving, and inheriting naational cultural heritage.	– Serving the countries and the regions first and then serving the global society. – Contributing to the economic development of the city and country and continuously improving the quality of people's life. – Serving the local community and leading the development of the local area and beyond.
I: Integration	*Resources and conditions:* – Extensive international cooperation networks. – Rich and high-quality academic resources. – Extensive alumni network which spreads around the world.	*Resources and conditions:* – Close connections and interactions with local communities. – Extensive cooperation with local enterprises and industry.

(*cont.*)

TABLE 2.6   A comparison of service between WCUs and RUs based on AGIL scheme (*cont.*)

AGIL scheme	WCUS	RUS
	Approaches and pathways: – Keeping active on the global stage and establishing international cooperation to jointly solve the challenging issues facing humankind (especially with an emphasis on health and medical issues). – Sharing high-quality campus resources with external community. – Participating actively in national and international public affairs. – Keeping in close touch with alumni around the world. – Conducting various voluntary activities. – Integrating technology into providing services.	*Approaches and pathways:* – Bringing more positive influences to the (broader) external communities through partnerships with industry, enterprises, governments and other organizations in local areas and other countries. – Enhancing social engagement through hosting various academic and cultural activities to enrich the academic and cultural life of local society. – Participating actively in national and local public affairs. – Providing technical support for the region and the state. – Providing more opportunities of continuing education for the local residents.
L: Latent Pattern Maintenance	– No significant differences.	– No significant differences.

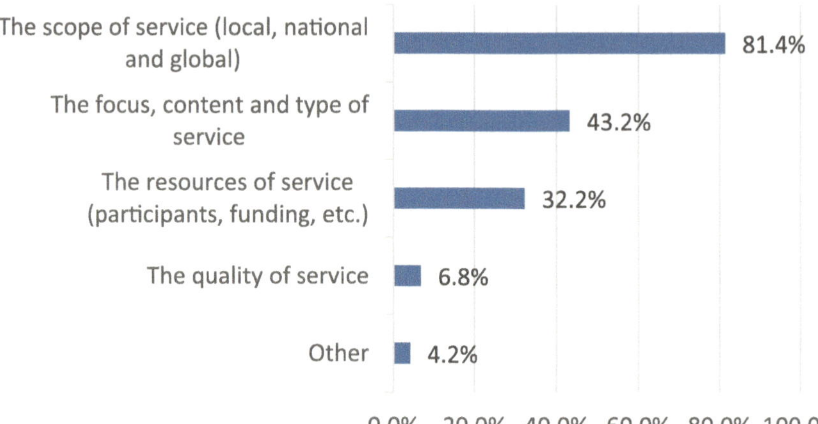

FIGURE 2.5   Responses of "the differences between WCUs and RUs in service" (multiple answers)

In the questionnaire, most respondents also agreed that the scope of service (81.4%) is significantly different between the two types of universities. Though the selection ratio of the other three dimensions does not exceed 50%, it is clear that in terms of the quality of services, respondents considered the difference between the two types of universities to be minimal (6.8%) (see Figure 2.5).

Though most respondents from all four locations invariably considered that "the scope of service" significantly differ between WCUs and RUs, there are also different opinions among respondents. For instance, most Chinese respondents believed that in terms of the focus, content, and type (70%) of service, WCUs and RUs are very different (see Figure 2.6).

3.2   *Dimensions of a WCU's Special Function*

For the second research question, only data from interviews and questionnaires are adopted, with interviews as the major data source. Among the 74 interviewees, the vast majority of respondents (N = 70) considered that WCUs have a *special function* that differentiates them from RUs. More than half of the respondents (N = 44) believed that serving the global common good is one of the dimensions of a WCU's special function; about one-third of the respondents (N = 24) suggested that acting as a global role model for research universities) is a dimension of a WCU's special function; more than 10 respondents mentioned that serving national soft power is also one of the dimensions of a WCU's special function.

3.2.1   Serving the Global Common Good

In the interviews, 44 (60%) participants considered "serving the global common good" is one of the dimensions of a WCU's special function. They believed

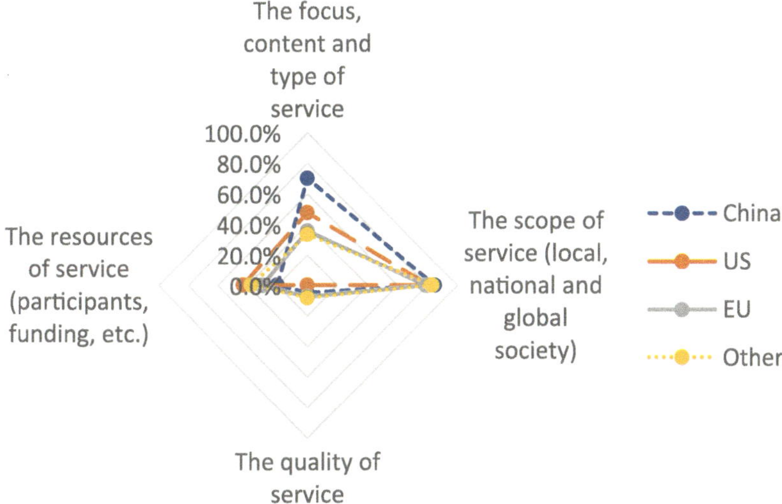

FIGURE 2.6   Choices of respondents from different countries/regions on the differences between WCUS and RUS in service

that the global common good is common to all people as benefits or interests. Specifically, participants argued that the reason these universities are labeled *world-class* is because of their vision and aspiration to serve the common good of the world.

> WCUS should serve the global common good … so the most important thing for them is to serve the whole world and humanity … If you add the term world-class for a university, then it must have the ability to benefit all humankind … promote global development … it must look at problems from a global perspective … focus on global issues … (WCP2)

Specifically, WCUS serving the global common good can be observed in the following six respects: (1) WCUS cultivate talents and leaders with global perspectives and future orientation, who can also guide people to think about broader global interests and human well-being; (2) WCUS generate transformative and leading scholarship, ideas and practices, which can not only advance the development of the world, but also lead the entire society culturally, philosophically, and morally; (3) WCUS construct global collaborative networks and then build a global academic community through global cooperation, which indicates that (networked) WCUS function positively and effectively as a whole, sharing talents, knowledge, and resources with each other, shouldering common responsibility in responding to global challenges and striving to achieve common goals; (4) WCUS are dedicated to revealing and solving complex problems in the global society, as they bring together top talents and academic resources, thereby having the capability and responsibility to help solve the major problems facing human society; (5) WCUs have a firm commitment to the sustainable development of the world, implying that when responding to the needs of the contemporary world and future development, WCUs endeavour to maintain a balanced and harmonious environment in resource development, technological development, and institutional reforms; (6) WCUs contribute to inclusive innovation and social mobility. Specifically, WCU contributions to inclusive innovation has two aspects: First, WCUs have the capability to predict the potential damage of new technologies for some people (how robots may influence auto workers' live), and prepare measures in advance to alleviate the possible harm, which is seen as the soft landing of new technologies. Second, WCUs work on the big problems where innovation is needed, but there is no profit motive, for example, the study of neglected diseases and tackling the problems faced by vulnerable groups. Also, promoting social mobility is a feature attributed to higher education and public WCUs that are open to first-generation university students by setting up specific scholarships for socially excluded groups.

> One of the incredible advantages we have as a WCU in serving these global common goods is the opportunity to partner with similar universities in a global network to really make a difference … and how could we bring those collective networks together to be even more impactful in improving human well-being, and so something like the Association of Pacific Rim Universities … it's both a privilege and responsibility of a WCU to be engaged in that kind of networking to tackle problems we have in common. (WUL2)

3.2.2 Global Role Model for Research Universities

While WCUs represent only a small proportion of higher education, other institutions often look to them as models; thus their influence is greater than their numbers would suggest. 24 interviewees believed that WCUs are global role models for research universities. This is mainly reflected in: (1) WCUs are the benchmark for both research-intensive universities and other universities aspiring to become research universities, especially in the process of developing strategic plans; (2) WCUs are not only the framers and maintainers of high-level academic standards, but also the pioneers of discovering and disseminating knowledge in new ways, and front runners of considering and solving scientific, technological, social, and cultural issues in a global context; (3) WCUs are often the guides and leaders of new ideas and practices; they are exemplars in a certain country and can also lead the spirit, value, culture, and practice of students, faculty and staff, universities, and society as a whole in a positive and promising direction.

> In order to be worthy of the title as "world-class", such institutions must have a sense of responsibility to the global common good. Their status as respected institutions inherently make them into role models, and by their actions, they set the standards and expectations of institutional behavior for others – in their purpose of operation, in ethical conduct, in commitment to values that underlie excellence … and most importantly, in considering scientific, technological, social, economic, cultural, and political issues in a global context. (RUL1)

At the same time, some scholars (N = 5) pointed out that regarding WCUs as a role model does not mean that all research universities must completely model a certain WCU. The global higher education system needs diverse and dynamic WCUs and their distinctive features and ideas should be maintained.

3.2.3 Serving National Soft Power

In the interview, a dimension of the special function mentioned by more than 10 interviewees also included serving a nation's *soft power*, that is, WCUs, by virtue of their own culture, values, spirit, and practices, influence and inspire the external environment, attract, and gather resources and talents at home and abroad, so promoting national development. At the same time, WCUs also disseminate the culture and values of the country where they are located, enhancing the soft power of these countries. This is mainly reflected in the following three aspects: (1) The brand effects of WCUs help their countries attract resources and talents; (2) WCUs enhance the academic strength and influence of their countries in the global community; (3) WCUs help to disseminate and export their countries' culture, practices, and political ideas. For example, international students in the American WCUs help to widely export the American culture and values, which at the same time makes American universities become the role model for many research universities around the world.

> It is undoubted that WCUs having the special function of serving the national soft power … but this may be achieved through cultural influence. In my opinion, a WCU increases the soft power of a country … If a country has a WCU, the attraction of this country will increase, the inward flow of talents will increase, and the economic investment received will increase as well. (EXP11)

Apart from this, some interviewees (less than ten) also mentioned other dimensions of a special function that WCUs may have, but due to the limited word count, this paper will not discuss them specifically.

After the semi-structured interviews, researchers conducted an online survey to triangulate the results. The survey listed three special dimensions of a special function of WCUs that were frequently mentioned by interviewees, that is, (1) serving the global common good; (2) acting as a global role model for research universities; and (3) serving national soft power.

For the three dimensions of a special function listed, the vast majority of respondents agreed that WCUs serve the global common good (70.3%) and act as a global role model for research universities (72.9%); only less than half of respondents agreed that WCUs serve national soft power (see Table 2.7). As the number of respondents chose serving the national soft power as a dimension of a special function is much less than the first two options, the result derived from the survey is not strong enough to support it as a dimension of a special function so it is not analysed in the following paragraphs.

Concerning regional differences in the responses, most respondents from China (80%) and other places (71%) agreed that WCUs serve a global common good, while a majority of respondents from the United States (76%) and Europe (79%) tended to consider that WCUs act as a global role model (see Figure 2.7).

Regarding the comparison between the university leaders and international (academic) experts, their answers are compatible with each other. More than 70% of both groups of respondents agreed that WCUs serve the global common good and act as a global role model for research universities (see Figure 2.8).

In general, results from the survey come close to the interview findings, with both interviewees and survey respondents considering that serving the global

TABLE 2.7　Respondents' perspective on WCUs' special functions (multiple answers)

Dimensions of a special function of WCUs	Number (respondents who chose the item)	Percentage
Serving the global common good	83	70.3
Global role model for research universities	86	72.9
Serving the national soft power	45	38.1
Other	9	7.6

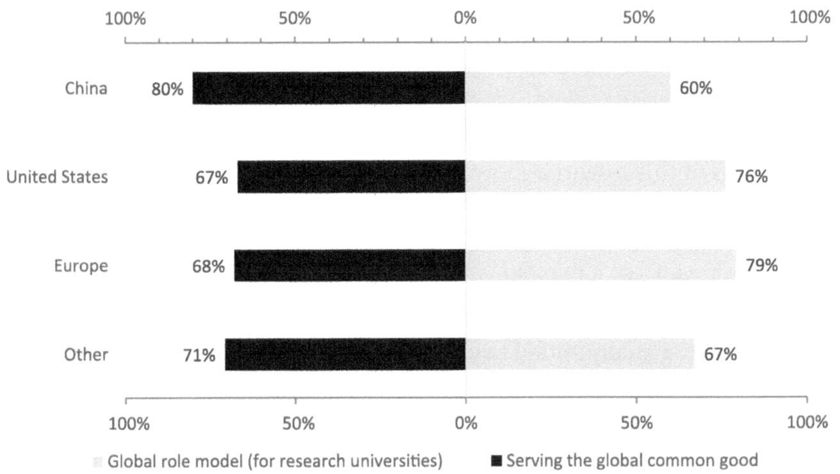

FIGURE 2.7   Respondents' views on the dimensions of a special function based on their geographic locations

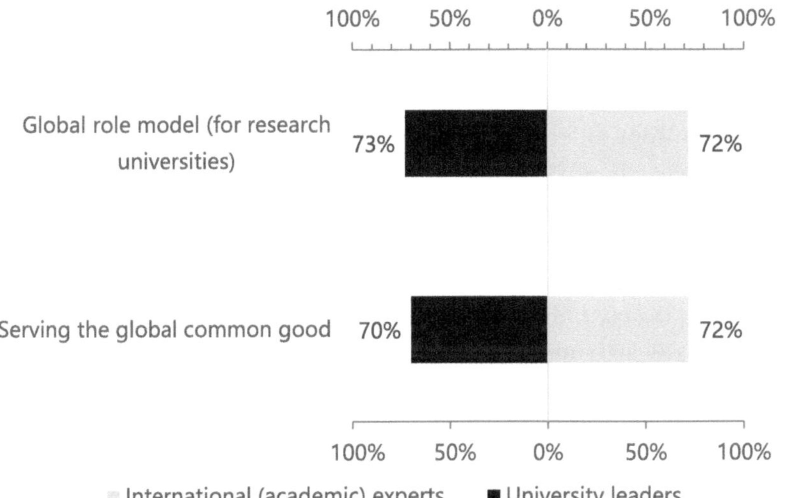

FIGURE 2.8   Comparison of responses between university leaders and international experts

common good and acting as a global role model for research universities are dimensions of a WCU's special function.

4   Discussion

The findings of this study show that there are differences in the three basic functions between WCUs and RUs and the majority of participants agree that

WCUs have a special function to serve the global common good and act as a global role model for research universities, which distinguish them from RUs.

4.1   *Differences in Three Basic Functions between WCUs and RUs*

The findings of this research show that there are differences in the three basic functions between WCUs and RUs. In terms of education, the aim or purpose of education (related to the types and levels of talents cultivated by universities), the approach and model of education and the resources of education (participants, funding, etc.) are significantly different between WCUs and RUs. For example, WCUs are committed to cultivating global leaders, educating top and future-oriented talents with digital literacy, paying more attention to research-led education. Also, in WCUs, there are more doctoral programmes than is the case with RUs. This is partly compatible with Song's (2003) idea that almost all WCUs emphasize the training of talents as well as global leaders, which fully reflects their pursuit of excellence in education. Also, it is the responsibility of WCUs to cultivate world-class talents, and the cultivation of leading talents has become an important indicator of the status and reputation of WCUs (Zhang, 2005).

The interviewees in this study proposed research as the function with the most significant differences between WCUs and RUs. The differences in research between these two types of universities are largely contingent on available resources, universities' self-positioning, and visions, which results in the differences in type, content and focus, level, and size of research. Zhang (2011) considers that the ability to generate excellence in research decade after decade reflects the continuing ability and competitiveness of WCUs. The level and quality of research and innovative ability are important signs that distinguish WCUs from RUs. Similarly, Reichert (2009) finds that in five European countries, the quality, level, and type of research are used to define whether a university is a top-tier research university or a non-elite research university. In his research, Slovak universities are most clearly stratified by their research ability and quality, being followed by British, French, Norwegian, and Swiss universities.

Regarding service, the most significant differences between WCUs and RUs lie in the scope of service. Based on the research findings, WCUs have an international perspective and deliver benefits to the international community, while RUs first serve their local community and their own countries. Apart from this, in this study, American interviewees highlighted WCUs' role in facilitating economic development. However, of particular note, not all interviewees in this study agreed with universities' direct contributions to economic development. An international expert in the interviews believed that WCUs should never be directly involved in activities that facilitate economic development, but to boost it indirectly by cultivating talents and delivering advanced research outputs. Otherwise, universities will become increasingly commercialized and their roles in enlightening citizens and promoting democratic and humanistic social values will be undermined.

Nevertheless, the above-listed differences do not necessarily indicate that WCUs are superior to RUs in terms of education, research, and service. First, as the results of this study show, the quality of undergraduate education is difficult to compare between the two types of universities. Interviewees proposed that undergraduates entering WCUs are already high-achieving students, so the added value provided by WCUs is not necessarily higher than that provided by RUs. Also, some interviewees (N = 5) even believed that the undergraduate education of RUs is better than that of WCUs. In fact, some RUs' official documents put claim to provide world-class education for their students, for example, the chancellor's message in the University of Tennessee-Knoxville indicates:

> For 225 years, the University of Tennessee has been committed to serving the people of Tennessee. Today, we continue to deliver on that promise with world-class education, life-changing research, and economic benefits for the state. I believe education is for everyone. A college degree means a better job, more opportunities, and the chance to create meaningful change for yourself, your family, and your community. (Plowman, 2019)

Huang (2017) suggests that conducting world-class undergraduate education is not a fundamental or important feature of WCUs, because the factors restricting and affecting the level of undergraduate education are extremely complex, and limited information and cases cannot fully explain how undergraduate education provided by WCUs is world-class undergraduate education. He believes that there are differences in education between WCUs and RUs, and the most obvious aspect is that WCUs place more emphasis on postgraduate education, especially doctoral education, and more emphasis on faculty engagement in world-class research. This is consistent with the findings of this research that WCUs attach more importance to the integration of education and research.

Secondly, as for research and service, RUs may perform better in conducting research and providing services related to their local society. RUs often have a strong commitment and close connection with local communities, which make these institutions play an indispensable role in their local community, providing direct and practical solutions to various local problems. This is supported by Tian and Liu's (2020) study that RUS' functions in pushing forward social progress at local, regional, and national levels cannot be neglected, as these universities can take full advantage of their long-standing and active engagement with local and regional enterprises, industry, and organizations, and sometimes they can also leverage their geographical advantages to actively carry out bilateral, multilateral, and regional exchanges and cooperation with neighbouring countries.

4.2　*The Unique Features of WCUS' Special Function*

The findings of this study show that WCUS have a special function that distinguishes them from RUS, mainly reflected in serving the global common good and acting as a global role model for research universities, which can be regarded as the two core dimensions of WCUS' special function. By and large, the unique feature of the special function proposed by interviewees and agreed by WCUS' leaders and academic experts is global orientation, meaning global positioning, global contribution, global influence, and global cooperation. This meshes with Mohrman's (2008) idea of the "Emerging Global Model" of research universities and Marginson's (2013) notion of a "Global Research University". Both concepts underline the global orientation of top research universities, including the development of global networks, global engagement, and global academic mobility. These two concepts are closely associated with the idea of WCUS, as Mohrman (2008) equates WCUS with the "Emerging Global Model" of research universities and Cheng et al. (2014) note that global research universities are generally recognized as WCUS. In general, these four unique features indicate that WCUS position themselves in the global community, strengthening and steering global cooperation to solve major challenges facing human society; they are role models for research universities worldwide, and during the process of spreading their academic and cultural influence, they also make global contributions. These universities are both key players in nation-states and as leaders in the global higher education system.

4.2.1　Global Positioning

The global positioning of a WCU's special function indicates their functional positioning, identity and principle of development. According to the research findings, the global positioning of WCUS' special function is reflected in a WCU's training of global talents and leaders, leading the development of global society, shouldering global roles and responsibility in tackling global problems, building a global academic community, striving for global sustainable development, performing as the framers and maintainers of global academic standards, etc. For instance, in an increasingly globalized context, many domestic problems faced by countries in the past, such as environmental pollution, water and food security, and resource shortage, are no longer national and regional issues, but common problems of global society. WCUs are global institutions in this globalized world, and through research activities and global cooperation, they position themselves at the forefront of seeking practical solutions to meet these severe challenges, illustrating the decisive role that WCUs are playing in global affairs. In this sense, research collaboration on common global challenges lifts WCUs above their more localized and captured functions as engines of national and individual prosperity, benefit, advantage, and prestige (Marginson, 2018). The global positioning of WCUs' special function determines the important role of WCUs in global society. They bring together the world's top talents and academic resources, and at the same time carry the high expectation of global society, which means that WCUs will be at the centre of responding to global challenges and a bridge to promoting world communication, which indicates WCUs' global responsibility and influence.

4.2.2 Global Contribution

The global contributions highlighted by WCUs' special function indirectly reflect WCUs' responsibility and capability. The research findings show that these global contributions include educational contributions, academic contributions, and social contributions. Educational contributions include WCUs educating and exporting global talents, leading university development models, and generating advanced educational ideas, concepts, and practices; academic contributions include WCUs generating transformative and leading global knowledge, formulating and maintaining high levels of academic standards; social contributions include WCUs providing effective solutions to global problems, conducting inclusive innovation, facilitating social mobility, and maintaining a firm commitment to sustainable development. Taking KU Leuven in Belgium as an example, one of the key dimensions in its strategic plan is to promote sustainability, which is reflected in its sustainable university management (for example, supporting and gearing faculty members towards travelling green and reducing building carbon emissions, etc.) and a strong stand in favour of the Sustainable Development Goals (SDG) in research and education (KU Leuven, 2019). KU Leuven's practices of sustainable development will soon lead to a new direction of university development, contributing to the realization of SDGs. This means that WCUs need to assume responsibilities beyond their national boundaries and make contributions that match their global influence. In other words, WCUs shoulder the responsibility and mission of leading the world's direction, cultivating global leaders, creating global knowledge, solving global issues, and serving global development (Wang, 2018).

4.2.3   Global Influence

The global influence reflected in WCUs' special function is closely related to the global positioning and global contribution mentioned above. Based on the research findings, the global influence of the special function of WCUs covers ideological influence, practical influence, academic influence, cultural influence, etc., which can be demonstrated in the following three respects. First, WCUs are global role models and they have a leading and guiding role in the ideas and practices for students, faculty and staff, universities, and society as a whole. WCUs are not only the framers and maintainers of high-level academic standards, but also the pioneers of discovering and disseminating ground-breaking knowledge and on various issues of global concern. Many WCUs have expressed that they will continue to positively influence global policies, cultures, and practices. For instance, in its strategic plan, King's College London declares that "our academics connect and collaborate with other universities, businesses, cultural institutions, healthcare providers, practitioners and policymakers, to ensure that our research is having global impact – changing practice and influencing understanding, behaviors, policy and culture" (King's College London, 2017). Kleinman and Vallas (2013) consider this kind of global influence in research is the form of collegialization – scientists in WCUs transcend national borders, form, and participate in international alliances or global research teams, playing an important role in responding to global challenges and tackling global issues. Second, WCUs' global influence can also be viewed as their attraction and soft power. Given the increasing competition among higher education systems in a globalized environment, many countries are attracted by a world-class image, reshaping their higher education sectors by learning and even copying the WCU model (mainly the Western-based WCUs) (Deem, Mok and Lucas, 2008). Also, WCUs have a "privileged voice" that is recognized by the global community due to their academic reputation for excellence. When solving major problems and proposing new ideas, these universities and their scholars are the most widely-recognized groups in the international community; therefore they set the academic trend that will be followed by other universities. Third, the global leaders cultivated by WCUs are future-oriented talents with a global perspective. These talents are spread all over the world, when advancing the national and global progress, they also convey ideas about the global common good that cross national borders, illustrating the global cultural influence of WCUs.

4.2.4   Global Cooperation

The global cooperation emphasized by WCUs' special function is not only the distinctive advantage of WCUs, but also a necessary condition for WCUs' special function to be formed and performed. According to the research findings, the global cooperation and collaboration of WCUs are not limited to academic exchanges and cooperation with various organizations, but also include their construction of and participation in the global collaborative networks (for example, various global university alliances). Through direct or indirect connections, WCUs can form global networks of collaboration. These global networks also form a global academic community where participants (WCUs) share talents, knowledge and resources, shoulder shared responsibility in solving global problems, and work towards common goals. Marginson (2019) proposes that WCUs, as "thickly" networked institutions, are more globalized than the national-local societies in which they are located, and they sustain an expanding worldwide space for research inquiry, academically codified thought, and the dissemination of knowledge. Also, the global collaborative network of WCUs implies WCUs that compete against each other vertically in university rankings also work together horizontally, indicating that there are synergies, but also tensions in WCUs' competition and collaboration (or in their national and global activities). Hence, in global higher education, the common good does not always come front and centre, but the expansion of WCUs' global networks indicates that the potential global commons has expanded (Marginson, 2018). This suggests that the global role and national responsibility of WCUs are not in conflict and highlights cooperation rather than competition among them, thereby transcending the internationalization function of universities proposed by Scott (2006), which internationalizes the basic three functions of universities to serve the body of nation-states and compete in the global marketplace.

4.3   *The Relationship between WCUs' Special Function and Their Basic Three Functions*

According to the findings of this research, WCUs' special function is closely related to their three basic functions of education, research and service. However, it is not covered by them. For instance, WCUs lead and participate in global cooperation to construct a global academic community to serve the global common good, which surpasses their three basic functions. First, global cooperation is different from international cooperation and exchanges in research and service. Global cooperation builds global collaboration networks, within which every WCU acts as a key node that plays the role of expanding the networks automatically. Both the direct or indirect connections with other members are the catalysts for larger, more formal collaborations among institutions around the world, resulting in a dynamic and global-wide collaboration network naturally. Such relationships and networks enable the development of a global academic community with shared goals, in which members jointly meet the severe challenges facing global society and guide the development of global society. Second, the global academic community with shared goals is not just a research community (mainly engaged in international research cooperation), but also shoulders social responsibility. For example, in some cases, wcus in the global academic community act as diplomatic "buffers" or "safe zone", which means that even if there are tensions between the countries where the wcus are located, cooperation and communication between universities will not be suspended. In this process, inter-university exchanges have created a space for dialogue to ease international relations beyond political and economic considerations. It can be seen that the global academic community formed through global cooperation breaks the barriers of national interests and is directed to the ultimate goal of serving the global common good.

Moreover, acting as a global role model for research universities is partly based on the excellence of education, research, and service of wcus, which is a reflection of the influence, attraction, and the soft power of wcus themselves, transcending the content of the three basic functions. According to the Russell International Excellence Group's (2012) report, conducting a large volume of excellent research is one of the ways wcus can gain role model status. Specifically, wcus deliver outputs that are crucial to a nation's knowledge base and innovative capacity, create the knowledge and scientific breakthroughs, underpin long-term economic growth and social well-being, thereby performing as leaders and models of rus worldwide. It can be seen that the role of wcus as global role models is not the content of their research function, but it is achieved by obtaining research excellence.

In this sense, the special function of wcus is partly based on their three basic functions while at the same time transcending them. In terms of the two dimensions of the special function, the global reach and far-reaching influence of serving the global common good, as well as the complexity and diversity of the practices in serving the global common good go far beyond the content, scope and practices of the three basic functions; also, acting as a global role model for research universities hinges on wcus' influence, attraction, leading, and guiding roles in higher education, transcending the content, scope, and practices of the three basic functions as well. Hence, with significant differences, a wcu's special function cannot be its three basic functions. However, as the special function and the three basic functions ar3 not defined under the same logical framework, it is also debatable to simply list the special function as a fourth function parallel to the three basic functions. In fact, a WCU's special function underlines the roles, effects, and influences of WCUs, as well as a strong commitment and sense of duty for WCUs to do or achieve something, distinguishing WCUs from RUs. Therefore, it is more reasonable to summarize it as WCUs' special function or unique mission.

4.4 *The Distinctiveness of WCUs for Their Special Function or Unique Mission*

In general, WCUs' special function or unique mission includes two major dimensions: serving the global common good and acting as a global role model (for research universities; and four unique features: global positioning, global contribution, global influence, and global cooperation. Though the global orientation and features of WCUs are distinctive, RUs also participate in global activities and make global contributions in certain fields (see 3 .1). However, the special function or unique mission is exclusively possessed by WCUs, because it is related to WCUs' distinctive advantages, including global obligation, global capability, and global reputation.

4.4.1 Global Obligation

WCUs' special function or unique mission is closely related to the obligations they are taking on, which means that the resources, competitiveness, and influence of WCUs determine that they should aim for the highest and take on greater and more important global obligations when compared with RUs. For example, WCUs educate global talents and leaders, tackle global problems, and act as the framers and maintainers of global academic standards, while RUs tend to attach more importance on the development of local society and their countries, giving more priority to serving the local society and the country than making global contributions. This is supported by Shin and Kehm's (2013) study that there is a phenomenon of mission differentiation in the global higher education system, which means that different universities have different positioning, priorities, and responsibilities, because not all universities can become WCUs. WCUs should gain global recognition, which can be summarized as: global reputation, global capability to solve global issues, well-developed strategies responding to global changes, global competitiveness, and a global value with local concerns (Liu, 2019). This indicates the global orientation of WCUs as well as the global obligation placed by their world-class status or identity. Therefore, even though RUs are functioning similar to WCUs in some respects, their global obligation is not as strong as that of WCUs, which determines that WCUs must have the special function or unique mission that is different from RUs.

4.4.2 Global Capability

WCUS' special function or unique mission comes down to a fact of capability matching, that is, only WCUS have the global capability to perform their special function or unique mission. For instance, solving global problems and acting as pioneers of knowledge production and technological innovation need basic research that is closely aligned with the real-world challenges, which requires world-class research teams, facilities, abundant funding and global research cooperation networks. Restrictions on funding and facilities often prevent RUS from conducting large-scale and basic research that is time-consuming and slow to generate economic benefits. In other words, RUS are pale in comparison to WCUS in terms of resources, support and global reach. According to Marginson (2011b), universities' global capacity and connectivity are conditions for global activities, in that once global capacity and global connectivity are established, the institution has the freedom to act globally. The global capacity of a university is contingent on its infrastructure, including financial resources, physical resources, cultural/linguistic and intellectual resources, organizational and regulatory mechanisms, etc. The global connectivity is established through partnerships, networks and the ongoing exchange of staff and students at a global level. These conditions are often found in WCUS, as they house global research capability and outputs in many fields, and they are globally networked, globally recognized and effective in local, national and global actions. Therefore, the global capability of WCUS is stronger than that of RUS, which is also a necessary condition for WCUS possessing and performing their special function or unique mission.

4.4.3 Global Reputation

WCUS' special function or unique mission also depends on their global reputation and the resulting influence and appeal. Based on the findings of this research, cooperating globally to build a global academic community and responding to major global challenges to serve the global common good need not only WCUS' global capability and connectivity, but also their global reputation and the resulting influence and appeal; functioning as a role model to lead the spirit, value, and practice of other universities and society are also closely related to the global reputation and resulting influence and appeal of universities. As interviewees in this study pointed out that, the global influence of WCUS gives them a privileged voice, which makes them come front and centre in understanding, uncovering, and solving challenging problems. Therefore, they play an important and powerful role in leading the social development. This global influence is partly enhanced by WCUS' global capability and connectivity, but also stems from their world-renowned reputation, which is enhanced by their long-cherished history, culture and contributions. Essentially, the term "world-class" relies very much on the perceived reputation of universities (Xavier and Alsagoff, 2013; Liu, 2019). Hence, the global reputation can be regarded as a determining factor of universities' world-class status or identity, while at the same time being a distinctive advantage of WCUs, bringing reputational impact for WCUs. Global reputation defines the rationale and effectiveness of WCUs in possessing and performing their special function or unique mission.

4.5 Globalizing as WCUs' Special Function or Unique Mission

In summary, according to the research findings, WCUs have the special function that is possessed exclusively by them when compared with RUs, which is embodied in WCUs serving the global common good and acting as a global role model for research universities. The unique features of WCUs' special function are global positioning, global contribution, global influence and global cooperation, which also indicate the "global orientation" of WCUs. WCUs' special function is closely related to their three basic functions (education, research and service) while transcends them. The global vision, far-reaching influence, as well as the complexity and diversity in its practices have exceeded the three basic functions. However, since the special function and the three basic functions are not defined under the same logical framework, it may be debatable to list the special function as the fourth function in parallel with the three basic functions. In fact, WCUs' special function underlines the roles, effects, and influences of WCUs as well as a strong commitment and sense of duty for WCUs to do or achieve something. Therefore, it is more reasonable to define it as WCUs' special function or unique mission. Also, this special function or unique mission exclusively possessed by WCUs is closely related to their distinctive advantages: global obligation, global capability, and global reputation.

In the light of this, this study defines the special function or unique mission of WCUs as *globalizing*, that is, in the face of the increasingly complex internationalization of higher education, continuously growing global challenges, and rapidly evolving information technology, world-class universities, relying on their distinctive advantages, including global obligation, global capability, and global reputation, serve the global common good and act as a global role model for research universities, and continuously improve the unique features of their special function or unique mission, including global positioning, global contribution, global influence, and global cooperation.

5   Conclusion

The findings of this study illustrate that there are differences in the three basic functions between WCUs and RUs, but these differences do not necessarily indicate that WCUs perform better than RUs in terms of education, research, and service. Meanwhile, the findings of this study suggest that WCUs have a special function or unique mission, with two core dimensions, serving the global common good and acting as a global role model for research universities, and four unique features, global positioning, global contribution, global influence, and global cooperation. The special function or unique mission of WCUs' is not covered by their three basic functions and differentiates them from RUs. Accordingly, this study defines it as *globalizing*. Just as Nicholas Dirks (2015), the previous chancellor of UC Berkeley, said: "The goal here is two-fold: the first, that universities represent the most successful experiments in global institution building; the second, that if universities work together to build global curricula and global platforms, for research and teaching, they might provide models and ideas that will predicate new ways of engaging – and reimagining – globalization itself". Therefore, among all universities, WCUs, at any one time, are being asked to stretch beyond the traditions of education, research, and service, and to reach out beyond their walls, real or metaphorical, in order to connect with the global world in ways that are novel, challenging, and impactful. Though WCUs' are not flawless, their special function or unique mission of *globalizing* should be cherished and enhanced both now and into the foreseeable future.

References

Altbach, P. G. (2009). Peripheries and centres: Research universities in developing countries. *Asia Pacific Education Review, 10*(1), 15–27.

Chen, C. (2004). Cong wen hua quan qiu hua kan shi jie yi liu da xue de jiao wang gong neng [Considering world-class universities' communication function from a perspective of cultural globalization]. *Wai Guo Jiao Yu Yan Jiu* [*Studies in Foreign Education*], *31*(3), 29–33.

Cheng, Y., Wang, Q., & Liu, N. C. (2014). How world-class universities affect global higher education. In Y. Cheng, Q. Wang, & N. C. Liu (Eds.), *How world-class universities affect global higher education* (pp. 1–10). Sense Publishers.

Creswell, J. W., & Plano Clark, V. L. (2011). *Designing and conducting mixed methods research.* Sage Publications.

Deem, R., Mok, K. H., & Lucas, L. (2008). Transforming higher education in whose image? Exploring the concept of the "world-class" university in Europe and Asia. *Higher Education Policy, 21*(3), 83–97.

Dirks, N. (2015, October 2). The future of world-class universities. *University World News.* Retrieved June 16, 2017, from http://www.universityworldnews.com/article.php?story=20151001004022774

Douglass, J. A. (Ed.). (2016). *The new flagship university: Changing the paradigm from global ranking to national relevancy*. Palgrave Macmillan.

Gu, J. M., & Liu, A. S (2011). Shi jie yi liu da xue de jia zhi zhui qiu [The pursuit of world-class universities]. *Jiao Yu Fa Zhan Yan Jiu* [*Research in Educational Development*], *17*, 54–57.

Huang, F. T. (2017). Shen me shi shi jie yi liu da xue de ben ke jiao yu [What is the undergraduate education of world-class universities]. *Gao Deng Jiao Yu Yan Jiu* [*Higher Educaiton Research*], *8*, 1–9.

Jiang, G. H., & Sun, C. (2000). Yi liu da xue yu ke xue gong xian [World-class universities and their scientific contributions]. *Guo Jia Jiao Yu Yan Jiu* [*Journal of Higher Education*], *2*, 65–68.

Jongbloed, B., Enders, J., & Salerno, C. (2008). Higher education and its communities: Interconnections, interdependencies and a research agenda. *Higher Education, 56*(3), 303–324.

King's College London. (2019). *King's strategic vision 2029*. Retrieved December 4, 2019, from https://www.kcl.ac.uk/aboutkings/strategy/index.aspx

Kleinman, D., & Vallas, S. (2001). Science, capitalism, and the rise of the knowledge workers: The changing structure of knowledge production in the United States. *Theory and Society, 30*(4), 451–492.

KU Leuven. (2019). *Strategic plan for KU Leuven*. Retrieved September 5, 2019, from https://www.kuleuven.be/english/about-kuleuven/strategic-plan/index.html

Lee, J. (2013). Creating world-class universities: Implications for developing countries. *Prospects, 43*(2), 233–249.

Liu, K. N. (2019). Guo ji ze ren yu hua yu quan: yi liu da xue guo ji hua jian she de shi ming yu fang xiang (How to recognize and evaluate the "global" features of world-class universities). *Jiang Su Gao Jiao* (*Jiangsu Higher Education*), *2019*(9), 29–34.

Liu, N. C. (2009, February). *Building up world-class universities: A comparison*. Presentation in 2008–2009, Research Institute for Higher Education, Hiroshima University.

Marginson, S. (2011a). Higher education in East Asia and Singapore: Rise of the Confucian model. *Higher Education, 61*(5), 587–611.

Marginson, S. (2011b). Global perspectives and strategies of Asia-Pacific research universities. In N. C. Liu, Q. Wang, & Y. Cheng (Eds.), *Paths to a world-class university: Lessons from practices and experiences* (pp. 3–28). Sense Publishers.

Marginson, S. (2013). Nation-states, educational traditions and the WCU project. In H. C. Shin & B. M. Kehm (Eds.), *Institutionalization of world-class university in global competition* (pp. 59–77). Springer.

Marginson, S. (2018). Global cooperation and national competition in the world-class university sector. In Y. Wu, Q. Wang, & N. C. Liu (Eds.), *World-class universities: Towards a global common good and seeking national and institutional contributions* (pp. 13–53). Brill Sense.

Mayring, P. (2014). *Qualitative content analysis: Theoretical foundation, basic procedures and software solution*. Retrieved December 4, 2019, from https://nbn-resolving.org/urn:nbn:de:0168-ssoar-395173

Mohrman, K., Ma, W., & Baker, D. (2008). The research university in transition: The emerging global model. *Higher Education Policy, 21*(1), 5–27.

Ouda, H., & Ahmed, K. (2015). Strategic approach for developing world-class universities in Egypt. *Journal of Education and Practice, 6*(5), 125–146.

Parsons, T., & Platt, G. M. (1973). *The American university*. Harvard University Press.

Parsons, T., & Smelser, N. (1956). *Economy and society: A study in the integration of economic and social theory*. Routledge.

Plowman, D. (2019). *A message from the chancellor*. University of Tennessee – Knoxville. Retrieved October 16, 2019, from https://chancellor.utk.edu/

Reichert, S. (2009). *Institutional diversity in European higher education: Tensions and challenges for policy makers and institutional leaders*. European University Association.

Ren, Y. H. (2012). *Da Xue Gong Neng De Zheng Ti Xing Ji Qi Chong Jian* [*The integrity of university function and its reconstruction*] (Doctorate thesis). Southwest University, Nanjing.

Russell International Excellence Group. (2012). Jewels in the crown: The importance and characteristics of the UK's world-class universities. *Russel Group Papers*. Retrieved June 16, 2017, from https://www.russellgroup.ac.uk/media/5227/jewelsinthecrown.pdf

Salmi, J. (2009). *The challenge of establishing world-class universities*. World Bank Publications.

Scott, J. C. (2006). The mission of the university: Medieval to postmodern transformations. *The Journal of Higher Education, 77*(1), 1–39.

Shin, J. C. (2013). The world-class university: Concept and policy initiatives. In J. C. Shin & B. M. Kehm (Eds.), *Institutionalization of world-class university in global competition* (pp. 17–32). Springer.

Shin, J. C., & Kehm, B. M. (Eds.). (2013). *Institutionalization of world-class university in global competition*. Springer.

Song, F. J. (2003). Da xue shi ming: ying mei zhu ming da xue de fen xi bi jiao [University mission: A comparison analysis of top universities in the U.S. and U.K.]. *Jiang Su Gao Jiao* [*Jiangsu Higher Education*], 2, 123–126.

Soukhanov, A. H., Ellis, K., & Severynse, M. (1992). *The American Heritage dictionary of the English language*. Houghton Mifflin Company.

Tian, L. (2019). World-class universities: A dual identity related to global common good(s). In In Y. Wu, Q. Wang, & N. C. Liu (Eds.), *World-class universities: Towards a global common good and seeking national and institutional contributions* (pp. 93–113). Brill Sense.

Tian, L., & Liu, N. C. (2020). The role of world-class and regional research universities in contributing to the New Silk Road. In W. C. Kirby, N. C. Liu, S. Marginson, & M. C.

van der Wende (Eds.), *The new silk road: Connecting universities between China and Europe*. Oxford University Press.

van der Wende, M. C. (2018). World-class universities' contribution to an open society: Chinese universities on a mission? In Y. Wu, Q. Wang, & N. C. Liu (Eds.), *World-class universities: Towards a global common good and seeking national and institutional contributions* (pp. 189–214). Brill Sense.

Wang, M. M. (2018). Guo ji ze ren yu hua yu quan: yi liu da xue guo ji hua jian she de shi ming yu fang xiang [International responsibility and the right to speak: The mission and direction of the internationalization of world-class universities]. *Xian Dai Jiao Yu Guan Li* [*Modern Education Management*], *11*, 59–64.

Wang, Q., Cheng, Y., & Liu, N. C. (2013). Building world-class universities: Different approaches to a shared goal. In Q. Wang, Y. Cheng, & N. C. Liu (Eds.), *Building world-class universities: Different approaches to a shared goal* (pp. 1–10). Sense Publishers.

Wu, D. G. (2018, June 19). Universities' talent training must have its own direction. *Guangming Ri Bao* [*Guang Ming Daily*], 13.

Xavier, C. A., & Alsagoff, L. (2013). Constructing "world-class" as "global": A case study of the National University of Singapore. *Educational Research for Policy and Practice, 12*(3), 225–238.

Zhang, K. (2005). Shi lun yi liu da xue de nei han fa zhan yu ren cai pei yang [A discussion on the development and talent cultivation of world-class universities]. *Zhong Guo Gao Jiao Yan Jiu* [*China Higher Education Research*], *9*, 26–27.

Zhang, X. H. (2011). Lun ke xue yan jiu zai gao xiao zhong de di wei yu gong neng [A discussion on the status and function of scientific research in universities]. *Guo Jia Jiao Yu Xing Zheng Xue Yuan Xue Bao* [*Journal of National Academy of Education Administration*], *5*, 37–40.

Zhao, J. G. (2007). Shi lun shi jie yi liu da xue zhi neng de duo yuan hua [A discussion on the diversification of world-class universities' function]. *Wen Jiao Zi Liao* [*Data of Culture and Education*], *28*, 56–58.

CHAPTER 3

The Global Science System and National Science Systems

Simon Marginson

Abstract

Since 1990, there has been a major growth in and diversification of science worldwide, and of cross-border collaboration between scientists. Many lower middle-income countries now have their own science systems and one quarter of all papers have international co-authors. Science combines the networked open global science system, characterized by bottom-up cooperation between researchers, with bordered national science systems which shape activity through the provision of resources and the regulation of scientific institutions. The global and national systems overlap but have differing dynamics. This chapter discusses the character of each kind of science system, noting that countries vary in the extent to which they expand national networks compared to their participation in global networks.

Keywords

higher education science – research – globalization – networks – geo-politics

1 Introduction

In the last thirty years, there has been major growth in worldwide scientific capacity, albeit uneven by nation. Between 1995 and 2018, in all OECD countries expenditure on research and development (R&D) in all sectors rose from 1.95% to 2.4% of GDP. Of the 32 OECD for which data are available, R&D as a share of GDP increased in 27 countries and declined in five countries. R&D as a proportion of GDP more than doubled in Austria, the Czech Republic, Greece, Hungary, the Republic of Korea (ROK), Israel, Lithuania, Portugal, and Turkey, and also in non-OECD regions, the People's Republic of China (PRC) and Taipei, China. The absolute level of R&D spending in higher education in constant price terms rose almost everywhere between 1995 and 2017. It multiplied by 5.6 times in ROK and 16.5 in PRC, more than doubled in the United States and Canada, and almost doubled in the United Kingdom and Germany. The research workforce has also grown. While data on researchers in higher education are incomplete, in the intermediate case of Germany, where research has grown but less rapidly than in East Asia, the number of full-time equivalent researchers working in higher education increased from 53,905 in the year 2000 to 141,434 in 2018 (OECD, 2020).

The growth of resources has been accompanied by a proportional growth in output. Between 2000 and 2018, the total number of papers listed in Scopus rose from 1.072 million in 2000 to 2.556 million in 2018, growth of 4.95% a year, rapid by historical standards (National Science Board [NSB], 2020, table S5A-2), while world GDP grew 2.5% per annum (World Bank, 2020).

There have been two striking features of the growth of science. First, it is growth in collaboration in two forms: national networks and global networks (Figure 3.1). Both kinds of externally joint-authored papers grew faster than papers joint-authored or sole-authored in single institutions. The Scopus data in Figure 3.1 show that from 1996 to 2018 the proportion of papers with co-authors from more than one institution within the same national system rose

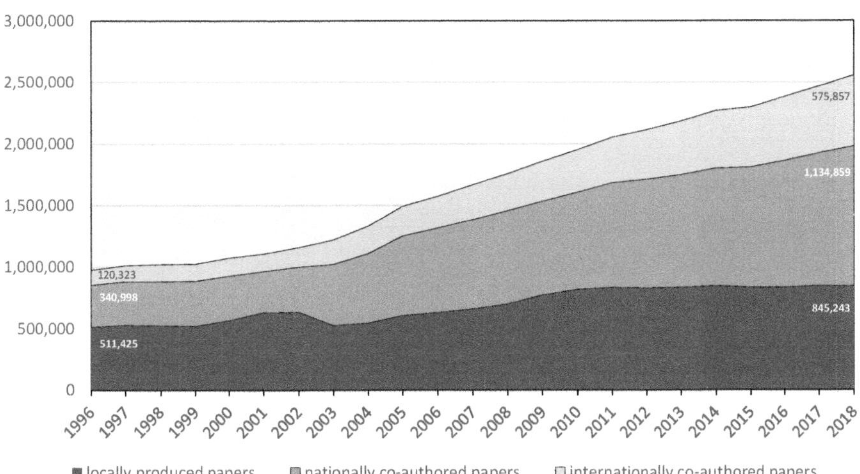

FIGURE 3.1   Number of published papers in Scopus, world, 1996 to 2018 (from NSB, 2020, table S5A-32). Note: Total papers rose from 972,746 in 1996 to 1,574,326 in 2006, 2,377,180 in 2016, 2,553,959 in 2018. Locally produced papers are authored in one institution, by one or more authors. Nationally co-authored papers involve more than one institution from the same country. Internationally co-authored papers involve authors from more than one country.

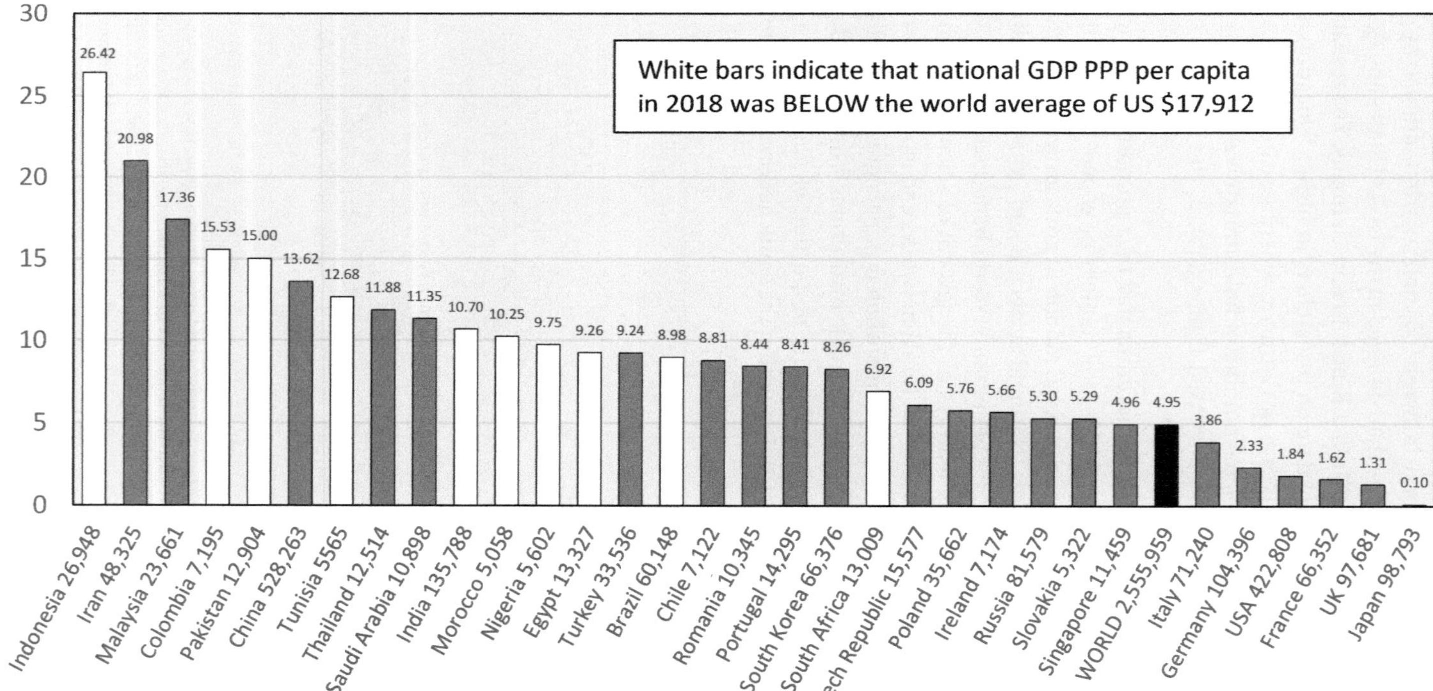

FIGURE 3.2   Annual rate of growth (%) between 2000 and 2018 in the number of published science papers, nations above the world average growth rate of 4.95% and over 5000 papers in 2018, plus the six largest nations in total papers in 2018, not already included (based on NSB, 2020, table S5A-2; World Bank, 2020). Notes: (1) Numbers next to country name are total 2018 papers. Countries with white bars have 2018 per capita income *below* world average. (2) PPP = Purchasing Power Parity. In joint papers national authorship is allocated on a weighted basis.

from 35.1% to 44.4%. The proportion of papers with co-authors from more than one country rose from 12.4% to 22.5%. Correspondingly (notwithstanding a small group of papers where institutional affiliation is not fully recorded) the proportion of papers authored or co-authored within one institution fell from 50.7% to 32.6% (NSB, 2020).

Internationally co-authored papers constituted only 1.9% of indexed articles in Web of Science in 1970 (Olechnicka et al., 2019, p. 78). The growth of cross-border collaboration to almost one quarter of all papers indicates the dynamism of the global science network. Nevertheless, the expansion of networked activity at the national level has also been important, particularly in certain emerging systems, as will be discussed below. Both the global science system and national science systems have grown at the same time.

Second, the growth of science has been accompanied by national diversification. New science countries have emerged with their own PhD-training, funded projects, and published outputs. Many are not wealthy. In 15 countries that published more than 5000 papers in 2018, papers grew faster in 2000–2018 than the world rate of 4.95% (Figure 3.2). In nine of these 15 fast-growing science countries, incomes per person were below the world average in 2018 of $17,912. They were lower middle-income countries. Science capacity is spreading across the world. In the year 1987, 20 relatively wealthy nations accounted for 90% of all published science. By 2017, a more mixed group of 32 nations made up the first 90%, indicating greater global diversification (Table 3.1).

TABLE 3.1   Deconcentration of country shares of world science paper output: 1987 to 2016

	1987	1997	2007	2017
Number of countries with 50% of world science papers	3 U.S., U.K., Germany	4 U.S., Japan, Germany, U.K.	5 U.S., PRC, Japan, Germany, U.K.	6 PRC, U.S., India, Germany, Japan, U.K.
Number of countries with 75% of world science papers	9	11	14	16
Number of countries with 90% of world science papers	20	23	26	32

Note: The data for 1987, 1997 and 2007 are from Web of Science; those for 2017 are from Scopus.
SOURCE: GROSSETTI (2013, P. 2225); NSB (2020, TABLE S5A-2)

This chapter focuses on publication and collaboration in science, especially the relation between the networked global system in science, primarily autonomous, bottom-up, and open in character, and the more heteronomous, bounded, and governed national systems of science. While the two science systems are heterogeneous, they overlap in the real world. The chapter draws on secondary data in relation to science, ultimately sourced from the Elsevier/Scopus and Clarivate Analytics/Web of Science collections, and as reworked by the U.S. National Science Board and others. It also discusses the findings of papers that constitute interpretations of scientific production and collaboration, primarily from scientometrics.

By *system* is meant a set of elements that together form an interactive whole within defined boundaries. As far as it goes, this simple definition of system is consistent with the sociological concept of a *field* (Bourdieu, 1993; Fligstein and McAdam, 2012) though it is more open-ended, without the theoretical baggage attached to the notion of a field. In his *Theory of Society* Luhmann states that the decisive step towards world society was "the full discovery of the globe as a closed sphere of meaningful communication" (Luhmann, 2012, vol. 1, p. 85). All social systems, including national and regional systems, are located within the single communicative system of a world society grounded in the natural ecosystem.

In the chapter *science* is understood as a combination of five partly-autonomous elements. First, researchers and research groups, largely self-organising, connecting episodically within networked systems of exchange. "Scientific knowledge is produced in almost every country across the globe. Scientists are organised in global epistemic communities that codify their knowledge in peer-reviewed articles published in specialist journals" (Wuestman et al., 2019). Relations combine the cooperative and competitive (Powell et al., 2017, p. 31). Second, organizations: universities, institutes, research centres, companies, and government laboratories, also networked. Third, infrastructures: tools, equipment, machines, information, and communications resources. Fourth, published knowledge that is generated, shared, codified, disseminated, stored, and reproduced. This published knowledge rests on a large infrastructure of conversations, tacit understandings, unpublished data, and draft papers, that together can be defined as *pre-science* knowledge. Fifth, the regulatory policies, rules, conventions, norms, languages, discourses, data protocols, and behavioural codes that are necessary to scientific activity and the institutions in which it is housed.

The focus here is on science rather than research. Although the chapter is concerned with the national scale as well as the global scale in science, it emphasizes those disciplines that are involved in global conversations, which are those grounded in the natural sciences. It engages less with the social sciences and little with the humanities. The chapter's relatively narrow focus on science is dictated by its inquiry into global relations. (This bias does not reflect an intrinsic preference of the author, who works in the humanistic end of the social sciences, where social theory, political economy, sociology and history meet education).

The next two sections discuss the global dimension in general and in science, and outline the global science system and national science systems. The section that follows considers the dynamics and trajectories of each kind of system in the light of the data and the literature. The conclusion reflects the relation between global and national in science.

2 The Global Dimension and Science

The term *global* as used here does not refer to the whole world and everything in it. The global dimension is specific to activities and relations constituting the worldwide or planetary ontology, that trend towards the evolution of the world as an integrated meta-system. *Globalization* refers to the combined processes of global convergence and integration (Held et al., 1999; Marginson, 2010; Conrad, 2016). These processes are partial and provisional. The existence of global phenomena does not mean everything is connected to everything else, or that global forces proceed independently of human agents, or that the global is always determining, or that global factors are necessarily privileged over local actors (Conrad, 2016, p. 158). Global relations provide conditions in which people act, as do relations within nation-states and regions, and as do the path-dependencies of kin and locality. Action in any scale can be determining.

Further, growing global openness, interconnectedness, and interaction are often interspersed with fragmentation, divergence, and autarky. Spatiality in human affairs is rarely neat or necessarily coherent. Half-bounded systems intersect with other systems and are scattered eclectically in larger spaces. The tendency is not always to greater integration: times of growing interconnectedness and interaction may be followed by times of disconnect and divergence (Conrad, 2016, p. 99). The two meta-tendencies, globalization, and de-globalization, can coincide. At present, global integration might be reversing in some domains such as trade, while moving forward in others, such as culture, as in the 1930s. A feature of the global science system is its fecund continuing expansion to an ever-growing number of sites, despite interruptions to globalization in politics and economics.

In social theory and in the literature on science (Choi, 2012, pp. 25–26), there are divergent views about the global and globalization. Some understand *global* as a normative term, others, including the present author, as a neutral descriptor. For some scholars, *globalization* is inherently top-down, combining global market formation with neo-imperial Western (especially American) hegemony, and a neoliberal policy sensibility, fostering the subordination and exploitation of emerging countries, maintaining neo-colonial relations and leading to cultural homogenization. Others see global convergence as associated with the narrowing of income gaps between countries, cultural hybridization, pan-national regional cooperation, and new potentials for human agency in mobility and cross-cultural learning. This chapter sees all of the above. Under particular circumstances, global integration can be associated with vertical or horizontal relations, homogeneity or diversity, and all of the imperial, regional, or shared forms. There are both hierarchy and flat networking in global science. The nature of global relations is an empirical question.

Arguably, the global dimension and its formation through globalization have three primary spatialities (Held et al., 1999; Marginson, 2010; Conrad, 2016).

First, there are interdependent systems at the world level, such as climate in the natural world, or integrated communications networks, or the global science system, which is discussed here and which affects the conditions in which national and local agents operate. One kind of global system, albeit a limited one, is that of the multilateral interaction between nation states (Held, 2003, pp. 73–86). Nations are enmeshed in many lines of association – tacit, informal, bilateral, and regional – and concede limited formal authority to the United Nations General Assembly as a collective body. The extent to which multilateral global governance constitutes a systemic whole in Lehmann's sense is open to question. It is a weakly bound whole if it is one. There are also organizations with a world-spanning mission, some of which are proto-systems, such the IMF as an agent of financial coordination.

Second, there are cross-border connections and relations, for example in trade, and in people mobility in the form of migration. Unlike global systems, these connections do not trigger an initial change in national structures, but when they become "regular and sustained" they may come to "shape societies in profound ways" (Conrad, 2016, p. 9). They become "embedded in processes of structural transformation" (p. 64). Held et al. (1999) refer to these repeated, embedded processes as "institutionalization", meaning the "regularization of patterns of interaction and consequently, their reproduction across space and time" (p. 19). Cross-border connections can have locally confined impacts, and may leave some places untouched, but as the world becomes increasingly integrated, the transformative potential of regular global connections is advanced.

Third, there is the worldwide diffusion of ideas, models, and behaviours, which is again transformative at scales below that of the global and may lead to a growing synchrony of events and sensibilities, and paralleling developments, in different parts of the world.

Science, including social science, is implicated in all three forms of the global (Helibron, 2013, p. 698). Scientific publication constitutes a worldwide system of codified knowledge in English. In science there is much cross-border data transfer and people mobility. Scientific knowledge and practices are highly visible and subject to rapid diffusion. The process of diffusion in turn provides favourable conditions for the evolution of the global science system. In this chapter, *global science* refers to only that part of science which enters into the common networked worldwide system of people, institutions, and published works. Here, global science is not confined to science at a level "above and beyond that of nations and regions" (Helibron, 2013, p. 692), or focused solely on recognizably global problems like climate. It includes all scientific knowledge developed in common cross-border conversations plus the infrastructures and activities that sustain those conversations.

Global connectedness in science has facilitated both the diffusion of common approaches and the building of networked science systems at both the global and national levels. The developmental logic of networks is explained by Castells in *The Network Society* (2000). As a network grows, each successive node is added at negligible cost. It adds value to the existing nodes by increasing potentially fruitful connections and cheapening the average unit cost of each connection across the network. Networks continually call new agents into being, expanding naturally towards complete inclusion of every possible node, while at the same time adding every possible edge, every possible link between existing nodes. Networks encourage the continual expansion of connections while facilitating both "flat" horizontal relationships and concentrations of network power. Castells (2001) remarks that the internet "allows metropolitan concentration and global networking to proceed simultaneously" (p. 225). Networks cluster at the principal nodes, empowering those nodes, while spreading inclusion. Networks combine an expansionary dynamic with an intensifying dynamic. The first dynamic generates flatness and inclusion. The second dynamic generates concentration and hierarchy. Often the outward expansion of the network and diversification of nodes is so rapid that for part of the time at least, the intensity of concentration declines. Arguably, this has happened in global science (Wagner et al., 2015). From time to time, the intensification process catches up and concentration and hierarchy are intensified. Whatever happens with concentration, the total number of connections keep growing. The two dynamics, horizontal and vertical, are not contrary. They are part of the same social process, just as the growth of high participation in systems of higher education enhances both horizontal social inclusion, and vertical institutional and social stratification, at the same time (Cantwell et al., 2018).

Science networks in the global system, and in national science systems, are distinct but not necessarily antagonistic. Each feeds the growth of the other. Such a national-global symbiosis is common to globalization. World historians (for example, Bayly, 2004) argue that the modern nation-state was incubated by global strategic competition between the late-eighteenth and the mid-nineteenth centuries. National leaders in Europe, America, and Japan saw the world as a field of comparison. They watched each other, imitated each other, and innovated to gain advantages over each other in military and industrial capability. The global did not necessarily dissolve the national. Rather, they each provided conditions for each other's development, in symbiosis or in tension. Likewise, since 1990, the internet has facilitated the evolution of a single system of published science, universally visible and instantly accessible, grounded in decentralized scientific networks, and which has become the main source of innovations in both science and knowledge-intensive industry. At the same time, emerging global science has fostered and encouraged the growth and spread of national science systems with their own research and doctoral training. Nations needed to connect effectively to the common pool of science and technology. To do this, they needed to share in the production of global science, or at least be able to interpret it. By building national science at home and encouraging scientists to collaborate abroad they are able to access that common pool.

In short, relations between national and global science have two-way effects. Global science makes national science more necessary, and opens national science to a larger body of work while stimulating in it a continuous dynamism both competitive and cooperative in form. Global science partly rests on and incorporates national science systems. It remakes those national systems. Nations are also potent. National science systems provide resources for global science. The stronger national and regional systems, and the communities of scientists they incubate, shape global relations in science, in a process of co-evolution.

3   Global and National Science Systems

On one hand there is the free interaction of individual scientists and scientific teams in the open space between institutions and between national systems. On the other hand, science is funded by many governments as a source of global survival and national competitive advantage, and is subject to national law and the policies shaping and regulating scientific institutions. This is the ambiguity of system in science. Two kinds of science systems operate simultaneously:

the global system and national systems (Figure 3.3). One outcome is that science is identifiably global in more than one way. It is both directly global in its own right, though free association in global space, and more indirectly global via the multilateral system of nations. Both of these forms of global science appear in the literature and can be mixed eclectically in the same papers. Perhaps the national and multi-lateral framing of science is more dominant in the literature. Yet it is impossible to understand freely associating global science, with its positive-sum potentials, solely through the lens of the multilateral system of zero-sum nation-states.

The ambiguity is not just discursive. The two kinds of science system are more than "imagined communities", to use Anderson's (1983) famous term for the nation. Each of the global science system and the national science systems are imagined relational communities but also has materiality. Though not everything in these systems can be directly observed, "systemness" is "an empirical question" (Etzkowitz and Leydesdorff, 2000, p. 113). Much can be measured, for example patterns of collaboration and citation. The complication is that in empirical terms the contents of the two categories, global science,

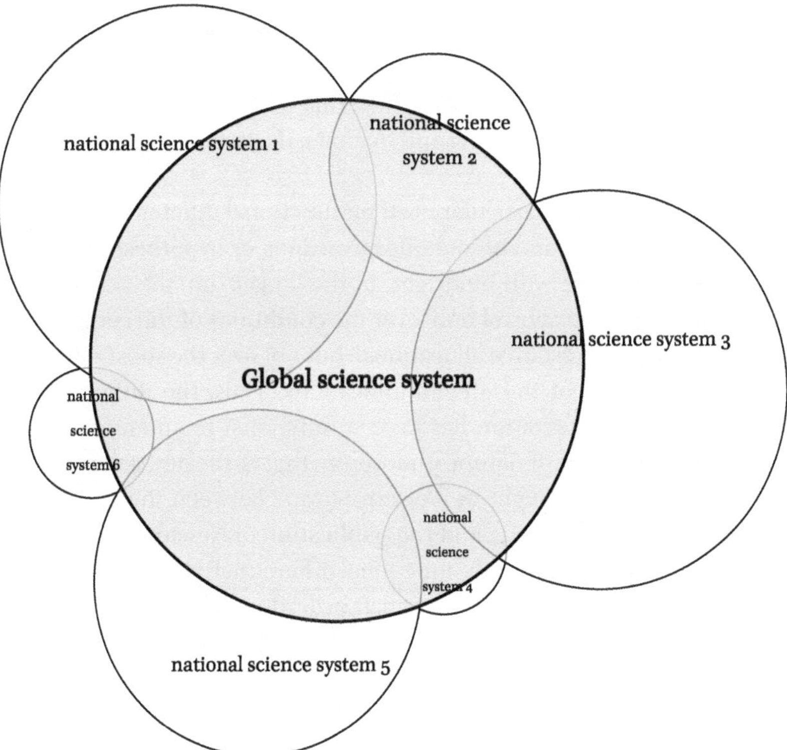

FIGURE 3.3   Model of global science system and national science systems

and national science are not entirely separate. They overlap. Networked global science is more than just global. Most of it is also part of national science systems. A large part of scientific work is plural in character, it has a double role, contributing simultaneously to globally networked science and to national science systems. Scientists wear two hats and many are well aware of it.

Global science and national science are practiced by many of the same people, moving in and out of different circles, or remaining within the same circles but with multiple and differing purposes and roles, continuously connected, with an unseen division of labour between global and national. Global science and national science are composed of partly differing mixes of elements. Though both global and national science consist of researchers in association, national science has something additional. Unlike global science, national science has a formal organizational personality and the nodes of the network, the individual researchers, are not wholly autonomous. National science is a closed set of activity with an agent at the centre, the nation-state. At the same time, because it is closed it is more limited than global science.

What is the essential difference between global and national science? Leydesdorff (2007) provides an explanation of the boundary between autonomous science and the state. In the last analysis science cannot operate when its contents are externally normalized, by a state, a church or any other power. It must be functionally differentiated. In terms of cognitive accumulation, contents, it must be self-referencing and that on a decentralized basis:

> Scientists have had a particular need for functional differentiation, since they need room for provisional interpretations or hypotheses that they may wish to change with hindsight. In the longer run, the sciences can allow for normative control only over the conditions of the communication (for example, resource allocations), but not over the substantive and reflexive contents of these communications. Thus, the differentiation from normative integration has been a functional requirement for the further development of natural philosophy, that is, the new sciences. This crucial conflict was fought in Western Europe between the appearance of Galileo's Dialogo in 1632 and the publication of Newton's Principia in 1687. From that time onwards, functional differentiation has been further institutionalized in the social system. (Leydesdorff, 2007, p. 382)

Along with scale, this explains the contrast between global and national systems of science *qua* science. The global system is a Leydesdorffian combination of autonomous units in the outer reaches, beyond external authority. In contrast, the national system combines the network of autonomous scientists with the external authority of the nation-state. It is always hybrid, always vulnerable to national normalization. Mostly the dual identity of scientists, global or national, provides them with the room to move, enabling them to evade the normalization of the specific content of their work. Nevertheless, they are routinely open to the ordering by policy makers of priorities between disciplines, the selection of major initiatives, and episodic funding vetoes that impact global science, as well as the national map of activity. Sometimes national governments intervene more closely at the project level.

3.1   *Global Science*

Global science is a global civil society functioning as a combined culture without a single organizational personality. Luhmann expresses the pure form of global science: "Subjects constitute the world. But intersubjectivity is by no means a subject" (Luhmann, 1996, p. 260). As global knowledge, science is something like a language, accumulating on a grass-roots basis with its own momentum and patterns of necessity and contingency, part fragmented and part unified, regulated by agreed conventions and standards that are managed in continuous negotiation on a voluntary basis and that change over time (King, 2011). It is not controlled from a single pivot. The autonomy of global subjects enables the autonomy of the global network, and the vice versa also applies.

The work of Wagner, Leydesdorff and colleagues is distinctive in both mapping the global system and breaking with "internalist" explanations (Conrad, 2016, p. 88) in which national societies are solely self-generating. Cross-border activity in science is also self-generating. In the argument of Wagner et al. (2015) national science activity is as much a function of global activity as vice versa, perhaps more so. They find that the global system is gaining material weight and may be partly displacing and destabilizing national science systems. They emphasize the decentralized, bottom-up, and self-evolving character of networked global science. Researchers from new countries freely enter the network and collaborate with others from emerging systems. The leading countries and institutions are not gate keepers. This draws attention to two salient characteristics of the global system. First, its grounding in researcher agency, in the autonomy of individuals. Second, its grounding in the partial autonomy, from states and capital, of the networked global system itself.

The autonomy of scientists is exercised under specific conditions. Scientists need freedom from constraint by national governments and institutional managers, what Berlin (1969) called negative freedom and Sen (1985) calls control freedom. They must be able to conduct their chosen inquiry subject only to the collective judgement of their peers. They also need effective or positive freedom, the capacity to act, including the capacity to access information, communicate and cooperate with others, conduct research, and publish results. In this respect national systems and individual universities can affect the content of globally networked activity without moving to the global pivot. Chinchilla-Rodriguez et al. (2018) note the "autonomy of science is mostly limited by the need to obtain funding and by the agendas of the organizations and nations that provide it" (p. 1486).

Scientists also need agency freedom, freedom of the will, the drive to determine their own pathway (Sen, 1985). A growing number of scientists feel an impetus to work across borders. Schott (1998) refers to the subjective stance of "outwardness" (p. 134). This is partly distinct from all of cognitive, financial, career-positional, status, or institutional factors (for example, Ryan, 2014, p. 357; Maisonobe et al., 2016; Kato and Ando, 2017). As Georgiou (1998) and Melin (2000) note, the widespread desire for collaborative networks long predated formal programmes designed to build international collaborations, such as European funding schemes. "Very often, there has to be a personal chemistry at play … sometimes even friendship" (Melin, 2000, p. 39). It is often friendship of a cross-cultural kind, which all else being equal, requires more effort than local friendships that share the same language or culture. A survey by Ryan (2014) finds that of the different kinds of motivation affecting research scientists, "internal self-concept" was the strongest and "instrumental" was the weakest (p. 355).

The second salient characteristic of the global system is its autonomy as a system. This starts with the autonomy of researchers in communicating with other researchers, a norm established worldwide in the twentieth century (Schott, 1998, p. 116), and extends to the autonomy of networked collaboration vis-a-vis national and institutional authorities. In "International collaboration in science and the formation of a core group" Leydesdorff and Wagner (2008) argue that "international collaboration in science can be considered as a communications network that is different from national systems and has its own internal dynamics" (p. 317). In "Growth of international collaboration in science: Revisiting six specialities", Wagner et al. (2017) note that global cooperation is not just driven by "big science", projects with multilateral budgets. "Many 'small science' projects at the international level are based upon the shared interests of otherwise unrelated parties, working independently of organizing imperatives or shared resources, to find reasons to cooperate despite geographic distance" (Wagner et al. 2017, p. 1634). The "spectacular growth of international collaborations may be due more to the dynamics created by the self-interests of individual scientists rather than to other structural, institutional or policy-related factors" (p. 1616).

Likewise, King (2011) describes the global system as "a largely privately governed network" (p. 359). It is an individualized matter "largely outside the control of governmental authorities" that constitutes "a move from scientific nationalism for most researchers" (pp. 360–361). Globally, science is driven by both intellectual curiosity and ambitions for "reputation and recognition" (p. 360). Crucially, the global system is "emergent", like an ecosystem. "It develops unpredictably on the basis of free individual exchanges" (p. 372). It is also its own normative system, "a constantly emergent social system" that is regulated by "standards that help constitute and coordinate scientific practices worldwide" (p. 362). These standards, which are common across science, while at the same time culturally specific and framed by the dominant countries and organizations, include language and notions of "autonomy, objectivity, testability, and peer judgment" (p. 371).

3.2 *National Science*

"The growth of the global network in science does not mean we are witnessing the death of the nation-state or even a reduction in its influence in scientific investments", as Leydesdorff and Wagner remark (2008, p. 324). However, unlike global science, national science networks are not solely self-generating, in that in some cases states or institutions drive and fund their creation. Hennemann and colleagues (2012) note that "important forces act on the national scale", including funding bodies, competition between universities, and the labour markets for science; while at the sub-national scale, companies influence scientific activities and research organizations "cluster in urban agglomerations" (pp. 217–218). National systems, often disproportionately patterned by large research grants in a small number of organizations, are affected by "socio-cultural features such as language and institutions (for example, common ethics, regulatory frameworks, legal ground, or fiscal idiosyncrasies)" (p. 223). There is also a part of science that is irreducibly national, not published openly, and outside of the global exchange. This includes much research on matters of national defense and security, not the basic science (which is mostly accessible) but the development of applications. The proportion of science that is in this zone may be increasing, though it is difficult to estimate. However, the point is that for all of the above reasons, the state matters.

Nations set boundaries on inclusion and insert motivations and objectives external to science itself. The national system of science filters the work of nationally-located scientists in global science, to the extent the agency of scientists, who carry a dual identity in the national and global systems, is nationally-defined, resourced, regulated and normatively shaped. National government, regulation and organization directly affect network evolution at national level. National collaboration is determined by policies, norms, directions, incentives, or specific cultures, which might differ between research fields or technologies, or both, and also between countries (Graf and Kalthaus, 2018, p. 3).

There is much focus on comparative national performance in both policy circles and scholarly literature. Studies have investigated the role of national researchers in both global collaboration and national collaboration, and the correlations to performance in terms of paper numbers and citations. Yet network analysis struggles to separate out the national system from the global system. This is not only because network analysis, when operating without social theory or sociology, is by itself insufficient to explain global and national science as relational social systems. There are also problems internal to the scientometric data.

First, the record of national systems is incomplete. Bibliometric data provide a comprehensive coverage of global activity, including national science linkages part of both the global and national science systems, but are less complete in recording national linkages not part of the global system, especially non-English language science. Second, while recorded papers in the English language literature appear as more or less global in terms of authorship and citation, the extent to which papers are part of a particular national conversation is mostly unclear. Once the growth of collaboration, internationally mobile researchers, dual identities and the multiple international basis of citations are taken into account, "it becomes increasingly difficult in bibliometric analysis to separate clear country effects" (Bornmann et al., 2018, p. 942; see also Adams, 2013, p. 2). While national science systems are more visible than the global system in terms of institutions, policies, rules, and economics, they are less visible in terms of the data on collaborative networks.

Many network-based studies identify national systems simply in terms of papers with national authors, thereby dividing up the world as a zero-sum between separate national systems. Logically, this eliminates the global system as such. In the zero-sum approach, it is solely the sum of the national parts. Yet while all science is thereby fitted into a national system and made global at the same time, border-crossing international collaborations are left in a grey zone, and the relational and cumulative character of knowledge is lost. Packalen (2019) uses an investigation of whether scientists build on novel or established ideas to compare national science system performance, oblivious to the fact that these allegedly separable parcels of performance derive from free flows of knowledge in which it is ultimately impossible to know where one state ends and another begins. Are collaborations simply a function of national attributes as Packalen's method suggests, or are they essentially global as Wagner and colleagues imply? Or both? If they are both – if the fact of multiplicity of system, identity, and purpose is admitted – where does that leave international citations of single nation papers? Such papers have a solely national identity, they are not cross-border authored, yet they are recognizably part of global knowledge and in that way different from those national papers that fall outside the global conversation.

Arguably, in a small group of countries, including the United States, the United Kingdom, Singapore, and Switzerland, the national science system is positioned at the heart of global science (Adams and Gurney, 2018). In those countries, a large part of the nation-to-nation co-authorships are utilized within the global science conversation in the same manner as are internationally coauthored work. However, this is not true of all nationally authored work. Bornmann et al. (2018) investigate the national identity of the citations used in science papers. They find that while papers from the United Kingdom drawing on national authors in their citation base are just as likely to be globally cited as are papers resting on global authors, that is not so in Germany and the Netherlands, where there is a category of nationally co-authored papers grounded in national litera-ture that are less likely to be globally cited. "The likelihood that the citing paper is highly cited decreases by 11% if that paper has cited at least one German paper" (p. 937). This points to partly bounded intra-national conversations:

> This may suggest that there is a potential separation between the domes-tic and internationally-engaged parts of the research base in those coun-tries ... Our results suggest a stratification in national publication systems in terms of international or domestic orientation of the knowledge base from which authors cite. (Bornmann et al., 2018, p. 941)

This study suggests one empirical pathway for further exploration of the character of national science systems.

4 Trajectories of Global and National Growth

Castell's (2000) theorization of networks suggests that they expand without limit until saturation is reached. The global science network, grounded in the autonomous links between scientists and largely free to evolve, expands contin-ually more or less as Castells describes. The rapid growth of global networking drives up the proportion of papers co-authored across borders, as repeatedly confirmed in scientometrics (for example, successive changes in the network indicators in Wagner and Leydesdorff, 2005; Wagner et al., 2015, p. 6; Wagner et al., 2017, pp. 1637–1640). This is the pure materiality of networked science.

National science networks are different. Their long-term trajectory does not solely follow a Castellian expansionary network logic. National networks expand most of the time, especially as a new science system is emerging, but they do not expand always or at the same rate as global networking. In mature science sys-tems, solely national co-authorship may stop growing altogether. As networks, national scientific linkages are both enabled and limited by non-network social phenomena including geo-politics, national policy, regulation, funding and institutional arrangements – more than is the case with global networks.

Emerging national science systems, fostered by nation-states, typically demonstrate accelerated growth in total papers (Figure 3.2). This early growth is furthered not solely by the expansionary logic of the science network but also by government policies, infrastructure, funding and targets. All emerging systems also grow their international collaborations as part of the capacity building process. Unless they remain both relatively small and largely dependent on international collaboration, they also manifest accelerated growth of nationally co-authored papers. Later, national systemic collaboration ceases to expand with the outward dynamic of a network. It seems that as nation-only network density increases, the national expansion of national systems hits the border. There is not the same scope for grass-roots growth of new nodes and additional edges as in the global science system. Meanwhile, national governments reach another kind of limit. The duration of accelerated nation-building in science is not fixed by a social law; it is determined by each government; but once a mature national system is achieved, all else being equal the policy drive to build national capacity is reduced. In addition, it is more difficult to manage the politics of funding new capacity. There is a trade-off between established institutional bases, with influence, and the creation of new capacity. Funding in a mature system tends to become mostly focused on existing science, such as concentrations in leading universities, less arbitrary and controversial than creating new winners. "Direct R&D subsidies ... only seem to encourage collaboration with already well-embedded actors" (Graf and Kalthaus, 2018, pp. 2, 11).

In sum, it can be theorized that as national science systems mature the growth of nation-only co-authorship will plateau and their total scientific output also grows more slowly. Only global collaborations keep operating as a network so that the quantitative expansion of networked activity becomes located largely in the global domain. Notwithstanding the ambiguity (national science is partly coincident with global science and partly separated from it), this theorized boom/plateau trajectory fits the patterns in actual national systems, as confirmed in the literature. "For the scientifically advanced nations, the internationally coauthored articles account for almost all the growth", state Wagner et al. (2015, p. 7). In a study of 1981–2012 papers in Web of Science, Adams exaggerates only slightly:

> Over more than three decades, domestic output – papers that list only authors from the home country – has flatlined in the United States and in Western European countries. The rise in total annual output for each

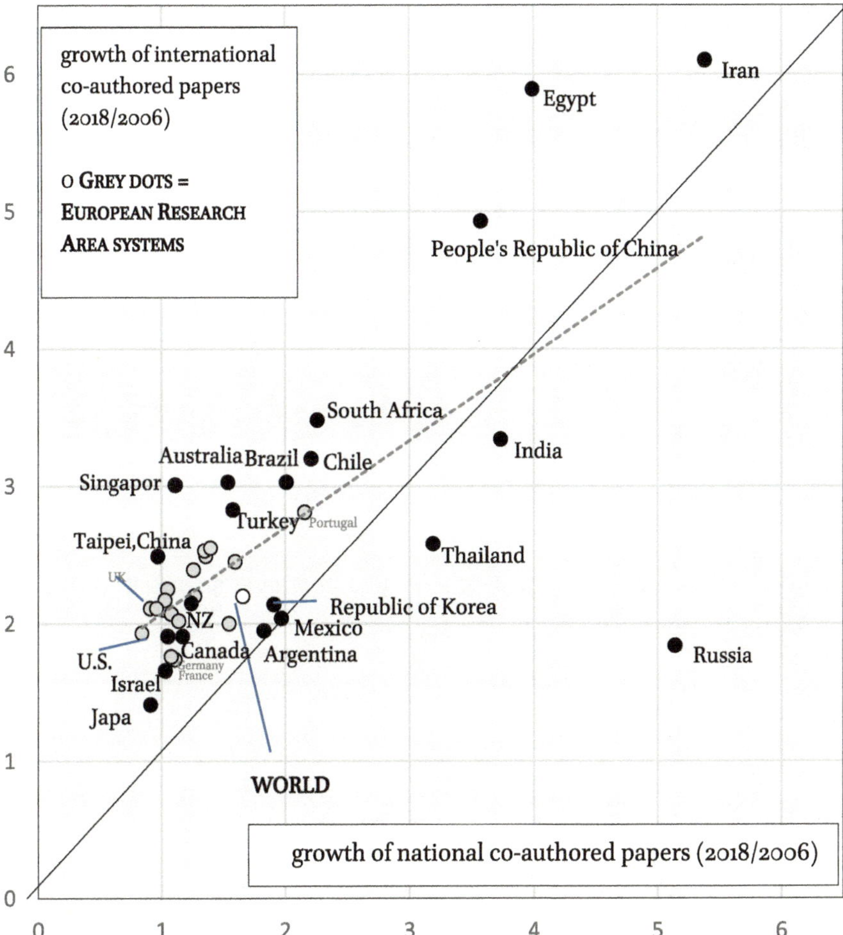

FIGURE 3.4   Growth of international co-authored papers compared to growth of nation-only
co-authored papers, world and major research systems: 2018 compared to 2006
(2006 = 1.00) (based on data from NSB, 2020, table S5A-32). Note: Grey dots are
countries engaged in European Research Area programmes in 2018. Data include
42 leading research countries selected from Scopus data by U.S. National Science
Board. Dotted line is line of best fit for the 42 cases plus the world (growth multiplier 2006–2018 of 2.2 for international co-authorship and 1.7 for national co-authorship). National systems above the dotted line exhibit relatively high growth
on international collaboration compared to domestic collaboration; countries
below the line exhibit relatively high growth in building national collaboration
compared to international. For ease of presentation the chart excludes outliers
Saudi Arabia (growth multiplier 17.8 for international /3.3 for domestic), Pakistan
(10.6/5.1) and Malaysia (8.4/7.8). NZ = New Zealand. WORLD refers to all science
countries and not just this group of 42 leading countries.

TABLE 3.2　Growth of international co-authored papers compared to growth of nation-only co-authored papers, world and 42 research systems: 2018 compared to 2006 (2006 = 1.00)

System	Multiplier all papers 2018/2006	Internationally co-authored papers 2006	Internationally co-authored papers 2018	Multiplier international 2018/2006	Nationally co-authored papers 2006	Nationally co-authored papers 2018	Multiplier national 2018/2006
National systems with rapid shift to internationally co-authored papers, compared to national (systems above the broken line in Figure 3.4)							
Malaysia	7.28	1,418	11,954	8.43	1,322	10,257	7.76
Iran	4.87	2,177	13,277	6.10	4,753	25,548	5.38
Pakistan	5.64	928	9,810	10.57	1,051	5,363	5.10
Egypt	3.92	1,727	10,176	5.89	1,482	5,918	3.99
PRC	2.87	25,753	126,868	4.93	78,749	280,881	3.57
Saudi Arabia	8.58	900	16,037	17.82	636	2,102	3.31
South Africa	2.65	3,218	11,188	3.48	1,693	3,828	2.26
Chile	2.65	2,534	8,097	3.20	1,252	2,761	2.21
Portugal	2.27	4,467	12,534	2.81	2,874	6,200	2.16
Brazil	2.23	8,116	24,610	3.03	16,811	33,783	2.01
Ireland	1.82	3,286	8,050	2.45	1,427	2,289	1.60
Turkey	1.82	3,426	9,698	2.83	11,500	18,158	1.58
Australia	1.97	16,709	50,584	3.03	13,404	20,628	1.54
Norway	1.96	4,967	12,687	2.55	2,896	4,051	1.40
Czechia	1.96	4,202	10,449	2.49	3,741	5,100	1.36
Denmark	1.95	6,578	16,670	2.53	3,391	4,577	1.35
Spain	1.62	17,638	42,137	2.39	17,546	22,042	1.26
Singapore	1.85	4,387	13,216	3.01	2,813	3,131	1.11
Austria	1.69	6,762	15,183	2.25	3,289	3,454	1.05
Sweden	1.58	11,377	24,740	2.17	6,390	6,604	1.03
Belgium	1.54	9,825	20,667	2.10	4,718	4,812	1.02
Taipei,China	1.19	4,629	11,542	2.49	14,348	13,852	0.97
U.K.	1.39	47,409	99,924	2.11	30,886	29,683	0.96
Finland	1.43	5,360	11,323	2.11	3,826	3,497	0.91

(cont.)

TABLE 3.2   Growth of international co-authored papers compared to growth of nation-only co-authored papers, world and 42 research systems: 2018 compared to 2006 (2006 = 1.00) (*cont.*)

System	Multiplier all papers 2018/2006	Internationally co-authored papers 2006	Internationally co-authored papers 2018	Multiplier international 2018/2006	Nationally co-authored papers 2006	Nationally co-authored papers 2018	Multiplier national 2018/2006
National systems with slow or no shift to internationally co-authored papers, compared to national (systems below the broken line in Figure 3.4)							
Russia	2.58	11,708	21,530	1.84	6,569	33,789	5.14
India	3.49	7,991	26,684	3.34	15,837	59,023	3.73
Thailand	2.85	2,512	6,486	2.58	1,812	5,787	3.19
Mexico	1.81	4,688	9,583	2.04	4,214	8,282	1.97
ROK	1.85	10,493	22,422	2.14	18,224	34,839	1.91
Argentina	1.68	3,080	6,004	1.95	2,311	4,231	1.83
Poland	1.70	7,480	14,950	2.00	8,840	13,689	1.55
Italy	1.59	22,793	50,243	2.20	23,863	30,410	1.27
New Zealand	1.67	3,833	8,258	2.15	1,956	2,434	1.24
Canada	1.42	26,787	51,287	1.91	18,808	22,001	1.17
Switzerland	1.61	14,618	29,476	2.02	4,748	5,424	1.14
France	1.27	34,982	60,916	1.74	24,207	26,865	1.11
Germany	1.38	46,596	82,089	1.76	33,488	36,010	1.08
Netherlands	1.51	16,280	33,713	2.07	10,499	11,341	1.08
U.S.	1.22	112,950	215,388	1.91	192,916	201,706	1.05
Israel	1.28	5,886	9,790	1.66	4,426	4,540	1.03
Japan	0.95	25,488	36,050	1.41	58,091	52,805	0.91
Greece	1.25	4,675	9,029	1.93	4,625	3,871	0.84
WORLD	1.62	262,099	575,857	2.20	684,143	1,134,859	1.66

SOURCE: BASED ON DATA FROM NSB (2020, TABLE S5A-32). FIRST GROUP OF SYSTEMS ARE ABOVE THE BROKEN LINE IN FIGURE 3.4.

country is due to international collaboration. The percentage of papers that are entirely "home grown" is falling. In emerging countries, by contrast, domestic output is rapidly expanding. (Adams, 2013, p. 558)

The pattern of boom/plateau in national capacity building is also apparent when comparative data are examined, as summarized in Table 3.2 and Figure 3.4.

4.1   *Data on National and Global Growth*

The data on nationally and internationally co-authored papers allow direct if partial comparisons of the two different trajectories of system evolution. The comparison confirms Castells's theorization. The global system and national systems have different patterns of growth because global growth is more faithful to a network logic. Figure 3.4 and Table 3.2 track the growth of each form of co-authorship between 2006 and 2018, in 42 leading science countries. Because of the gaps in coverage (not all national science is included) and the overlap between national and global systems (part of the global is national, only part of the national is global), these data do not conclusively sort the global and national science systems. Nevertheless, they show which national systems exhibit robust growth of national collaboration, suggesting accelerated national capacity building in emerging systems; and which systems exhibit very pronounced growth of international co-authorship, which can happen in either emerging systems or established systems. They also identify the nation-by-nation relation between the growth trajectories of global and national collaboration.

Figure 3.4 shows which nations are moving faster than others in one direction or the other – for example, it distinguishes emerging countries that especially use international collaboration as their way forward from those equally or more committed to national network building. (In these data single authors with more than one institutional affiliation are recorded as a collaboration, with varying effects on the data depending on the country.)

Between 2006 and 2018 the number of papers involving international collaboration at world level multiplied by 2.20 while national collaborative papers multiplied by 1.66. Figure 3.4 and Table 3.2 indicate that international co-authorship increased in all 42 countries while solely national co-authorship increased in all but five countries. The broken line in Figure 3.4 normalizes patterns across the 42 countries. The location of the dot for "World", relative to the normalizing broken line, indicates that there was a more rapid growth of international co-authorship in the leading 42 nations in Figure 3.4, relative to the growth of national co-authorship, than in science as a whole. Above the broken line, scientists increased the volume of international collaboration, relative to the increase in national collaboration, by more than did scientists in the 42 countries overall. That is, they increased international linkages, relative to domestic linkages, at a faster rate than did their peers. Over half the European countries were above this line, indicating increasingly intensive collaboration within the European Research Area, which functions almost like a large national system.

The number of nationally collaborative papers more than doubled in the case of scientists from Malaysia, where it multiplied by 7.76, Iran (5.38), Russia (5.14), Pakistan (5.10), Egypt, India, PRC, Saudi Arabia, Thailand, Chile, Portugal and Brazil. In all these emerging systems national government was building national scientific capacity during the period, albeit with varying degrees of effort. The data pinpoint those countries where national collaboration was a relatively high priority, compared to international collaboration. In the three countries below the unbroken line in Figure 3.4, national co-authorships grew more rapidly than international: Russia, India and Thailand. In Russia national collaborations were boosted by scientists in the Academy of Sciences who newly affiliated with universities during 2006–2018. There was also near balance between the two kinds of growth in ROK, Mexico, Argentina, Iran and Malaysia. In all eight of these systems the relative priority given to national collaboration exceeds that in most countries. PRC and Egypt, and in Europe, Portugal, where science has emerged more recently than in most other Western European countries, have also engaged in especially robust national network building, while at the same time expanding international collaboration more rapidly than national collaboration.

In emerging systems advanced internationalization appears near mandatory. In all such systems in Figure 3.4 except those of Russia, Mexico and Argentina (each of which might dispute the use of the term "emerging"), international co-authorship grew rapidly between 2006 and 2018. It multiplied by three times or more in the cases of scientists in Saudi Arabia (17.62), Pakistan (10.57), Malaysia (8.43), Iran (6.10), Egypt (5.89), PRC, South Africa, India, Chile, Brazil, Australia and Singapore (NSB, 2020, table S5A-32). Only the last two on this list were mature systems throughout the period. In Saudi Arabia international collaborations were boosted by mass signings of part-time foreign research leader faculty to improve the position of Saudi higher education institutions, especially King Abdulaziz University, in global rankings (see Gringas, 2014). The data also identify a group of emerging countries where international co-authorship has developed especially rapidly compared to the growth of domestic co-authorship: Brazil, Chile, Turkey, Saudi Arabia, Pakistan and South Africa.

The longer established science systems in Western Europe, North America and Japan saw relatively slow growth of nation-only co-authored papers between 2006 and 2018. In some mature systems – Greece; Finland; Japan; the United Kingdom; and Taipei,China – national co-authorship declined in absolute terms and the near pure network dynamics continued to play out only in global science. In most European countries the number of internationally co-authored papers by national scientists at least doubled, and among U.S. scientists, national co-authorship multiplied by 1.05 while international co-authorship multiplied by 1.91.

In Europe all of global, regional and national effects can be compared. Frenken (2002) investigates the integration of European science by comparing actual networks to a potential random distribution. He finds that in 1993–2000, prior to the data in Figure 3.4, collaboration within Europe became more evenly distributed, there was less bias in partner selection; large robust national systems exhibited the highest degree of integration; and there was a "strong bias towards intra-national collaboration" (p. 345). European integration was not at the expense of intra-national collaboration (p. 358). The United Kingdom, Germany and France, with the most scope to develop new links within the region, "exhibited the highest degrees of integration in Europe ... large countries benefit from scale effects that trigger European collaboration" (pp. 354–355). One reason was that their languages were more widely used than was the case in small systems (p. 356). Frenken et al. (2009) confirms the earlier results and finds that all else equal, scientists in the larger national systems were also the most prone to collaborate internationally (p. 224). The "strong correlation between the size of a country and the level of its integration" (p. 354) is visible also in the United States where national science is exceptional in both its extent of integration with other countries' science and in the robust identity and scope of the intra-national collaborative network. These outcomes "point to the persistence of national science systems" (Frenken, 2002, p. 345) and conform that national systems can be both internally robust and externally engaged.

Among the established systems in Figure 3.4, Singapore; Taipei,China; and Australia saw the most pronounced shift in priorities towards international networking. Networking within Taipei,China decreased (0.97) while its international networking multiplied by 2.49. In Australia the numbers were 1.54 and 3.03 (NSB, 2020, table S5A-32). The global/national distinction is not important in Singapore: nation-only collaborations between its two globalized universities are well placed in global science. International networking grew more modestly in Japan, where the growth figure of 1.41 for international networking was the lowest for all countries in Table 3.4 in the 2006–18 period, and in France, Germany and Israel.

These interpretations are consistent with other findings in the literature. Maisonobe at al. (2016) who investigate patterns of collaboration within and between cities between 2000 and 2007, highlight the growth of intra-national collaborations in systems in which science at scale was then recent: PRC; Taipei,China; India; Iran; Turkey; Greece; the Czech Republic and Brazil. They also identify a pronounced growth of international collaboration in the English-speaking countries (p. 1029). Notwithstanding the inclusion of

Greece and Taipei,China, where national networking slows after 2007, among the national capacity-building systems, these findings are generally compatible with Table 3.2 and Figure 3.4. Kwiek (2020, p. 9), who focuses largely on Europe, notes that between 2009 and 2020 the worldwide proportion of papers that involved international collaboration rose by 5.9% while the proportion of papers that were nationally collaborative rose by 4.7%. In EU28 countries the international collaboration share rose by 10.6% while national collaboration share fell by 0.5%, though in most EU countries the absolute number of these papers rose as Figure 3.4 suggests. Kwiek also notes that the EU13 countries, that joined more recently and whose science systems have mostly emerged later than those of the original EU15, the national collaboration share rose by 2%, consistent with many other emerging systems.

National policies articulate network dynamics through negative as well as positive effects. Desultory national funding and coordination (for example, India and Poland); or, in mature systems, the cessation or slowdown of funding growth amid the global expansion of science (for example, in Japan and Taipei,China), may limit not only what nation-building in science can achieve but also the material capacity of scientists to collaborate globally. The limitation is more decisive at national than global level because leading researchers who generate a disproportionate share of highly cited science typically operate partly independent of their national systems.

In much of the scientometric literature, the rate of international collaboration is seen as correlated to performance. It is not so simple. This leads to varying judgments. Graf and Kalthaus (2018) identify an increase in degree centralization, meaning the concentration of networked activity in key countries. They also find that over time all high publishing systems come to join what they define as the central group at global level, including emerging PRC, ROK and Taipei, China (p. 7). However, they also remark that European countries are more intensively networked with other leading systems than are the Asian countries, which have a relatively larger focus on national collaborations. While scientists in Taipei,China and ROK "are very well connected nationally they are not as strongly connected internationally" as are systems of similar size and capacity in geographical Europe or European cultural outlier countries. "In general, Asian countries seem to have a higher degree of internal interaction than European countries in the last period" (p. 7). On this basis Graf and Kalthaus argue that despite their major growth in papers the Asian systems "do not fully exploit their knowledge sourcing potentials" (p. 12).

Yet as noted, the high rate of collaboration in Europe is partly determined by European funding and if Europe is treated as a single country for comparative purposes its rate of collaboration with the rest of the world converges with that of North America and Asia. Further, as Chinchilla-Rodriguez et al. (2019) note, there is no one single pattern in emerging countries with growing influence in science. East Asian countries and regions including PRC, Taipei,China and ROK, and some large systems elsewhere such as Iran and India, have a high ratio of national collaborations to international collaborations. Smaller countries like Azerbaijan, Peru and Panama "depend almost exclusively on international collaboration for their output, with low degrees of domestic collaboration and sole authorship" (p. 5). Some countries with relatively low rates of international collaboration, including PRC, Iran and Brazil, exhibit both robust national collaboration and regional leadership (p. 6). Nor does national science necessarily mean low citations. Adams (2013) found that in PRC, the top 10% of national-only papers had citation rates at double the world average (p. 558).

Like all national systems, emerging science countries must build robust capacity in order to both meet national policy objectives and enable nation-based scientists to participate effectively in global networks. However, emerging nations vary markedly in the relation between national collaboration building and international collaboration. International collaboration also varies in the extent to which it is sustained autonomously and realized as augmented national capacity. Small countries may have little choice but to be heavily dependent on internationalization. Larger ones can vary the extent to which they focus on establishing robust cooperation at national level across the range of research fields.

5   Conclusions

In sum, what then connects and combines the heterogeneous global and national science systems? First, they provide positive conditions for each other. International cooperation in science rests on nationally ordered infrastructures, while at the same time its fruits are seen to advance national development in science (Georghiou, 1998). These are the points most discussed in the literature. Second, there is the division of labour. The national and local scales foster science organically, providing it with a stable legal, institutional and financial framework and social circles, and connecting it to applications in policy, industry and community; while the global scale motivates collaboration, calibrates activity within a system of value, distributes status in science, and structures many of the leading conversations. Marginson (2018) discusses the case of PRC, showing how a global-national symbiosis was achieved by combining on one hand policy centralization and robust national system development, with on the other hand participation in global science. Researchers connected national science to the expanding global circuit, whose rapid growth after 1990 thereby helped to power national development of the national scientific infrastructure.

This combination was made possible because the national government provided scope for grass-roots initiative and open global connections, while at the same time the global system, especially in the United States, built open connections with science in PRC from the other end.

Science is always both global and national. If the global system generates status that trumps national esteem, the communities of scientists in the stronger research nations, however internationalist in outlook, are also shaped by a national-cultural solidarity that they maintain when they are inside world conversations. For example, there is close cooperation between the United States and PRC in science (Lee and Huapt, 2019). Researchers from these nations together published 55,382 science papers in 2018, much the largest country-to-country collaboration in world science. Yet each country exhibits an unquestionable potency of national identity and networks. The global science system and the national science system are held together by people and institutions with multiple presence in different scales. Leading scientists play global and local roles and are also nationally significant.

Wagner et al. (2015) are right to state that global and national networks shape each other (p. 11). However, it is more arguable whether there is a "growing divide between international and domestic research", or an "intellectual separation" (Adams, 2013, p. 559), or that the goals of international collaboration have become "decoupled" from national science (Wagner et al., 2015, p. 5). The point rather is that whatever its size, globally networked science is beyond the control or even the "gaze" of nation-states (King, 2011, p. 359). With the growth of globally connected activity the domain of science that has slipped, not beyond the influence of governments but beyond their full control, has grown. Without nations in any way withering in influence, the potential of global society is expanding.

Governments never effectively ordered science and globalization has expanded the scope for science to determine itself. How much that will happen is another question. The extent to which the relations between global science and national science are zero-sum or positive sum is a case by case matter. It varies across geo-political space and time. There are no laws of motion here. The outcomes accumulate, determined by the ongoing interactions between the heterogeneous agencies of national governments and networked scientists.

Acknowledgement

The research for this chapter took place in the ESRC/OFSRE Centre for Global Higher Education funded by the U.K. Economic and Social Research Council (award number ES/M010082/1).

References

Adams, J. (2013). The fourth age of research. *Nature, 497*, 557–560.

Adams, J., & Gurney, K. (2018). Bilateral and multilateral coauthorship and citation impact: Patterns in UK and US international collaboration. *Frontiers in Research Metrics and Analytics, 3*(12). https://doi.org/10.3389/frma.2018.00012

Anderson, B. (1983). *Imagined communities* (2nd ed.). Verso.

Bayly, C. (2004). *The birth of the modern world 1780–1914: Global connections and comparisons*. Blackwell.

Berlin, I. (1969). Two concepts of liberty. In I. Berlin (Ed.), *Four essays on liberty* (pp. 118–172). Oxford University Press.

Bornmann, L., Adams, J., & Leydesdorff, L. (2018). The negative effects of citing with a national orientation in terms of recognition: National and international citations in natural-sciences papers from Germany, the Netherlands, and the UK. *Journal of Informetrics, 12*, 931–949.

Bourdieu, P. (1993). *The field of cultural production*. Columbia University Press.

Cantwell, B., Marginson, S., & Smolentseva, A. (Eds.). (2018). *High participation systems of higher education*. Oxford University Press.

Castells, M. (2000). *Rise of the network society* (2nd ed.). Blackwell.

Castells, M. (2001). *The internet galaxy*. Oxford University Press.

Chinchilla-Rodriguez, Z., Miguel, S., Perianes-Rodriguez, A., & Sugimoto, C. (2018). Dependencies and autonomy in research performance: Examining nonoscience and nonotechnology in emerging countries. *Scientometrics, 115*, 1485–1504.

Chinchilla-Rodriguez, Z., Sugimoto, C., & Lariviere, V. (2019). Follow the leader: On the relationship between leadership and scholarly impact in international collaborations. *PLOS ONE, 14*(6), e0218309. https://doi.org/10.1371/journal.pone.0218309

Choi, S. (2012). Core-periphery, new clusters or rising stars? International scientific collaboration among "advanced" countries in the era of globalisation. *Scientometrics, 90*, 25–41.

Conrad, S. (2016). *What is global history?* Princeton University Press.

Etzkowitz, H., & Leydesdorff, L. (2000). The dynamics of innovation: From National System and "Mode 2" to a Triple Helix of university-industry-government relations. *Research Policy, 29*, 109–123.

Fligstein, N., & McAdam, D. (2012). *A theory of fields*. Oxford University Press.

Frenken, K. (2002). A new indicator of European integration and an application to collaboration in scientific research. *Economic Systems Research, 14*(4), 345–361.

Frenken, K., Hardeman, S., & Hoekman, J. (2009). Spatial scientometrics: Towards a cumulative research program. *Journal of Informetrics, 3*, 222–232.

Georgiou, L. (1998). Global cooperation in research. *Research Policy, 27*, 611–626.

Graf, H., & Kalthaus, M. (2018). International research networks: Determinants of country embeddedness. *Research Policy*. https://doi.org/10.1016/j.respol.2018.04.001

Gringas, Y. (2014, July 18). How to boost your university up the rankings. *University World News*. Retrieved June 23, 2020, from https://www.universityworldnews.com/post.php?story=20140715142345754

Grosetti, M., Eckert, D., Gringas, Y., Jegou, L., Lariviere, V., & Milard, B. (2013). Cities and the geographical deconcentration of scientific activity: A multilevel analysis of publications (1987–2007). *Urban Studies, 51*(1), 2219–2234.

Heilbron, J. (2013). The social sciences as an emerging global field. *Current Sociology, 62*(5), 685–703.

Held, D. (2003). *Global covenant: The social democratic alternative to the Washington Consensus*. Polity.

Held, D., McLew, A., Goldblatt, D., & Perraton, J. (1999). *Global transformations: Politics, economics and culture*. Stanford University Press

Hennemann, S., Rybski, D., & Liefner, I. (2012). The myth of global science cooperation – Collaboration patterns in epistemic communities. *Journal of Informetrics, 6*, 217–225.

Kato, M., & Ando, A. (2017). National ties of international scientific collaboration and researcher mobility found in Nature and Science. *Scientometrics, 110*, 673–694.

King, R. (2011). Power and networks in worldwide knowledge coordination: The case of global science. *Higher Education Policy, 24*, 359–376.

Kwiek, M. (2020). What large-scale publication and citation data tell us about international research collaboration in Europe; changing national patterns in global contexts. *Studies in Higher Education*. https://doi.org/10.1080/03075079.2020.1749254

Lee, J., & Haupt, J. (2019). Winners and losers in US-China scientific research collaborations. *Higher Education*. https://doi.org/10.1007/s10734-019-00464-7

Leydesdorff, L. (2007). Scientific communication and cognitive codification: Social systems theory and the sociology of scientific knowledge. *European Journal of Social Theory, 10*(3), 375–388.

Leydesdorff, L., & Wagner, C. (2008). International collaboration in science and the formation of a core group. *Journal of Informetrics, 2*, 317–325.

Luhmann, N. (1996). On the scientific context of the concept of communication. *Social Science Information, 35*(2), 257–267.

Luhmann, N. (2012). *Theory of society, Vol. 1* (R. Barrett, Trans.). Stanford University Press.

Maisonobe, M., Eckert, D., Grossetti, M., Jegou, L., & Milard, B. (2016). The world network of scientific collaborations between cities: Domestic or international dynamics? *Journal of Informetrics, 10*, 1025–1036.

Melin, G. (2000). Pragmatism and self-organization: Research collaboration on the individual level. *Research Policy, 29*, 31–40.

Marginson, S. (2010). Space, mobility and synchrony in the knowledge economy. In S. Marginson, P. Murphy, & M. Peters (Eds.), *Global creation: Space, mobility and synchrony in the age of the knowledge economy* (pp. 117–149). Peter Lang.

Marginson, S. (2018). National/global synergy in the development of higher education and science in China since 1978. *Frontiers of Education in China, 13*(4), 486–512.

National Science Board. (2020). *Science and engineering indicators 2020.* Retrieved June 23, 2020, from https://ncses.nsf.gov/pubs/nsb20201

Olechnicka, A., Ploszaj, A., & Celinska-Janowicz, D. (2019). *The geography of scientific collaboration.* Routledge.

Organization for Economic Cooperation and Development. (2020). *Science and technology indicators.* Retrieved June 23, 2020, from https://stats.oecd.org/Index.aspx?DataSetCode=MSTI_PUB

Packalen, M. (2019). Edge factors: Scientific frontier positions of nations. *Scientometrics, 118,* 787–808.

Powell, J., Fernandez, F., Crist, J., Dusdal, J., Zhang, L., & Baker, D. (2017). Introduction: The worldwide triumph of the research university and globalizing science. In J. Powell, D. Baker, & F. Fernandez (Eds.), *The century of science: The global triumph of the research university* (pp. 1–36). Emerald Publishing.

Ryan, J. (2014). The work motivation of research scientists and its effect on research performance. *R&D Management, 44*(4), 355–369.

Schott, T. (1998). Ties between centre and periphery in the scientific world-system; Accumulation of rewards, dominance and self-reliance in the centre. *Journal of World-Systems Research, 4,* 112–144.

Sen, A. (1985). Well-being, agency and freedom: The Dewey Lectures 1984. *The Journal of Philosophy, 82,* 169–221.

Wagner, C., & Leydesdorff, L. (2005). Network structure, self-organisation, and the growth of international collaboration in science. *Research Policy, 34,* 1608–1618.

Wagner, C., Park H., & Leydesdorff, L. (2015). The continuing growth of global cooperation networks in research: A conundrum for national governments. *PLoS ONE, 10*(7), e0131816. https://doi.org/10.1371/journal.pone.0131816

Wagner, C., Whetsell, T., & Leydesdorff, L. (2017). Growth of international collaboration in science: Revisiting six specialties. *Scientometrics, 111,* 1633–1652.

World Bank. (2020). *Data and statistics.* Retrieved June 23, 2020, from https://data.worldbank.org/indicator

Wuestman, M., Hoekman, J., & Fenken, K. (2019). The geography of scientific citations. *Research Policy.* https://doi.org/10.1016/j.respol.2019.04.004

CHAPTER 4

Do Rankings Promote Academic Excellence?

Redefining World-Class Universities

Jamil Salmi

Abstract

The introduction in 2003 of the Academic Ranking of World Universities on the global higher education scene, at the initiative of Shanghai Jiao Tong University, has had a profound and long-lasting impact on governments and universities alike. Governments have financed ambitious investment programmes to upgrade their universities. Universities, in turn, have eagerly joined this new "brain race". Too often, the rankings have become the milestones to guide institutional strategic plans and influence the motivation and behaviour of university leaders and academics. While many universities all over the world have indeed improved their research performance over the past decade, there are many signs that the kind of academic excellence promoted by the rankings is often side-tracking universities from contributing to progress in several crucial dimensions of human life, such as the inclusion of minorities, scientific truth, social justice, and sustainability. The Shanghai Principles launched in 2017 were an attempt in this direction, as a reminder to world-class university leaders of the social responsibility of their institutions of higher learning. Echoing the philosophy of the European Magna Charta Universitatum signed in 1988, the 2017 Shanghai Principles focus on social inclusion, scientific truth, ethical values, responsible research, and global solidarity as moral pillars for world-class universities.

Keywords

world-class universities – rankings – academic excellence – missing dimensions

1 Introduction

In the past, the role of government in nurturing the growth of elite research universities was not a critical factor. On the contrary, Oxford and Cambridge evolved over the centuries of their own volition, with variable levels of public funding, but with considerable autonomy in terms of governance, definition of mission, and strategic direction. Similarly, the history of the Ivy League universities in the United States reveals that, by and large, these elite institutions grew to prominence as a result of incremental progress rather than deliberate government intervention.

However, the advent of international rankings almost twenty years ago – pioneered by the first Academic Ranking of World Universities (ARWU, also called the Shanghai ranking) by Shanghai Jiao Tong University in 2003 and the subsequent emergence of competing global league tables (THE, HEEACT, QS, etc.) – has changed the university landscape in an irreversible way. Today, the creation of world-class universities has become part of the political agenda in many countries as a matter of national pride. A growing number of governments have launched excellence initiatives in one form or the other, consisting of large injections of additional funding to boost their university sector. This reflects an awareness that flagship institutions cannot emerge rapidly without a favourable policy environment, direct public initiative and significant financial support, if only because of the high costs involved in setting up advanced research facilities and capacities.

In an increasingly global and competitive world, governments want to make sure that their top universities are actually operating at the cutting edge of intellectual and scientific development. A growing priority has therefore been to identify the most effective method for inducing substantial and accelerated progress in a country's top universities. While a few nations have opted for establishing new universities from scratch, many countries have adopted a strategy combining mergers and upgrading of existing institutions.

Much progress has been achieved in the past twenty years. Countries that did not have a single university among the top ranked institutions are now present. New universities set up from scratch have shot to prominence, and old universities that were living complacently off their past glory have jumped to the fore again. It would appear that the global rankings have indeed played a positive role in boosting academic excellence in research.

But is it progress in the right direction? How can we reconcile advances in research power with lack of progress in tackling humanity's major challenges, such as hunger, poverty, disease, and environmental decay? Have the top-ranked universities become more inclusive or elitist? Are societies using the vast knowledge generated by world-class universities to make choices based on scientific evidence and rational political debate? Are the leading universities contributing to the construction of ethical and democratic societies?

Against this background, the main purpose of this chapter is to assess how the relatively limited definition of academic excellence driven by international rankings has influenced the behaviour and performance of existing and aspiring world-class universities. While the first section of the chapter analyses how international rankings have shaped national and institutional policies for the development of world-class universities, the second part assesses the main results that can be observed. The third and final section of the chapter explores important elements that are missing from the rankings' approach to the promotion of academic excellence, such as equity, truth, ethics, social commitment, and sustainability.

2   Impact of Rankings on Policies and Behaviours

> One thing is certain; rankings do not leave institutions and stakeholders indifferent. If their publication is eagerly anticipated by students, they are often dreaded by university administrators. International rankings generate pride and anger; the press and political parties are eager to use them as weapons against the government.
>
> SALMI AND SAROYAN (2007, p. 40)

2.1   *National Level*

When Vladimir Putin was reelected as president of Russia in 2012, one of his first declarations was a call for the transforming of the country's universities into world-class institutions, with the specific goal of having five Russian universities in the top 100 – hence the name Project 5-100 for the Russian Excellence Initiative. In November 2015, the President of India observed in an official address to the country's vice-chancellors that "India cannot aspire to be a world power without having a single world-class university". This was followed by the launch, in 2017, of the Institutes of Eminence programme. In May 2019, the Deputy Prime Minister of Poland signaled that "rankings ... have their import in the public domain. Rankings that contain indicators describing different entities or countries are used for benchmarking purposes, to see how well – or poorly – our country or our institution scores compared with the others". This was one of the factors leading to Poland's decision to invest in the emergence of world-class universities through its Excellence Initiative-Research University programme.

These kinds of public statements and initiatives are characteristic of the influence that the global rankings have had on the political scene of many countries in the past two decades, especially in East Asia and Europe. While the first excellence initiatives during the 1990s had more of an endogenous character, reflecting a long-term policy concern about boosting the contribution of universities to national economic development, especially in the Nordic countries and the People's Republic of China (PRC), the most recent wave seems to have been primarily induced by external considerations linked to the perception of a competitive disadvantage relative to the more stellar performance of foreign universities, as measured by the global rankings (Salmi, 2016).

Besides stimulating public investment in the university sector, the rankings have also induced healthy national conversations about the performance and contribution of universities. In France, for example, where the publication of the first Shanghai ranking had caused a mix of indignation and consternation because no French university appeared in the top 50, one of the country's leading education economists, François Orivel (2004), wrote a very lucid article analysing the reasons why French universities were not internationally competitive. One of the principal factors identified was the fact that French universities are not allowed to select the most academically qualified high school graduates. A unique feature of the French tertiary education system is the dual structure which separates the *Grandes Écoles* (top schools), which recruit the best students through very competitive national examinations, and the universities, to which all secondary school graduates have automatic access. Since the Grandes Écoles are predominantly elite professional schools that conduct little research, most doctoral students in the research universities do not come from the most academically qualified student groups, unlike the top British, Japanese or U.S. universities.

The other important factor is the existence of a large network of independent public research institutes (CNRS, INSERM, INRA, CEA, CNES, etc.) that, though embedded into the universities, operated until a few years ago more as competitors than collaborators. The resulting fragmentation of research capacity and resources has undermined the capacity of French universities to build centres of scientific excellence with a critical mass of researchers working on similar or complementary scientific areas (Le Prestre et al., 2018).

In Japan, similarly, the rankings have prompted a retrospective analysis of institutional performance and forward-looking benchmarking, leading to goal setting in support of ambitious national and institutional visions. This had led, in turn to the launch and implementation of important reforms toward quality improvement (Yonezawa et al., 2002).

Perhaps less beneficial have been policy decisions narrowly focused on the rankings. In Brazil, for instance, when the Government launched the Science without Borders programme in 2011 to send thousands of students to the best universities in the world, it initially restricted eligibility to receive Brazilian students with full scholarships to the top 100 universities globally, without realizing that some universities could enjoy some of the best niche disciplinary programmes in the world without being among the top 100 institutions. In countries as diverse as Brunei Darussalam, Chile, Colombia, Kazakhstan, Mongolia, Qatar, Saudi Arabia and Singapore, the agencies offering scholarships for studies overseas have restricted eligibility to students admitted in highly-ranked universities. In the same vein, donor agencies and foundations that provide scholarships for students from developing countries are increasingly looking at the results of rankings to establish their list of eligible destination institutions.

The global rankings have also influenced national decisions about university partnerships and immigration visas. In 2011, for example, India's University Grants Commission announced that Indian universities could no longer enter into partnership agreements with foreign universities that are not in the top 500 (Downing and Ganotice Fraide, 2016). A growing number of governments are even taking the results of global rankings into consideration to issue fast track visas to foreign graduates of top universities. The U.K. Treasury, for instance, considers the eligibility of foreign graduates to MBA programmes on the basis of the *Financial Times'* ranking. In the same vein, Denmark, the Netherlands, North Macedonia and Russia are looking at international rankings to make decisions about degree recognition and visa eligibility.

Finally, it is worth mentioning that, in some cases, governments unhappy with the results of their universities have tried to put political pressure on the ranking organizations themselves, alternatively threatening and cajoling. As a result, the team who originally designed and continues to prepare ARWU had to move its activity from Shanghai Jiao Tong University (SJTU) to an independent consulting firm in order to protect SJTU's leadership and the Chinese government from undue political pressure of diplomatic proportions from both industrial and developing nations.

2.2   *Institutional Level*

The sway of international rankings has perhaps been even stronger at the institutional level. A major positive development has been the growing reliance on the rankings for strategic planning and quality improvement purposes.

> In the 2014 report published by the European Universities Association (EUA), "Ranking in Institutional Strategies and Processes (RISP)", it was stated that two thirds of those who participated in the survey agreed that ranking results had influenced them when making their strategic, organizational, managerial and academic actions and decisions. (Downing and Ganotice Fraide, 2016, pp. 241–242)

Universities that look at detailed ranking data for benchmarking purposes, whether within a single country, across countries and over time, can use the results to inform their strategic thinking and planning. Areas of weakness and strength can be identified in that manner, and corrective actions can be defined. This is a healthy activity as long as universities do not agonize over their rank per se, or set themselves a specific rank to beat or achieve, but rather focus on specific indicators in order to better understand the determinants of their performance and work towards improving the quality of teaching, learning and research as may be the case.

Less helpful are the shortcuts that universities have sometimes taken in their quest to rise quickly in the rankings without necessarily building capacity in a genuine manner. Some universities approach academics in other institutions and pay them to add a second university affiliation, or they encourage them to provide positive feedback through the reputation surveys conducted by some of the global rankings, such as THE and QS. A number of Australian universities have hired "ranking managers" to provide guidance on how to better position their institution (MacGregor, 2013). The Russian Academy of Science recently ordered the retraction of at least 869 Russian scientific articles for plagiarism (Dixon, 2020). Observers have accused Saudi universities of artificially inflating their scientific output by contracting, on a part-time basis, highly-cited foreign researchers who accept to publish under the affiliation of the Saudi institution (Bhattacharjee, 2011). Another worrisome practice is the increasing reliance on rankings to determine new university partnership opportunities. Finally, some universities have entered into contractual relationships with commercial rankers with the expectation of boosting their standing in the respective rankings.

3 Performance of World-Class Universities after Twenty Years of ARWU

Analysing the results of the Academic Ranking of World Universities (ARWU) prepared by Shanghai Jiao Tong University (SJTU) may be the best way of assessing how world-class research-intensive universities have performed over the past twenty years for two reasons. First of all, ARWU is a stable ranking that offers the longest running set of data (2004–2019) without any change in the methodology of the ranking. Second, ARWU shares with the Leiden ranking the characteristic of working only with objective and transparent indicators that are publicly available, which makes it possible to duplicate and validate their results, unlike other rankings that give a substantial weight to the results of subjective reputation surveys.

The first set of data (Table 4.1) shows the country ranking based on the position of the highest ranked university of that country among the top 100

TABLE 4.1   Country rankings based on the ARWU results for the top 200 universities (2004 and 2019)

	2004			2019	
Country ranking	Country	Rank of top university in country	Country ranking	Country	Rank of top university in country
1	U.S.	1	1	U.S.	1
2	U.K.	3	2	U.K.	3
3	Japan	14	3	Switzerland	19
4	Canada	24	4	Canada	24
5	Switzerland	27	5	Japan	25
6	Netherlands	39	6	Denmark	26
7	France	41	7	France	37
8	Germany	45	8	Sweden	38
9	Sweden	46	9	Australia	41
10	Australia	53	10	PRC	43
11	Denmark	59	11	Germany	47
12	Russia	66	12	Netherlands	49
13	Norway	68	13	Norway	59
14	Finland	72	14	Finland	63
15	Austria	86	15	Belgium	66
16	Israel	90	16	Singapore	67
17	Italy	93	17	Israel	85
			18	Russia	87

Note: The countries in bold are those with an excellence initiative.
SOURCE: ARWU (HTTP://WWW.SHANGHAIRANKING.COM/)

universities in the world. At that level, few significant differences can be seen over the past sixteen years. Seventeen countries had at least one university in the top 100 back in 2004; the 2019 ranking includes 18 countries. At the top, Japan and Switzerland traded places (#3 and 5), and the Netherlands lost six places (from #6 to 12). Three countries that were not in the top 100 in 2004 have now joined: PRC (#10), Belgium (#15) and Singapore (#16). Conversely, two countries fell off, namely Austria and Italy. The only countries with noteworthy increases (at least 8 places) are Denmark (+20), Australia (+9) and Switzerland (+8). At the bottom, PRC had the strongest jump, from 201–300 to 101–150. Three higher education systems that were not present in 2004 have joined the top 200:

Hong Kong, China; Ireland; and Taipei,China. Three countries saw their position decrease markedly: Austria, Israel and Italy. However, in as far as this table reflects only what happened to the highest ranked university in each country, it is hard to infer any causal relationship with the existence of an excellence initiative in the respective countries, except perhaps in the case of Beijing University and the University of Copenhagen, which both had a significant jump.

Following the evolution of the WCU concentration index over the years gives a more precise picture of progress and decline. Figures 4.1 and 4.2 calculate the WCU concentration index as the number of universities each country places among the top 100 globally relative to its population (using the Logarithmic value of the population).

Table 4.2 summarizes the results of the comparison between the two figures. The most significant change is the progress made by small countries.

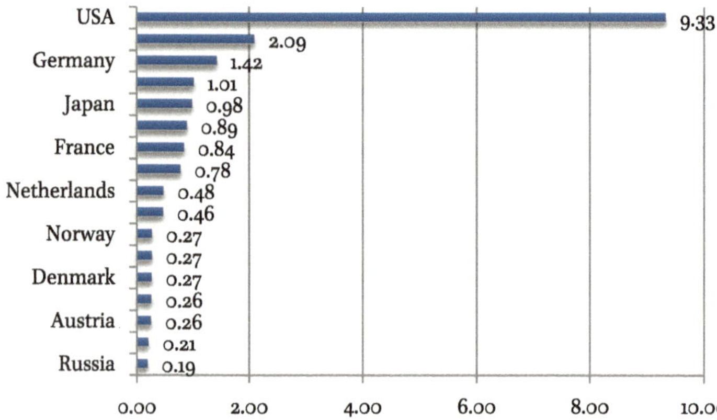

FIGURE 4.1　WCU concentration index (2004) (Source: ARWU and World Population Data)

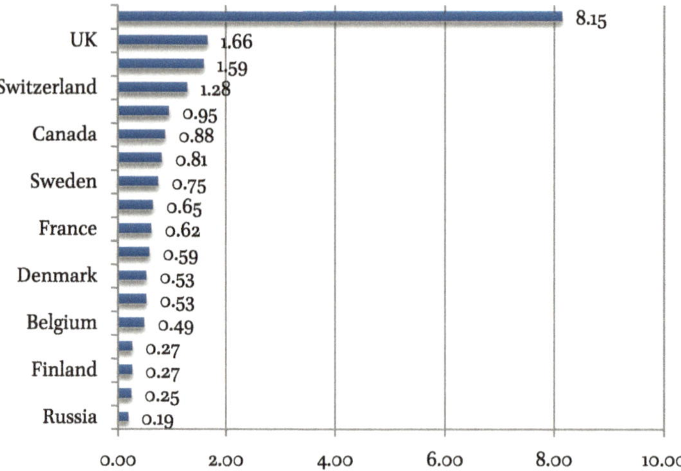

FIGURE 4.2　WCU concentration index (2019) (Source: ARWU and World Population Data)

TABLE 4.2   Comparison of 2004 and 2019 results

2004			2019		
Country	Number of universities	Country rank	Country	Number of universities	Country rank
U.S.	51	1	U.S.	45	1
U.K.	10	2	U.K.	8	2
Germany	7	3	**Australia**	7	3
Sweden	4	4	Switzerland	5	4
Japan	5	5	Netherlands	4	5
Canada	4	6	**Canada**	4	6
France	4	7	**Germany**	4	7
Switzerland	3	8	Sweden	3	8
Netherlands	2	9	PRC	4	9
Australia	2	10	**France**	3	10
Norway	1	11	**Japan**	3	11
Finland	1	12	**Denmark**	2	12
Denmark	1	13	**Singapore**	2	12
Israel	1	14	Belgium	2	14
Austria	1	15	**Finland**	1	15
Italy	1	16	**Norway**	1	15
Russia	1	17	**Israel**	1	17
–	–	–	**Russia**	1	18

Note: The countries in bold are those with an excellence initiative.
SOURCE: ARWU AND WORLD POPULATION DATA

While 5 out of the 7 leading countries in 2004 were large countries (United States, United Kingdom, Japan, Germany and France), the picture had changed substantially by 2019, with four small population countries among the top 6 (Australia, Switzerland, Netherlands and Canada). Despite two rounds of excellence initiative, Germany moved down from third to seventh position, and France came down from 7th to 10th. By contrast, Australia climbed in an impressive manner from 10th to third. The United States and the United Kingdom lost 8 universities altogether. Japan moved down from 5th to 11th.

Finally, it is instructive to look at which universities have most improved and most regressed in the ranking over the 16-year span.[1] While there has hardly been any change among the top 20 universities in the world, Table 4.3 shows

TABLE 4.3   List of top 100 universities with highest progress since 2004

University	Country	# of positions gained
Shanghai Jiao Tong University	PRC	368
Zhejiang University	PRC	280
Nanyang Technological University	Singapore	277
Tsinghua University	PRC	207
Peking University	PRC	197
Monash University	Australia	177
Technion Institute of Technology	Israel	165
Erasmus University Rotterdam	Netherlands	107
The University of Texas M. D. Anderson Cancer Ctr.	U.S.	107
Swiss Federal Institute of Technology Lausanne	Switzerland	97
The University of New South Wales	Australia	81
The University of Western Australia	Australia	76
The University of Queensland	Australia	71
University of Geneva	Switzerland	67
Aarhus University	Denmark	65
University of Groningen	Netherlands	60
Ghent University	Belgium	59
National University of Singapore	Singapore	58
The University of Manchester	U.K.	45
University of Sydney	Australia	45
The University of Melbourne	Australia	41
KU Leuven	Belgium	40
University of Copenhagen	Denmark	33
University of Bonn	Germany	29
King's College London	U.K.	26
Stockholm University	Sweden	24
University of North Carolina at Chapel Hill	U.S.	23

SOURCE: ARWU

that the highest jumps were achieved by four top Chinese universities, Singapore's Nanyang Polytechnic, and several Australian universities. Substantial progress was also achieved by two Swiss universities, two Danish universities, two U.S. institutions, two Belgium universities, and one university each from Israel and the Netherlands.

As indicated by Table 4.4, the great majority of universities that have lost significant numbers of places are from the United States. One university each from Australia, Canada and Russia also appear in the table. This does not mean in any way that these universities are not great academic institutions any more, only that their academic output has increased less rapidly than other universities in the top 100.

It is difficult to assess in a conclusive way the extent to which past and present excellence initiatives explain the success or demise of individual universities. The availability of additional resources is certainly a necessary condition. These higher levels of funding may come from excellence initiatives, as in the case of Australia, PRC, Denmark and Singapore, or from high levels of public funding in a sustained way, as in Switzerland. But various studies have confirmed that it was not sufficient to explain the relative progress of countries and universities (Salmi, 2017; Usher and Ramos, 2018).

Perhaps more important than financing, various works point to the crucial role of governance in explaining the success of world-class universities (Aghion at al., 2009; Salmi, 2011). An adequate governance structure and favourable regulatory conditions help promote innovative behaviour among tertiary education institutions. Universities that are fully autonomous are not constrained by externally imposed regulations and can, as a result, manage their resources – financial, or human – with more flexibility in their search for academic excellence.

TABLE 4.4   List of top 100 universities with greatest decline since 2004

University	Country	# of positions lost
Rice University	U.S.	−20
Moscow State University	Russian Federation	−21
The Australian National University	Australia	−23
University of California, Irvine	U.S.	−25
The Ohio State University – Columbus	U.S.	−27
University of Florida	U.S.	−28
McGill University	Canada	−29
Carnegie Mellon University	U.S.	−33
University of Pittsburgh	U.S.	−41
University of California, Davis	U.S.	−48
Pennsylvania State University – University Park	U.S.	−55

SOURCE: ARWU

Among the various governance dimensions, leadership seems to be one of the most important drivers of transformation and progress at the institutional level, resulting in higher levels of performance and international visibility (Altbach et al., 2018). This is heavily influenced by the mode of university leaders selection. Several countries, Denmark and Finland for instance, have moved in recent years from a popular election process among members of the academic community to a professional selection approach led by empowered, independent university boards, following the tradition of Australia, Canada, Ireland, the United Kingdom and the United States. Analysing the leadership selection modalities for the top 100 universities in ARWU over time provides a useful illustration in that respect (Table 4.5). It shows the number of top 100 universities whose leader is selected through a professional search increased from 71 to 77 between 2004 and 2019, while the number of ranked universities with some form of election process went down from 28 to 18.

The case of Denmark is particularly relevant in that context. It is one of the few countries that has embodied its excellence initiative in an overall governance reform aimed at making the universities more flexible, including shifting from the democratic election of the university rector to an international professional search led by a newly-configured university board with a majority of independent external members. This high degree of alignment between the additional financial resources and the new governance framework explains, to a large extent, the rapid rise of the leading Danish universities in ARWU. Between 2004 and 2019, the University of Copenhagen gained thirty-three spots, from 59 to 26. Even more impressive was the progress of Aarhus University, the nation's second top university, which emerged from the 101–150 group in 2004 to climb to number 60 in 2019.

By contrast, the number of top ranked universities from France and Germany, two countries where the Excellence Initiative did not include significant changes in the governance arrangements, went down from 7 to 4, and 4 to 3, respectively, over the last sixteen years. These governance considerations also help to understand the absence of Southern European and Latin American universities from the top 100 (Salmi, 2014).

4   Missing Dimensions of Academic Excellence[2]

A university is not about results in the next quarter, it is not even about who a student has become by graduation. It is about learning that moulds a lifetime; learning that transmits the heritage of millennia; learning that shapes the future .... Universities make commitments to the timeless, and

TABLE 4.5   Selection modalities of leaders of top 100 universities in ARWU (2004–2019)

Professional search led by university board	Collegial election	Government appointment
2004		
U.S. (51)	Japan (5)	Russia (1)
U.K. (9)	Switzerland (2)	
Australia (2)	Germany (7)	
Canada (4)	France (4)	
Netherlands (2)	Sweden (4)	
Switzerland (1)	Belgium (2)	
Denmark (1)	Norway (1)	
Israel (1)	Austria (1)	
	Italy (1)	
	Finland (1)	
Total: 71	*Total: 28*	*Total: 1*
2019		
U.S. (45)	Japan (3)	PRC (4)
U.K. (8)	Switzerland (2)	Russia (1)
Australia (7)	Germany (4)	
Canada (4)	France (3)	
Netherlands (4)	Sweden (3)	
Switzerland (3)	Belgium (2)	
Denmark (2)	Norway (1)	
Israel (1)		
Finland (1)		
Singapore (2)		
Total: 77	*Total: 18*	*Total 5*

SOURCE: ARWU

these investments have yields we cannot predict and often cannot measure ... [that] we pursue ... in part 'for their own sake', because they define what has over centuries made us human, not because they can enhance our global competitiveness.

DREW FAUST, President of Harvard University (2007 Inaugural speech)

The poet and literary critic T. S. Elliot once asked: "Where is the wisdom we have lost in knowledge?" The same question could be probed about the pursuit of academic excellence by universities, under the influence of the global rankings. What are the rankings actually measuring? Many researchers have documented how, under the guise of measuring research output in various forms, the rankings are mainly selling international visibility (Bekhradnia, 2016; Hazelkorn, 2017; Rauhvargers, 2013).

The narrow focus on research excellence means that other equally important facets of a university's mission may be lost. At least five questions must be raised in that respect: How do world-class universities contribute to the social mobility agenda? How effective are they in upholding scientific evidence principles? Are they promoters of ethical behaviours? How relevant is their research to help solve societal problems? Do they contribute to the global sustainability agenda?

4.1   *Equity*

> Equality of opportunity: the impertinent courtesy of an invitation offered to unwelcome guests, in the certainty that circumstances will prevent them from accepting it.
>
> R. H. TAWNEY

In the search for academic excellence, many top universities have become more selective, which bears the risk of keeping talented students from low-income or those from low cultural capital families away. This trend brings about more elitism and greater disparities in tertiary education. The best-ranked institutions in India, the Indian Institutes of Technology, are the most selective tertiary education institutions in the world, with an admission ratio of one to three percent. The Ivy League universities are the most selective universities in the United States, admitting one out of every 10–15 candidates. Research has shown that the average SAT score of students accepted into top U.S. universities, which is closely correlated with their socio-economic background, has risen steadily in recent years (Gladwell, 2011). Table 4.6, which contrasts the proportion of Pell Grants beneficiaries enrolled in selective and less selective top U.S. universities, offers concrete evidence of the lack of inclusion of many world-class universities.[3] At the same time, these universities run considerable budget surpluses year after year, which would allow them to offer more scholarships and grants to low-income students. Between 2012 and 2015, for example, Harvard University's average annual surplus amounted to $1.2 billion, Yale's was $970 million and Stanford's $840 million (Carnevale and van der Werf, 2017).

The socio-economic distribution of students at leading public universities in California shows clearly that achieving world-class status is not incompatible

TABLE 4.6   Proportion of low-income students at top U.S. universities

More inclusive universities	Proportion of Pell Grant recipients	Less inclusive universities	Proportion of Pell Grant recipients
University of California-Los Angeles	35.9%	Stanford University	15.6%
University of California-Berkeley	31.4%	University of Pennsylvania	14.4%
University of Southern California	23.4%	Duke University	14.0%
Ohio State University-Columbus	22.4%	Northwestern University	14.0%
New York University	21.5%	Harvard University	13.0%
Columbia University	21.4%	Yale University	11.9%
University of Missouri-Columbia	21.4%	California Institute of Technology	11.3%
University of North Carolina-Chapel Hill	21.3%	University of Notre Dame	11.2%

SOURCE: CARNEVALE AND VAN DER WERF (2017)

with being more inclusive; quite the opposite. UCLA and UC-Berkeley are ranked 11th and 5th in the world in the 2019 ARWU, while having one of the highest proportions of low-income students among research-intensive universities.

Similarly, in the United Kingdom, policy makers and researchers have observed for many years the non-abating elitist nature of the top universities. David Lammy, who was Minister for Higher Education from 2007 to 2010, has been calling for a centralized admission system in the United Kingdom to improve access.

> Oxford and Cambridge are "two institutions that are wholly unrepresentative of the country at large and taking the overwhelming majority of their students from a small, privileged minority in the south of England … In 2012, both Oxford and Cambridge granted 79% of offers to children in the top two social classes – the sons and daughters of barristers, doctors and chief executives – a figure that rose to 82% and 81% respectively in 2015. There are more offers made to students from one school – Eton –

than students on free school meals across the whole country ... Only one in four Cambridge colleges made offers to black British students in every year between 2010 and 2015. Of those, many made just one or two offers apiece. And each year over that period, a quarter of colleges failed to make any offers at all to black British applicants. (Lammy, 2017)

Figure 4.3, which shows the proportion of Black students at Oxford and Cambridge, illustrates the huge gap compared to the average proportion across British universities.

A 2018 study by the Higher Education Policy Institute revealed that, among the 132 universities operating in the United Kingdom, the bottom ten in terms of social equality at admissions – using their address as a proxy of socio-economic level – were Cambridge (worst case), St Andrews, Bristol, Oxford, Aberdeen, Edinburgh, University College London, Durham, Robert Gordon, and the London School of Economics (SI, 2018). Five of these are among the top 100 universities in ARWU.

Another proxy to measure the degree of social selectivity of British universities is to look at the proportion of incoming students who attended a government high school, in a country where most children from elite families are enrolled in private schools (ironically called public schools). Table 4.7 presents data for eight U.K. universities appearing in the top 100 of ARWU, showing a significantly higher proportion of incoming students from elite private schools. The University of Manchester is the only outlier, five percentage points below

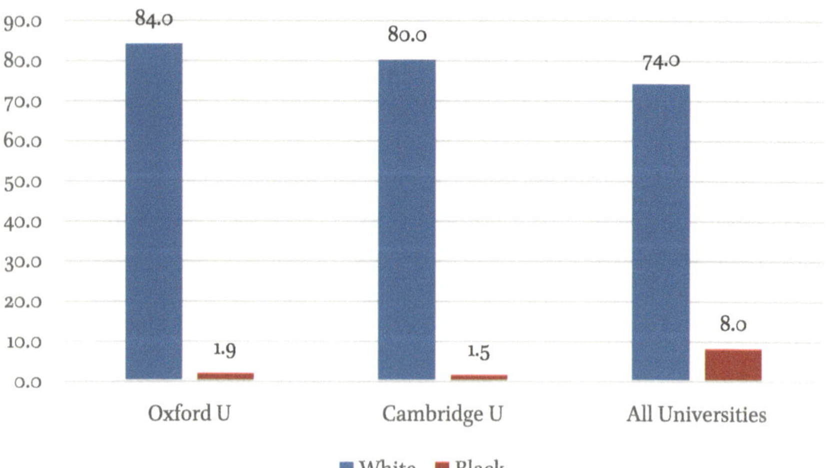

FIGURE 4.3   Proportion of black students (2018) (Source: Higher Education Statistics Authority)

TABLE 4.7   Proportion of students from state schools enrolled in top 100 British universities (2018–2019)

University	ARWU rank	Proportion of students from state schools
University of Cambridge	3	65.3%
University of Oxford	7	60.6%
University College London	15	65.9%
Imperial College London	23	67.1%
The University of Edinburgh	31	65.4%
The University of Manchester	33	85.4%
King's College London	51	77.8%
University of Bristol	64	67.6%
National average	–	**90.2%**

SOURCE: ARWU AND HIGHER EDUCATION STATISTICS AUTHORITY

the national average. Oxford University is the most elitist institution among the eight top U.K. universities.

By contrast, the Nordic countries are able to place universities in the top 100 with admission systems that are much more open than those of U.S. and U.K. universities. Using parental education as a proxy of income, Table 4.8 presents the probability of attending tertiary education relative to the level of educational attainment of one's parents in select countries having universities in the top 100. The odds ratio shown in the second column represents the likelihood of attending tertiary education of people whose parents have themselves completed tertiary education relative to individuals whose parents have only below upper secondary education. For example, looking at the OECD average, students from the most educated families are 4.5 times more likely to attend tertiary education as students from poorer families. Finland has the most egalitarian higher education system in Europe. Switzerland and the United States stand at the other extreme, with a probability almost 7 times higher.

4.2   *Truth*

... at present universities are confronted with a societal change so fundamental it is hard to know how it will turn out. The very essence of a university, is seems, is under threat. Throughout the history of universities, the

TABLE 4.8   Likelihood of participating in tertiary education relative to parents' educational attainment (2012)

Countries	Probability of attending tertiary education (odds ratio)
Australia	4.3
Canada	2.6
Denmark	3.0
Finland	1.4
Netherlands	2.8
Norway	2.0
Sweden	2.3
Switzerland	6.8
United Kingdom (England)	6.3
United States	6.8
OECD average	**4.5**

SOURCE: OECD EDUCATION AT A GLANCE (2014, TABLE A4.1B)

> exercise of reason, the pursuit of knowledge and the search for truth have enjoyed the respect and support of society. But no longer. Or at least no longer to the extent to which universities have always taken such respect for granted. It is hard to think of any earlier time when the very concept of truth itself has been undermined and constrained as at present.
>
> BRINK, former vice-chancellor of the University of Newcastle (2018)

The Covid-19 pandemic has revealed, in the most dramatic way, the importance of relying on scientific evidence to drive public policy and save human lives. In the post-truth world, building up and spreading critical thinking are absolutely essential. Universities have the responsibility to teach how to distinguish real evidence from fabricated information. Truth-seeking skills, the foundation of a genuine liberal arts education, should be at the core of every curriculum. In the current populist times, politicians and demagogues appeal more to emotion than reason, spreading pseudoscience, denial of facts, and conspiracy theories about a wide range of topics including climate change, infectious diseases and vaccines (Knobel, 2020). Today more than ever, universities should put emphasis on epideictic, the branch of rhetoric that explains why emotion and personal belief can be manipulated at the detriment of reason and facts.[4]

Digital platforms and social media, originally presented as the ultimate empowering tools, are becoming the greatest threat to free thought and democracy in history. The very idea of something going viral is an expression of the mob more than of the individual. The fact that search engines mostly rank search results based on the number of linked sites reinforces group thinking, not individuality. The entire logic of the Web works toward popularity rather than accuracy. As observed by Kaplan (2018), the fight for democracy has become synonymous with the fight for objectivity. In a recent interview, the former British Minister for Higher Education David Lammy observed that, in "the age of populism" academics have a duty to "stand brave and tall and communicate quite strongly the dangers that could lie ahead for the global world" (THE, 2019).

World-class universities should lead in upholding the academic tradition of free and fair debate that has been undermined by relativism and political correctness. They are well-placed to offer a safe space to present and assess a diversity of views and also engage with society in public debates on complex issues. The rector of the University of Belgrade, Ivanka Popovic, suggested in 2019 that the fight against fake news could become the fourth mission of the University, acting as the conscience of society.

Multi-disciplinary perspectives are often necessary for that purpose. Universities are among the few institutions that have this expertise, which is essential to nourish objective reflection, and to influence public policies on the basis of facts and scientific evidence. As van der Zwaan (2017, p. 182) wrote, "In the future, the university may well derive its most important form of legitimacy from its visibility and leadership in society. Despite the fact that public discourse is showing less and less interest in complexity, tackling complex problems is one of the university's key strengths".[5]

As part of their contribution to the public good, world-class universities can use multiple channels to communicate with the outside world and reach a large audience locally, regionally and globally. A good example of such practice is the yearly Lorne-Trottier Public Science Symposium Series, launched by McGill University in 2016, to communicate science responsibly to the public in these troubled times. Imperial College London has set up a free eight-week online course on the Coursera platform, called "Science Matters: Let's Talk about COVID-19".

An important challenge in that respect is the growing tension between the search for excellence and constraints to full academic freedom, which has traditionally regarded as a fundamental characteristic of universities.

> The essentiality of freedom in the community of American universities is almost self-evident … To impose any straitjacket upon the intellectual leaders in our colleges and universities would imperil the future of our

> Nation ... Scholarship cannot flourish in an atmosphere of suspicion
> and distrust. Teachers and students must always remain free to inquire,
> to study and to evaluate, to gain new maturity and understanding. (U.S.
> Chief Justice Earl Warren in 1957, quoted in Currie et al., 2006, p. 23)

Several excellence initiatives have been launched in countries with limited
democracy – PRC, Hungary, Iran, Russia, Saudi Arabia, Turkey and Viet Nam
to name a few and – it remains to be seen whether top universities can operate with sustained outstanding results where academic freedom is restricted.
While it is a somewhat lesser constraint in the hard sciences – although government control of the Internet constrains the scope of research of all scholars
alike – it certainly hinders the ability of social scientists to conduct scientific
inquiries on issues that may be seen by authoritarian governments as politi-
cally sensitive. For example, Hungary recently eliminated funding for gender
studies (Oppenheim, 2018). In 2015, the Chinese Minister of Education told
universities to shun textbooks that promote Western values, indicating that
academics should refrain from criticizing the Communist Party (Li, 2015). The
principle of "freedom of thought" was recently removed from the Charter of
three leading Chinese universities, including Fudan (The Guardian, 2019).
These new restrictions may undermine the efforts of Chinese universities to
improve their research performance.

4.3   *Ethics*

> No culture can rest on a crooked relationship to truth.
> ROBERT MUSIL

Considering that the graduates of the most prestigious universities in the
world are destined to occupy important authority functions in government
and industry, it is important to ask the question raised by the Belgian philosopher Pascal Chabot (2017, p. 56), "doesn't a great power require an education
that leaves space to doubt, philosophize and for a long ethical initiation?"

Another central question is the extent to which world-class universities promote ethical behaviours in the way they operate as institutions and in their
relationship with the outside world. This starts with upholding high principles within the university community itself to prevent and punish academic
dishonesty. Oxford University, for example, has a strict Code of Honor for this
purpose, which spells out the expectations pertaining to the standards of ethics and integrity in research, ethical and legal obligations, and potential conflicts of interest. The code further provides a definition of misconduct, sets out

the responsibilities of the university members, and covers the confidentiality related to investigations in potential instances of misconduct. It also defines the process for handling potential instances of misconduct, comprising the specific steps to be followed as well as the link of university internal procedures to other processes, such as legal ones.[6]

World-class universities must define and enforce strict standards with respect to fraud in examinations and research, as well as any form of aggressive behaviours on campus, including sexual violence, discrimination, harassment and bullying. Australia's chief scientist, Alan Finkel, made a recent plea for closer involvement of research grant agencies in monitoring research integrity that is being tested by the rankings-induced push to publish (Finkel, 2019). Observers have complained about the frequent use of non-disclosure agreements by British universities to suppress reports of misbehaviour by harassment victims (Murphy, 2019).

An aspect that the rankings are not well-designed to assess is whether the graduates are well prepared ethically, besides their general education and professional training. For instance, after the 2007–2008 financial crisis triggered by the subprime mortgage crisis, itself caused by the unregulated use of derivatives, many voices challenged the lack of emphasis on corporate responsibility in the programmes of business schools.

American business schools trained many of the people who had their hands on the tiller when the nation's economic ship ran aground. Now, those in leadership positions at top schools are asking themselves what degree of responsibility they bear. The schools had critics before the economic crisis cost millions of Americans their jobs and their retirement savings. Now, the critics are louder, and the questions they raise are being taken more seriously. 'This is a time of great introspection for this institution', says Jay Light, dean of the Harvard Business School.[7]

A recent study undertaken in Colombia, South America, is quite telling in that regard. The think tank that led this investigation looked at the highest university degree obtained by 110 famous politicians or business people who had been charged with corruption or other serious crimes in the previous two years and correlated this information with the university where they studied in Colombia. Table 4.9 shows the top universities appearing in this kind of "criminals ranking" from the viewpoint of their graduates, together with the academic excellence ranking prepared by the Colombian Ministry of Education (MIDE ranking). It is worrisome to observe that the top three ranked universities, according to the Government of Colombia's own ranking of academic excellence, are respectively number three, five and seven in the corruption ranking. The professions with the highest concentration of corrupt people

TABLE 4.9   Corruption ranking and excellence ranking in Colombia (2017)

University	Corruption ranking	Excellence ranking	Status
Universidad Externado de Colombia	1	15	Private
Universidad Pontificia Javeriana	2	7	Private
Universidad Los Andes	3	1	Private
Universidad Santo Tómas	4	49	Private
Universidad Nacional de Colombia	5	2	Public
Universidad Libre	5	50–100	Private
Universidad del Rosario	7	3	Private
Universidad de Antioquia	8	6	Public
Universidad del Norte	8	11	Private

SOURCE: OBSERVATORIO DE LA UNIVERSIDAD COLOMBIANA (2017) AND COLOMBIAN MINISTRY OF EDUCATION

were lawyers (43%) and business people (28%). As Don Winslow ironically observed in his novel The Border, "What is the difference between a hedge fund manager and a cartel boss? Wharton Business School" (p. 105).

Third, world-class universities have a duty to avoid conflict of interest in their dealings with the political and business world to preserve their intellectual independence. As the rector of the Free University of Brussels declared in his 2002 commencement address, "in democratic societies, universities must absolutely keep their independence, towards both government and the private sector. The press that is controlled by financial interests with profit targets has lost much of its counter power legitimacy … We must ensure that universities serve society not only through education and research but also indirectly through their critical views" (de Maret, 2007, p. 96).

One of the relevant elements in that respect is transparency in setting and applying strict rules regarding the type of research activities universities want to be involved in and from which donors they are willing to accept fund raising contributions. The University of Hong Kong, for example, has traditionally shied away from receiving any donations from companies manufacturing arms and tobacco products. By contrast, MIT's image was recently damaged when it became public that the Media Lab had accepted financial donations from the condemned sexual offender and mogul Jeffrey Epstein. Both Harvard University and MIT have been criticized in recent years for their financial ties with the Government of Saudi Arabia.

Lastly, in recent years, a few universities have tried to reexamine their past with a critical eye and acknowledge their close association with ugly moments in their country's history, such as slavery, apartheid or discrimination towards native population groups. In the United States, Brown University, Yale, and Georgetown have struggled to come to terms with their slave-owning beginnings. Even the land-grant universities have been challenged to recognize that the Morrill Act of 1862, which appropriated land to fund them at the beginning of their history, was in fact the result of land grabbing from Native American people by the U.S. government to create endowments for new universities.

> The Morrill Act was a wealth transfer disguised as a donation ... An investigation ... found that the act redistributed nearly 11 million acres, which is almost the size of Denmark. The grants came from more than 160 violence-backed land cessions made by close to 250 tribal nations. When adjusted for inflation, the windfall netted 52 universities roughly half a billion dollars. (Ahtone and Lee, 2020)

In the United Kingdom, University College London set up a database of British slave-owners, which has been influential in pushing universities in Bristol, Edinburgh, Glasgow, London and Liverpool to take a hard look at how they benefited from slavery and the slave economy (The Economist, 2020). In South Africa, the #RhodesMustFall movement that started in 2015 at Cape Town University has led to heated debates and violent actions against historical symbols of apartheid at the country's former white universities and widespread efforts to decolonize the curriculum. Finally, in Australia, Canada and New Zealand, a growing number of colleges and universities have launched "reconciliation initiatives" with the aim of offering increased opportunities to students and staff from Aboriginal groups, honoring Aboriginal peoples and their culture, forging deeper links with their communities, and developing intercultural dialogue and collaboration. In the wake of the 2020 incidents of racist police behaviour in North America, a number of Canadian academics have called severing research partnerships with law enforcement authorities to "confront the underlying racism and colonization of police violence" (Quan, 2020).

4.4   *Commitment*

The main aspect that the global rankings identify well is the ability of world-class universities to conduct excellent "blue sky" research. But the high publication count and superior H-index of researchers affiliated with top universities do not say much about the relevance and impact of their research, nor do they measure the extent to which universities engage actively with society and the economy to help solve real problems and address global challenges. Each university follows a distinct path in that respect, and the rankings are not designed to capture these differences. In fact, research has shown that the search for global visibility often pushes world-class universities to collaborate with other highly-ranked institutions in other corners of the world instead of engaging closely with their local community (Hazelkorn, 2020a).

In this respect, the contrast between the experiences of Oxford and Cambridge in the development of linkages with the local economy is very illustrative. Both universities share a similar history and stem from the same academic culture. They are both considered among the best universities in the world. And yet, when it comes to the impact on their respective city, Oxford and Cambridge have followed divergent paths and achieved strikingly different results. Oxford remains an old-fashioned university city, whereas Cambridge has become the "most exciting technology cluster in Europe". What begun in the 1970s with the creation of business parks to welcome entrepreneurial academics and their doctoral students has evolved into a hub of 4,000 knowledge-intensive firms in electronics, pharmaceutics, biotechnology and other frontier domains. It is today the most dynamic place in Europe where professors, Nobel Prize scientists and angel investors plot their next startup. With a productivity level 30% higher than London's, Cambridge generates more patents than its next six British rivals taken together, it hosts more billion-dollar firms than cities ten times bigger, and it boasts near full employment.

The secret to Cambridge's success seems to lie in a balanced approach combining enlightened policies to provide the right infrastructure and economic environment, and a laissez-faire attitude that trusts human ingenuity and serendipity. On the one hand, the university, the city council and the neighbouring authorities have worked in a coordinated way to create a favourable ecosystem by setting up science parks and incubators, encouraging the development of business and housing estates, attracting investors and lobbying the government for more open immigration policies. On the other hand, they have kept away from imposing strategic priorities and micromanaging the city's economic development. The city does not decide what type of high-tech industry is more likely to become tomorrow's industry, and the university gives incentives to academics interested in setting up companies, making the membrane between its laboratories and private firms as porous as possible. This has resulted in dynamic partnerships where firms provide advice free of charge and invite students to help them, while academics and angel investors work together to chaperon new companies (The Economist, 2015).

This does not mean that Oxford University's research output is less relevant; quite the opposite. For example, a team of medical researchers from Oxford has been at the forefront of the development of a vaccine against Covid-19. In fact, the proliferation of university-based initiatives throughout the world during the pandemic has come as a welcome reminder of the importance of their civic engagement role.

> Armies of students in health-related fields are volunteering in hospitals and other public places as needed. Engineering students are creating face shields for first responders and health workers. Chemistry students are producing sanitizers and the chemical agents that hospitals need. Academic staff have also sprung into action. University labs are producing coronavirus test kits. Medical faculties are donating their ventilators, facemasks and other personal safety equipment. (Sursock, 2020)

While the rankings are not constructed to take this relevance dimension into consideration, an exception is the new ranking of university contributions to the Sustainable Development Goals (SDGs), introduced in 2019 by Times Higher Education (THE).[8] The so-called "impact ranking" is based on submissions made by interested universities, providing data, evidence and examples against at least three SDGs of their choice and SDG-17 (international cooperation). THE received submissions from about 500 institutions in the first year and 858 in 2020. As reported by Ellen Hazelkorn and Angel Calderon (2020), the methodology assesses activity against four dimensions: teaching, research, stewardship, and outreach. Research data from Elsevier account for 27% of the weight used to measure the respective contribution of each SDG. The overall score is calculated on the basis of the three highest SDG scores plus each university's performance against SDG-17.

Comparing the list of top 100 universities in the SDG ranking and with those in ARWU yields interesting information. None of the top 20 world-class universities, as identified by ARWU, appear in the SDG ranking, most likely because they did not show any inclination to participate. In total, only 12 among the Shanghai top 100 are in the top 100 THE impact ranking. As revealed by Table 4.10, they all rank higher in the impact ranking, except for the University of Toronto, the University of Tokyo, and the University of Helsinki. For lack of access to the actual data used by THE to assess these universities' contribution, it is not clear whether their lower rank is due to the fact that they conduct more blue-sky research or to data problems.

Like any ranking, this SDG ranking has several methodological flaws. There is a strong element of built-in subjectivity stemming from the difficulty for THE to validate the accuracy and comparability of the information submitted by the universities (Hazelkorn, 2020b). The actual results and weights used to arrive at the ranking are not published by THE. Also, the number of universities included in the ranking is very small compared to the global universe of institutions. One reason for this is that preparing a complete submission requires a lot of work and information, which few universities in the world have the capacity to do. As observed by Calderon (2020), "… Of the 164 institutions which were able to submit data on all 17 SDGs, 95 were from high-income economies, largely drawn from the East Asia and the Pacific and Western Europe regions. There were 124 institutions from lower middle-income economies which submitted data on at least four SDGs and which were therefore given an overall rank". As a result, the ranking is heavily biased in favour of universities in high-income and middle-income countries.

Notwithstanding the methodological limitations of the THE impact ranking, it has the significant merit of calling world-class universities' attention to the importance of being relevant to the outside world. In a recent article advocating for a new form of multilateralism to prevent universities from becoming irrelevant, the general secretary of the Association of Pacific Rim Universities summarized the responsibility of universities in the new era after the Covid-19 pandemic well:

> To address the public interest, we need to emphasize higher education as a public good which aids social mobility and inclusion, seeks to align teaching and research with global challenges and honors public service and social commitment. (Tremewan, 2020)

4.5   *Sustainability*

The last but not least important dimension to consider is the extent to which the operation of world-class universities is environmentally responsible. The University of Indonesia produces a sustainability ranking (Greenmetric ranking) based on a number of factors, including the carbon footprint of each institution linked to its electricity consumption, water usage, waste management, and education and research activities in the field of climate change.[9] Only 5 universities appearing in the Shanghai top 100 ranking are also included in the Greenmetric ranking: Oxford University (2), University of California-Davis (3), University of North Carolina in Chapel Hill (21), McMaster University (51), and Washington University in St-Louis (60). In several parts of the world, universities are becoming producers of renewable energy. Universidad Autónoma del Occidente in Colombia, Strathmore University in Kenya, and RMIT University in Australia are leaders in that respect.

TABLE 4.10   Comparison of SDG and ARWU

Universities	THE impact rank (2020)	ARWU (2019)
University of Sydney	2	80
University of British Colombia	7	35
University of Manchester	8	33
King's College London	9	51
McMaster University	17	90
Monash University	18	73
University of North Carolina in Chapel Hill	22	33
University of Toronto	28	24
University of Edinburgh	30	31
Penn State	35	98
University of Tokyo	77	25
University of Helsinki	80	63

SOURCE: THE (2020) AND ARWU (2019)

This is, however, an area that a rising number of universities have been concerned with, adopting relevant steps to achieve carbon neutrality, including through reducing conference travel. The recent Climate Change Coalition initiative, announced by the University of California president, Janet Napolitano, brings together the research efforts of 13 leading Canadian, Mexican and U.S. universities committed to pooling their scientific knowledge and resources in this area.[10] In 2019, networks representing more than 7,000 higher education institutions from all over the world announced a "climate emergency" and committed to implement a three-pronged plan to work with their students to address the environmental crisis: (i) transforming their campuses into carbon-neutral zones by 2030, (ii) mobilizing resources for research and training in the area of climate change, and (iii) increasing teaching and learning activities on sustainable environment in the curriculum and community outreach programmes (O'Malley, 2019).

Finally, a growing number of universities have divested their endowment funds from investment in fossil fuel firms after sustained student campaigns. In the United Kingdom, for instance, the University of Glasgow was the first one to take this initiative in 2014, followed by Warwick, Sheffield, King's College London, Edinburgh, Oxford and Durham. It is estimated that about half the U.K. universities have moved in that direction (Ibrahim, 2020).

The movement has been slower in the United States. Hampshire College was the first institution to adopt such policy, back in 2011. The University of California system announced a similar move in May 2020, becoming the largest to do so in the country. Harvard University, by contrast, has resisted calls from faculty and students to adopt a similar policy (Asmelash, 2020). Academics and administrators in Australia have put increasing pressure on the national pension fund (Unisuper) to divest from firms with a negative impact on the environment (Richards and Pietsch, 2020).

5 Conclusion

> Beware of false knowledge; it is more dangerous than ignorance.
> GEORGE BERNARD SHAW

The introduction in 2003 of the Academic Ranking of World Universities on the global higher education scene, at the initiative of Shanghai Jiao Tong University, has had a profound and long-lasting impact on governments and universities alike. Many countries have started to look at the rank of their universities as a proxy of scientific performance and national pride. They have financed ambitious investment programmes to upgrade their universities, in some cases even creating new institutions with the explicit aim of achieving world-class status.

Universities, in turn, have eagerly joined this new brain race. Too often, the rankings have become the new milestones to guide institutional strategic plans and influence the motivation and behaviour of university leaders and academics. While many universities all over the world have indeed improved their research performance over the past decade, there are many signs that the kind of academic excellence promoted by the rankings is often side-tracking universities from contributing to progress in several crucial dimensions of human life, such as inclusion of minorities, scientific truth, social justice, and sustainability.

In the middle of the 2020 pandemic, it is sadly ironic to observe that two of the nations in the world with the highest numbers of Covid-19 deaths are the United States and the United Kingdom. These are the countries with supposedly the best universities in the world, with historians who study pandemics, virologists who research viruses, public health experts advising governments, and the greatest number of Medicine Nobel Prize winners in the past century (94 and 28, respectively). What happened there illustrates vividly the disconnect between scientific power and actual policy action, and the difficulties faced by the leading universities in constructing bridges between the world of scientific knowledge and the political, social, and cultural arenas.

The pandemic, the resulting economic crisis, and the explosions of social frustration at the deeply ingrained structural racism in the United States make it all the more urgent and imperative to look at the missing dimensions in the definition of academic excellence fueled by the global rankings. There is a strong need for a more comprehensive concept of academic excellence that does not focus narrowly on scientific publications in elite journals.

The Shanghai Principles launched in 2017 by de Maret and Salmi were an attempt in this direction, as a reminder to world-class university leaders of the social responsibility of their institutions of higher learning (de Maret and Salmi, 2018). Echoing the philosophy of intellectual independence, academic freedom, and institutional autonomy defended by the Magna Charta Universitatum signed in 1988 by 388 heads of European universities, the 2017 Shanghai Principles focus on social inclusion, scientific truth, ethical values, responsible research, and global solidarity as moral pillars for world-class universities. These dimensions may be difficult to measure through the rankings, but they are fundamental to the mission of world-class universities.

In a world full of grand challenges, no one has captured better the noble mission of universities as beacons of knowledge and wisdom as Alfred North Whitehead, the 20th century philosopher and mathematician:

> The tragedy of the world is that those who are imaginative have but slight experience, and those who are experienced have feeble imaginations. Fools act on imagination without experience. Pedants act on knowledge without imagination. The task of the university is to weld together imagination and experience.

Acknowledgement

This chapter is a more developed version of a chapter included in Hazelkorn, E. (Ed.). (2021). *Research handbook on university rankings: History, methodology, influence and impact.* Edward Elgar Publishers.

Notes

1 For this analysis, the author included only universities showing a rise or decline greater than 20 places. In the case of universities for which ARWU did not specify a single rank but

included them in a range, the mid-range value was considered. For example, if a university appeared in the 101–150 range, it was assessed as being ranked #125.

2   This section builds on earlier work by Pierre de Maret (Emeritus Rector of the Free University of Brussels) and the author. See de Maret et al. (2018).

3   Pell Grants are the main federal financial-assistance programme for low-income students in the United States. The recipients can use their Pell Grant for tuition or other college-related costs. About two of every five undergraduate students receive a Pell Grant.

4   In Finland, training to detect fake news starts in primary school. https://www.theguardian.com/world/2020/jan/28/fact-from-fiction-finlands-new-lessons-in-combating-fake-news

5   This echoes Edgard Morin's observation that it is "necessary to make connections among various threads of knowledge rather than just store it".

6   See https://hr.admin.ox.ac.uk/academic-integrity-in-research

7   See https://www.npr.org/templates/story/story.php?storyId=103719186

8   See https://www.timeshighereducation.com/rankings/impact/2020/overall#!/ page/0/length/25/sort_by/rank/sort_order/asc/cols/undefined

9   See http://greenmetric.ui.ac.id/

10 See http://www.climateactionprogramme.org/news/13-top-universities-form-climate-change-coalition

References

Aghion, P., Dewatripont, M., Hoxby, C., Mas-Colell, A., & Sapir, A. (2009). *The governance and performance of research universities: Evidence from Europe and the U.S.* National Bureau of Economic Research Working Paper No. 14851, April 2009. Retrieved June 14, 2020, from https://www.nber.org/papers/w14851

Ahtone, T., & Lee, R. (2020, May 7). Ask who paid for America's universities. *The New York Times*. Retrieved June 14, 2020, from https://www.nytimes.com/2020/05/07/opinion/land-grant-universities-native-americans.html?nl=todaysheadlines&emc=edit_th_200508

Altbach, P., Reisberg, L., Salmi, J., & Froumin, I. (Eds.). (2018). *Accelerated universities: Ideas and money combine to build academic excellence*. Brill Sense.

Asmelash, L. (2020, May 20). The University of California has fully divested from fossil fuels. It's the largest school in the US to do it. *CNN*. Retrieved June 14, 2020, from https://edition.cnn.com/2020/05/20/us/university-of-california-divest-fossil-fuels-trnd/index.html

Bekhradnia, B. (2016). *International university rankings: For good or ill?* HEPI.

Bhattacharjee, Y. (2011). Saudi universities offer cash in exchange for academic prestige. *Science, 334*(6061), 1344–1345.

Brink, C. (2018). *The soul of a university*. Bristol University Press.

Brooks, R. L. (2005). Measuring university quality. *Review of Higher Education, 29*(1), 1–22.

Calderon, A. (2020, May 9). Sustainability rankings show a different side to higher education. *University World News*. Retrieved June 14, 2020, from https://www.universityworldnews.com/post.php?story=2020050409591134

Carnevale, A. P., & van Der Werf, M. (2017). *The 20% solution: Selective colleges can afford to admit more pell grant recipients.* Georgetown University Centre on Education and the Work Force.

Chabot, P (2017). *Exister, résister. Ce qui dépend de nous.* PUF.

Currie, J., Petersen, C., & Mok, M. H. (2006). *Academic freedom in Hong Kong.* Lexington Books.

De Maret, P. (2007). *Le tour du potier. Six leçons sur l'université et le monde.* Le livre Timperman.

De Maret, P., & Salmi, J. (2018). World-class universities in a post-truth world. In Y. Wu, Q. Wang, & N. C. Liu (Eds.), *World-class universities: Towards a global common good and seeking national and institutional contributions* (pp. 70–87). Brill Sense.

Dixon, R. (2020, January 17). Putin wanted Russian science to top the world. Then a huge academic scandal blew up. *The Washington Post.* https://www.washingtonpost.com/world/europe/putin-wanted-russian-science-to-top-the-world-then-a-major-academic-scandal-blew-up/2020/01/16/f58239ec-34b9-11ea-898f-eb846b7e9feb_story.html

Downing, R., & Ganotice Fraide, A. (2016). *World university rankings and the future of higher education.* Information Science Publishing, IGI Global.

Finkel, A. (2019, November 21). It's time for granting agencies to tackle bad science. *University World News.* Retrieved June 14, 2020, from https://www.universityworldnews.com/post.php?story=20190916114836558

Gladwell, M. (2011). The order of things: What college rankings really tell us. *The New Yorker.* Retrieved June 14, 2020, from http://www.newyorker.com/reporting/2011/02/14/110214fa_fact_gladwell?currentPage=all

Hazelkorn, E. (2020a). Higher education in the age of populism: Public good and civic engagement". *International Higher Education, 100*(Winter), 6–7. Retrieved June 14, 2020, from https://www.internationalhighereducation.net/en/handbuch/gliederung/#/Gliederungsebene/789/Winter-Issue-No.-100-(2020)

Hazelkorn, E. (2020b, March 21). Should universities be ranked for their SDG performance? *University World News.* Retrieved June 14, 2020, from https://www.universityworldnews.com/post.php?story=20200317145134326

Ibrahim, Z. (2020, January 13). Universities divesting from fossil fuels have made history, but the fight isn't over. *The Guardian.* Retrieved June 14, 2020, from https://www.theguardian.com/education/2020/jan/13/universities-divesting-from-fossil-fuels-have-made-history-but-the-fight-isnt-over#img-1

Kaplan, R. D. (2018, March 2). Everything here is fake. *The Washington Post.* Retrieved June 14, 2020, from https://www.washingtonpost.com/opinions/everything-here-is-fake/2018/03/02/064a3d4a-18c6-11e8-8b08-027a6ccb38eb_story.html?utm_term=.67d 2d9799d26

Knobel, M. (2020). The critical role of communication in a post-truth world. *International Higher Education, 100*(Winter), 9–10. Retrieved June 14, 2020, from https://www.internationalhighereducation.net/en/handbuch/gliederung/#/Gliederungsebene/789/Winter-Issue-No.-100-(2020)

Lammy, D. (2017, October 20). Seven years have changed nothing at Oxbridge. In fact, diversity is even worse. *The Guardian.* Retrieved June 14, 2020, from https://www.theguardian.com/commentisfree/2017/oct/20/oxford-cambridge-not-changed-diversity-even-worse-admissions

Le Prestre, P., et al. (2018). France's quest for excellence in higher education. *Journal of the European Higher Education Area, 1*(1), 79–94.

Li, J. (2015, January 22). Communist party orders Marxism course for universities. *South China Morning Post.* Retrieved June 14, 2020, from https://www.scmp.com/news/china/article/1682774/communist-party-orders-course-marxism-chinas-universities

MacGregor, K. (2013, June 23). Concerns growing over 'gaming' in university rankings. *University World News,* p. 227. Retrieved June 14, 2020, from https://www.universityworldnews.com/post.php?story=2013062216300718

Murphy, S. (2019, April 17). UK universities pay out £90m on staff "gagging orders" in past two years. *The Guardian.* Retrieved June 14, 2020, from https://www.theguardian.com/education/2019/apr/17/uk-universities-pay-out-90m-on-staff-gagging-orders-in-past-two-years

Observatorio de la Universidad. (2017). Retrieved June 14, 2020, from http://www.universidad.edu.co/index.php/noticias/14583-las-universidades-colombianas-en-las-que-estudiaron-los-cuestionados-y-acusados-de-corrupcion

O'Malley, B. (2015). Minister blasts patchy quality of university teaching. *University World News.* Retrieved June 14, 2020, from https://www.universityworldnews.com/post.php?story=20150909182252437

O'Malley, B. (2019, July 10). Networks of 7,000 universities declare climate emergency. *University World News.* Retrieved June 14, 2020, from https://www.universityworldnews.com/post.php?story=20190710141435609

Oppenheim, M. (2018, October 24). Hungarian Prime Minister Viktor Orban bans gender studies programs. *The Independent.* Retrieved June 14, 2020, from https://www.independent.co.uk/news/world/europe/hungary-bans-gender-studies-programmes-viktor-orban-central-european-university-budapest-a8599796.html

Orivel, F. (2004, May). Pourquoi les universités françaises sont-elles si mal classées dans les palmarès internationaux? *Dijon: Notes de l'IREDU.*

Quan, D. (2020, June 3). To continue to partner with police … is to be complicit: These academics want Canadian universities to cut ties with law enforcement. *The Star.* Retrieved June 3, 2020, from https://www.thestar.com/news/canada/2020/06/02/to-continue-to-partner-with-police-is-to-be-complicit-these-academics-want-canadian-universities-to-cut-ties-with-law-enforcement.html

Rauhvargers, A. (2013). *Global university rankings and their impact – Report II.* European University Association.

Richards, L., & Pietsch, T. (2020). Climate change is the most important mission for universities of the 21st century. *The Conversation.* Retrieved June 14, 2020, from https://theconversation.com/climate-change-is-the-most-important-mission-for-universities-of-the-21st-century-139214

Salmi, J. (2014, January 29). The governance challenge for Ibero-American universities. *Inside Higher Education.* Retrieved June 14, 2020, from https://www.insidehighered.com/blogs/world-view/governance-challenge-ibero-american-universities

Salmi, J. (2017). Excellence strategies and the creation of world-class universities. In E. Hazelkorn (Ed.), *Global rankings and the geopolitics of higher education: Understanding the influence and impact of rankings on higher education, policy and society.* Routledge.

Salmi, J., & Saroyan, A. (2007). League tables as policy instruments: Uses and misuses. *Higher Education Management and Policy, 19*(2), 1–38.

Study International – SI. (2018, April 9). The most and least equal universities in the UK. *SI News.* Retrieved June 14, 2020, from https://www.studyinternational.com/news/most-least-equal-universities-uk/

Sursock, A. (2020, May 16). The vital role of civic engagement for universities. *University World News.* Retrieved June 14, 2020, from https://www.universityworldnews.com/post.php?story=20200515072822480

Swarns, R. L. (2019, October 30). Is Georgetown's $400,000-a-year plan to aid slave descendants enough? *The New York Times.* Retrieved June 14, 2020, from https://www.nytimes.com/2019/10/30/us/georgetown-slavery-reparations.html

The Economist. (2020). British universities are examining how they benefited from slavery. *The Economist.* Retrieved June 14, 2020, from https://www.economist.com/britain/2020/02/08/british-universities-are-examining-how-they-benefited-from-slavery

The Guardian. (2019, December 18). China cuts "freedom of thought" from top university charters. *The Guardian.* Retrieved June 14, 2020, from https://www.theguardian.com/world/2019/dec/18/china-cuts-freedom-of-thought-from-top-fudan-university-charter

Times Higher Education. (2019, June 10). In conversation with David Lammy MP. *Times Higher Education.* Retrieved June 14, 2020, from https://www.timeshighereducation.com/news/conversation-david-lammy-mp

Tremewan, C. (2020, May 30). A new multilateralism for our own endangered species. *University World News.* Retrieved June 14, 2020, from https://www.universityworldnews.com/post.php?story=20200529083803102

Usher, A., & Ramos, M. (2018). *The changing finances of world-class universities*. Centre for Global Higher Education Working paper No. 41. Retrieved June 14, 2020, from https://www.researchcghe.org/perch/resources/publications/wp41.pdf

van der Zwaan, B. (2017). *Higher education in 2040: A global approach*. Amsterdam University Press.

Yonezawa, T., Nakatsui, I., & Kobayashi, T. (2002). University rankings in Japan. *Higher Education in Europe, 27*(4), 373–382.

CHAPTER 5

World-Class Universities' Search for Quality, Reputation or Prestige?

Luiz Cláudio Costa

Abstract

A high quality university, or "world-class" university, is an important indication of a country's capacity to be a key participant in a global economy. That is why so many countries are trying to develop world-class universities. Today, more than 15 years after the launching of the first edition of the Academic Ranking of World Universities, the impact of rankings on higher education has increased exponentially. Several countries have a programme to improve the position of their universities in the rankings. In addition, several universities around the world struggle to be well-placed in the rankings as it implies growing in reputation and prestige. However, is it possible to reconcile a search for a better position in rankings with the search for a high quality learning environment?

Keywords

world-class university – rankings – reputation – prestige – quality

• • •

Knowledge is the key to economic development. Nations that ignore this fact suffer, while those that recognize it flourish.

HANUSHEK and WOESSMAN (2015, p. 1)

• • •

Just as castles provided the source of strength for medieval towns, and factories provided prosperity in the industrial age, universities are the source of strength in the knowledge-based economy of the twenty-first century.

LORD DEARING (2002)[1]

∴

1   Introduction

The awareness that developing human capital is crucial for the sustainable economic growth of a country is centuries old. In the seventeenth century, Sir William Petty, a British economist, suggested that the development of a nation depends directly on the skills of its labour force. Over two centuries later, in today's knowledge economy, we are more aware than ever that education prepares people with the skills that make them more productive in their work. Perhaps even more important, education conveys the knowledge for innovation and technological progress and thereby ensures future prosperity. Although many factors enter into a nation's economic growth, the cognitive skills of its population are the most essential to long run prosperity (Hanushek and Woessman, 2015).

Several articles, books and papers have been published in the last years, showing that education is the motor of economic growth, and without economic growth, there is little hope to reach the desirable outcomes of sustainable development in terms of social, environmental and human improvements. More recently, Eric Hanushek and Ludger Woessmann show that almost all of the variation in economic growth rates across nations can be explained by differences in knowledge capital. In their study, they show that what is important for economic growth is not school attainment, but quality education, which at the end of the day is the knowledge and skills of the population (Hanushek and Woessmann, 2015).

With the increasing awareness of the importance of knowledge capital for the development of a country, quality higher education has become an important indication of a country's capacity to be a key participant in the global economy. There is today a much stronger expectation that investment in higher education can yield economic and social returns (Hazelkorn, 2012; Blackmore, 2016).

Therefore, universities around the world are under a lot of pressure from society, governments and students to demonstrate quality, greater social accountability, entrepreneurship and relevance.

Universities can contribute to a country's development in three critical dimensions: the knowledge and skills of its graduates; the application and exploitation of research capability; and the enterprise and entrepreneurial culture it develops amongst its students (Wilson, 2012).

A report analysing what was needed to be done in the United Kingdom regarding skills in order to maximize economic prosperity, productivity and social justice, concluded that the United Kingdom's skill base at that time had improved, but was behind those of many countries that were increasingly competitive. The report highlighted the necessity for a strong focus on "economic valuable skills", so that a decisive shift would be achieved by 2020 (HM Treasury, 2006; Blackmore, 2016).

In our globally competitive economic environment, to have a high-quality higher education system has become crucial for a country's economic and social sustainable development. That is why so many countries are trying to develop a world-class university.

A world-class university is supposed to perform highly influential research, embody a culture of excellence, have good quality facilities, and retain a brand name that transcends national borders and therefore is able to attract, secure and retain talent and investment. A world-class university can provide a country with a highly skilled and enterprising workforce; constant innovation in products and service development; a thriving culture of entrepreneurship; and dynamic, leading-edge scientific and technological development (Wilson, 2012).

One important step, if it is not the most important one, for a university to be recognized as world-class is to be placed in the upper levels of the most influential world university rankings (Blackmore, 2016).

2 Global Rankings and Higher Education

Global rankings started in 2003, when the Academic Ranking of World Universities (ARWU) was created (Liu and Cheng, 2005). Since then, the impact of international rankings, both on individual institutions and on national higher education systems, has been substantial, and they have become one of the most important instruments to demonstrate prestige in academic life (Blackmore, 2016; Hazelkorn, 2017).

Hazelkorn (2017) gives a significant example that illustrates the instantaneous impacts of rankings in the domain of higher education. In the spring of 2004, a few months after the release of the first edition of ARWU, the Irish Minister of Education and Science, Noel Dempsey, speaking as President of the European Council of Education Ministers, said:

> Last year, the Shanghai Jiao Tong University's Institute of Education ranked the world's top 500 universities on academic and research performance. For the European Union, the news is not all that good. The study shows that 35 of the top 50 Universities in the World are American …

Today, more than 15 years later, the impact of rankings on higher education has increased exponentially. Several countries have a programme to improve the position of their universities in the rankings. In addition, several universities around the world struggle to be well-placed in the rankings as it implies growing in prestige.

Despite the criticisms, university rankings are very significant in the field of higher education, affecting on the organizational behaviour of single universities and with implications at the system level (Goglio, 2016).

University rankings have contributed to the discussion about the importance of higher education for economic and social development of a country and moved it from domestic affair to a wider comparative framework. In a more direct way, thanks to rankings, we have today, as never before, a systematic and reliable collection of national and international data on higher education institutions (Rauhvargers, 2014; Goglio, 2016).

There is no doubt about the influence of rankings worldwide. Students, media, society, employers, universities and governments are among those who use rankings, one way or another. Universities also use rankings for strategic planning and to shape priorities.

The influence of ranking is not homogenous across all universities. Some of the top universities have to invest money and human resources not to lose their position, and to be recognized as a world-class university. On the other hand, universities in a lower position or not included in the rankings are under a lot of pressure to improve their position, which means to be visible worldwide (Goglio, 2016).

3   Rankings and Higher Education Quality

In an environment where rankings are annually released, the pressure from society and governments on universities to become a world-class university has been increasing exponentially. Universities around the world struggle to be a world-class university, as it implies a growing reputation.

A survey of higher education institutions showed that 84% of universities have a mechanism to review their position in rankings on a regular basis (Hazelkorn, 2017; Altbach and Hazelkorn, 2017).

Being in the top 50 or top 100 is now part of a national or institutional strategy. To become a world-Class university is a target for several higher education institutions. In 2017, there were around three million searches for "university rankings" and over 95 million for "world-class universities" on Google (Hazelkorn, 2017).

Obviously, the first step for a university to improve its position in the most prestigious rankings is to understand how they work and what indicators they use. After that, the university needs to take actions that will reflect an improvement by its own indicators.

Figure 5.1 presents the indicators used by the most prestigious rankings to evaluate university quality. It seems to be quite clear from Figure 5.1 that if a university intends to improve its position in the rankings or to become a world-class university it needs to work on their research indicators.

So, one important question to be asked is, if a university works towards a better position in rankings by improving their performance in those indicators, will it have a high quality-learning environment?

As we have seen, in most of the rankings, research indicators are taken to be a proxy for teaching quality (Vught and Westerheijden, 2010; Teichler, 2011). However, as has been long pointed out, this relationship is not straightforward and a high scoring university in research does not automatically imply high quality level of teaching (Dill and Soo, 2005).

It is well known that, for several reasons, it is still a challenge for rankings to refine indicators in order for the quality of teaching and learning of undergraduates to be, in a more direct way, considered by a university to become a world-class university.

One of the assumptions by the rankings is that if a university has good research indicators, they reflect prestige and reputation, and this will increase its ability to attract and retain distinguished faculty members, and the "best and brightest" students, and therefore they will have a high quality-learning environment. Is this always true?

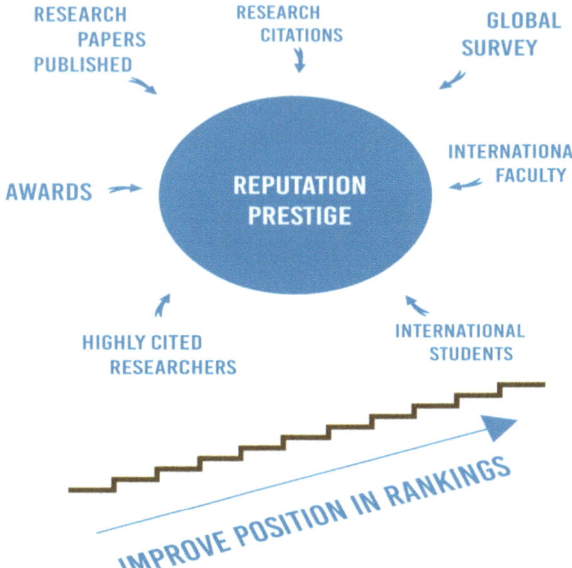

FIGURE 5.1
Indicators used by the most prestigious rankings in order to evaluate university quality

One example of the unwanted side effects of rankings is that some universities, in order to improve their position in rankings, are hiring highly cited scholars or Nobel Prize winners with part-time or temporary affiliations, but with low commitment to a high quality-learning environment (Kehm, 2014; Kehm and Erkkilä, 2014).

Let us bring out some examples for discussion. If a university hires a Nobel Prize winner, it will probably improve its position in rankings. May we say that it will directly improve its teaching quality? Or, if a university has in one year several papers published in a high-ranking journal, will it directly affect its teaching quality? There are not straightforward answers to these questions. In order to deepen the issue, we can talk about quality.

Undoubtedly, defining quality in higher education is difficult. That is why people have been asking, for more than 40 years, "what the hell is quality" (Pirsig, 1974; Ball, 1985). Quality is a relative term and depends upon individual and stakeholders perspectives. In higher education, we should consider students, employers, employees of the sector and providers (Schindler et al., 2015). Despite the difficulties, defining quality is an important prerequisite for defining quality assurance. After all, one must know what quality is before determining how to ensure it (Schindler et al., 2015).

In this paper, considering that the first mission of universities is to graduate highly skilled professionals, we will consider the transformative quality (Shindler et al., 2015) presented in Figure 5.2.

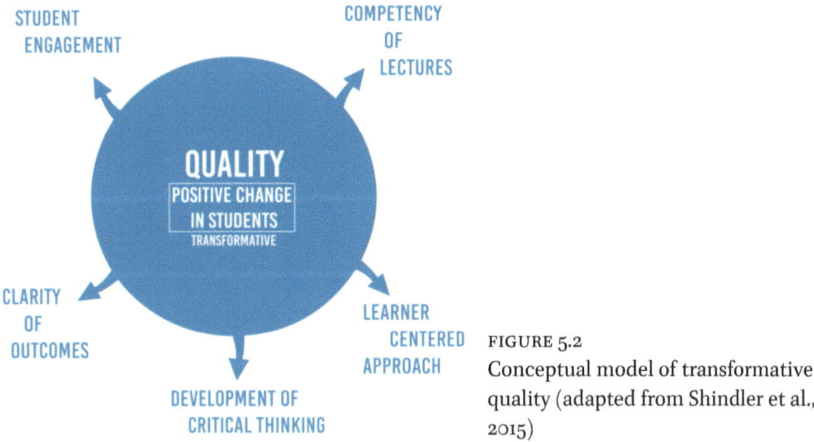

FIGURE 5.2
Conceptual model of transformative quality (adapted from Shindler et al., 2015)

Therefore, if we consider the indicators used by rankings for universities in order to improve their position in the rankings or to be considered a world-class university (Figure 5.1), we can see that they are not directly linked with transformative quality, and if they are, it is in a very special and indirect way

FIGURE 5.3
Improving reputation and
prestige with little impact,
if any, in its transformative
quality

(Rauhvargers, 2011). As an example, it seems quite clear that there is no direct link between the number of Nobel Prize winners among universities graduates with teaching quality (Rauhvargers, 2011). This means that universities can improve their position in the rankings without necessarily improving transformative quality (Figure 5.3).

However, if a university has a plan to improve its position in the rankings associated with a strategic plan for a high quality-learning environment, the hiring of a highly cited scholar or a Nobel Prize Winner can be a very important action.

To do so, universities need to look at rankings and try to improve their position in them and consequently its prestige and reputation, not only by looking at indicators, but also by working towards the development of a high quality-learning environment.

Universities can take strategic actions that can be measured by new indicators. As an example, universities could have a policy that an award winner or a Nobel Prize winner from its academic staff must have contact with their undergraduate students. Therefore, they can create an indicator such as the number of students taught by an award winner/total number of students. The same political can be done with the highly cited researchers. In addition, universities could have a strategic policy that highly cited researchers and award winners must give a number of seminars for undergraduate students in an academic year.

Working in these ways, universities could review, look for gaps and revise the ranking indicators in consideration of a conceptual model of transformative education (Figure 5.2), and identify a set of observable quality indicators that they can use to assess quality, as shown in the schematic concept in Figure 5.4.

I am quite convinced that higher education systems around the world are better prepared to face the future challenges worldwide with the presences of rankings than they were before. The correct use of rankings can help universities have a more objective idea of their performance in a local and global perspective, and even more importantly, rankings can serve as a guide to indicate what is needed to be done to improve the quality of their learning environment.

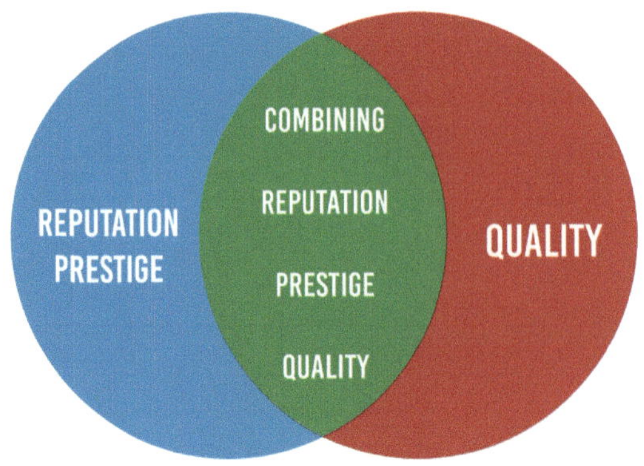

FIGURE 5.4
Working towards reputation,
prestige and quality

If we consider the higher education environment as it was before 2003, without global rankings, we will see that the universities that had global prestige at that time are almost the same as the ones as the "Top Ten" of the most traditional rankings today. The difference is that, before rankings, they were recognized by tradition, or "they are good because they are good", but now we have some indicators to compare them.

In addition, it is important to take in consideration that before global rankings, a great part of the prestige and reputation of the universities recognized globally were due to its research activities, and not because their teaching quality.

After rankings, we at least know what has been considered for one university to be placed at the top. Of course, the indicators used are not perfect and they are not able to consider all the important actions a university does, but at least we can analyse them, criticize, refine, and, in some cases, use them to improve higher education quality.

Of course, we do know that there is no one single model of excellence as there is no such thing as a perfect university ranking. However, we need to realize that rankings are much more than a set of indicators and have much more to tell us than just a university position on it.

Building a quality higher education system is a permanent job. I am optimistic that looking into the future challenges facing higher education, and using the rankings in the right way, we will be able to strengthen cooperation and make a joint effort in pushing forward the quality of higher education.

As we have said before, higher education is a determinant for the sustainable development of society, and I am sure that during the next ten years the pressure on universities and governments towards high quality higher education will continue to increase. In addition, there will be a massive increase in the number of students looking for a place in higher education, and there is no doubt about that they will look at rankings in order to make their decision.

Therefore, I strongly believe that we need to move away from the "love and hate ranking issue". What we need to discuss, given that "rankings are here to stay", is how they can be used to help create a better higher education system worldwide.

Note

1 Lord Dearing was the fifth Chancellor of the University of Nottingham (1993–2000) and is the author of the Dearing Report into higher education.

References

Altbach, P., & Hazelkorn, E. (2017, January 8). Why most universities should quit the rankings game. *University World News*, p. 442. Retrieved May 02, 2017, from http://www.universityworldnews.com/article.php?story=20170105122700949

Ball, C. (1985). What the hell is quality? In C. Ball & D. Urwin (Eds.), *Fitness for purpose: Essays in higher education*. Society for Research into Higher Education and NFER-Nelson.

Blackmore, P. (2016). *Prestige in academic life: Excellence and exclusion*. Routledge.

Dill, D. D., & Soo, M. (2005). Academic quality, league tables, and public policy: A cross-national analysis of university rankings systems. *Higher Education, 49*(4), 495–533.

Goglio, V. (2016). One size fits all? A different perspective on university rankings. *Journal of Higher Education Policy and Management, 38*(2), 212–226.

Hanushek, E. A., & Woessmann, L. (2015). *The knowledge capital of nations: Education and the economics of growth*. MIT Press.

Hazelkorn, E. (2012). Understanding rankings and the alternatives: Implications for higher education. In S. Bergan, E. Egron-Polak, J. Koheler, L. Purser, & M. Vukasović (Eds.), *Handbook of internationalization of European higher education*. Raabe Verlag.

Hazelkorn, E. (2017). *Rankings and higher education: Reframing relationships within and between states*. Working Paper No. 19. Centre for Global Higher Education.

HM Treasury. (2006). *Prosperity for all in the global economy: World class skills*. Final report (Leitch Review of Skills). HMSO.

Kehm, B. M. (2014). Global universities rankings: Impacts and unintended side effects. *European Journal of Education, 49*(1), 102–112.

Kehm, B. M., & Erkkilä, T. (2014). Editorial: The rankings game. *European Journal of Education, 49*(1), 3–11.

Liu, N. C., & Cheng, Y. (2005). The academic ranking of world universities. *Higher Education in Europe, 30*(2), 127–136.

Pirsig, R. M. (1974). *Zen and the art of motor-cycle maintenance: An inquire into values.* Willian Morrow and Company.

Rauhvargers, A. (2011). *Global university rankings and their impact.* European University Association.

Rauhvargers, A. (2014). Where are the global rankings leading us? An analyses of recent methodological changes and new developments. *European Journal of Education, 49*(1), 29–44.

Shindler, L., Puls-Elvidge, S., Welzant, H., & Crowford, L. (2015). Definition of high quality in higher education: A synthesis of the literature. *Higher Learning Research Communications, 5*(3), 3–13.

Teichler, U. (2011). Social contexts and systemic consequence of university rankings: A meta-analyses of the ranking literature. In J. Shin, R. Toutkoushain, & U. Teichler (Eds.), *University rankings: Theoretical basis, methodology and impacts on global higher education.* Springer.

Vught, F., & Westerheijden, D. (2010). Multidimensional ranking: A new transparency tool for higher education and research. *Higher Education Management and Policy, 22*(3), 1–26.

Wilson, T. (2012). *A review of business-university collaboration.* HM Government. Retrieved May 7, 2020, from https://www.gov.uk/government/uploads/system/uploads/attachment_data/file/32383/12-610-wilson-review-business-university-collaboration.pdf

CHAPTER 6

Accelerating Asian Systems of Higher Education

Moving from Middle to High Income

Gerard A. Postiglione and Brajesh Panth

Abstract

This paper examines selected aspects of higher education in Asia. It emphasizes the importance of urbanization in designing an ecology of higher education institutions, especially for the middle-income economies. It highlights the leading centers with strong research universities and the importance of interregional educational and academic cooperation in the greater Asian region.

Keywords

urbanization – Asian models – institutional differentiation – quality higher education

1 Introduction

To position itself as a global economic hub by the middle of the century, Asia will need to cement its reputation for excellence in higher education. It accounted for 40.9% of global GDP in 2016, an increase of 11.5% since 2000. Three countries, the People's Republic of China (PRC), India, and Japan, accounted for about 70% of Asia's total output in 2016 (Asian Development Bank [ADB], 2017). For Asia to constitute more than half of global GDP by 2050, it must raise the quality, diversity, and autonomy of its institutions of higher education (ibid.).

All but a few of Asia's economies are middle or high income. Despite this, there are still many millions living below the poverty line. The Asian economy will grow faster with greater access to quality higher education for women, poor rural communities, and ethnic minorities.

Asia's higher education systems continue to make extraordinary gains. For rising economies to avoid the middle-income trap, their higher education systems are aiming to address several challenges, including how to manage explosive enrollment growth; recruit qualified staff; improve instructional quality; diversify the curriculum; accelerate skills-based programmes; make breakthroughs in basic research; commercialize research results; strengthen cost-based assessment; broaden the sources of finance; and propel a culture of innovation.

2 Transformation in Asian Higher Education

Asian higher education is part of a global transformation of higher education toward internationalization, social relevance, quality assurance, and graduate employment. This section identifies distinct forces that are reshaping universities globally, but especially in Asia.

2.1 *Reshaping Universities: Urbanization*

The rapidly growing population of Asia stands at 4.1 billion people, or 55% of the global population (United Nations Population Fund [UNFP], 2000). Asia is home to 54% of the world's urban population. By 2030 its urban population is projected to 2.6 billion (UNFPA, 2000; United Nations [UN], 2019). More than 60% of the increase in the world's urban population over the next three decades will occur in Asia, particularly in PRC and India, but also in Bangladesh, Pakistan, the Philippines, and Viet Nam. Urban ecosystems are underdeveloped (ADB, 2017). As the most rapidly urbanizing region in the world, Asia can capitalize on the finding that cities with a top research university are far more likely than those without one to innovate in new production processes.

2.2 *Reshaping Universities: Tech Disruptions*

The technological and economic disruptions shaping Asia require an array of tertiary education institutions that have different missions but operate as a higher education ecosystem. According to McKinsey and Co., the forces that has reshaped Asia in the 2010–2020 included the rise of emerging markets, the impact of technology on market competition, and accelerated flows of trade, capital and people (McKinsey, 2015, 2017, 2018). As part of a diverse set of mission oriented tertiary education institutions, high quality universities are at the pinnacle of a developing country's engagement with technological acceleration and deepened global connectivity and interdependency in the coming decade of 2020–2030. New technologies (i.e. artificial intelligence, big data and algorithms, facial recognition, biosensors, augmented reality, gamification, block chain, cloud computing, etc.) can be used to improve how student learning is programmed and evaluated, how higher finance is managed, and how knowledge networks are organized.

2.3 *Reshaping Universities: Stakeholder Engagement*

Each country's development trajectory requires a particular configuration of higher education institutions (HEIs). Such a configuration, coordinated by a national committee of higher education, is composed of a wide variety of stakeholders, including amphibious entrepreneurs and amphibious academic scientists, those individuals who cross borders between university and industry and facilitate the creation of new organizational forms that drive innovation (Powell and Grodal, 2005). Such a committee can provide guidance and steering to HEIs to improve relevance, interdisciplinary collaboration, and the transportation of commercially-derived practices back into the academy.

2.4 *Reshaping Universities: Differentiation and Recalibration*

Advice is needed on the kind of configuration each country needs, as it includes research universities, regular universities, liberal arts colleges, colleges of applied science, polytechnics, community colleges, technical-vocational colleges, technical training colleges, and open universities, all with the capacity to employ technology for e-learning that is cost efficient and able to support higher education over a lifetime. Each institution has a unique mission and together they form a tertiary education ecosystem that can respond in a coordinated way.

2.5 *Reshaping Universities: Schools as Preparatory Institutions*

Mass higher education calls for a reconsideration of the role of schools as institutions for teaching and learning. Colleges and universities are the main institutions entrusted with the task of preparing schoolteachers and providing them with continuing professional education. It is critical for there to be a closer link between the modes of teaching and learning across all levels of the education system. This means a continual realignment to strengthen the links with schools. Academies of teacher education located within high quality universities can provide international best practices in teacher education, (not just teacher training) that recognizes changes in the culture of learning more disposed to innovation and entrepreneurship.

2.6 *Reshaping Universities: Massive Upward Reskilling*

Most Asians will be living in cities where there is an urgent need of advanced knowledge and higher order skills to address how best to sustain human development. For a start, colleges and universities have to address intensified regional and global demands of the labor markets and changing workplaces. In 2018, a Microsoft study found that, driven by digital economy and artificial intelligence, 85% of the jobs in Asia will change by 2021. Half will become higher value work roles and require massive reskilling (Microsoft, 2018). This calls for strategic investment.

2.7   *Reshaping Universities: Mission, Market, and Margin*

Within a system of higher education, high quality universities are mission-centred, market-smart, and margin-conscious. To be mission-centred encompasses a clear declaration of what value the institution produces for the community that it serves. To be market-smart means to devise ways to work with the market by adding value but not having its value determined by the market. To be margin-conscious means to ensure that financial decisions are founded on a sophisticated formula of preserving the value of the institutional mission rather than by overly simplistic, political, or ad hoc factors (Massey, 2016).

3   Finding Valuable Models

Asia has become a region of rising significance in higher education. It is widely accepted that the Asian higher education system is quantitatively strong, but qualitatively weak. Its global influence pales in comparison to that marshalled by its economy. Several countries, including Japan, the Republic of Korea (ROK), and Singapore, which have world-ranked universities, also manage to have high quality systems of higher education. Twenty universities in Asia rose into the ranks of the world's top 200. PRC's Hong Kong Special Administrative Region (Hong Kong, China) has four of the world's top 200 universities and a qualitatively strong higher education system. There is no one single model that can provide lessons on how to organize higher education for a region with four billion people.

The traits of leading systems of higher education are well known. There are sound reasons why Asia, with a rich educational heritage and many of the best students in the world, has not yet attained its potential in higher education. Great systems of higher education have diverse institutions that offer high-quality academic and vocational choices with many inter-connected pathways that provide opportunities that invigorate learning. At the very least, great systems spare no effort to open the minds of students and broaden how they think – the key organizing principle of a great system of higher education. The best systems give students the opportunity to acquire skills to innovate and live effectively in a changing world so they can live a productive and satisfying life.

No doubt Asia will remain an influential player in the world community. It will take longer to achieve global prominence in higher education. Should it manage to use its strengths to address its weaknesses, the sheer scale of the Asian higher education will yield enormous global impact.

With regard to colleges, polytechnics, and research universities, there are valuable lessons to be learned from the experiences, Hong Kong, China; Japan; ROK; and Singapore, all of which have world-class ranked universities (Altbach & Salmi, 2011). Leading research universities of science and technology in major cities like Beijing, Hong Kong, Seoul, Singapore, Shanghai, Taipei, and Tokyo can serve as useful examples for creating high quality research universities in Asia's emergent high tech cities, including Bangkok, Bengaluru, Guangzhou, Ha Noi, Jakarta, Kuala Lumpur, Lahore, and Manila. There is already a wealth of experience to offer for the creation of high quality universities across other urban centres. Asia's high quality universities offer valuable insights for policy and planning about how to establish new institutions, as well as how to strengthen existing ones that are mission-centred, market-smart, and conscious of opportunities.

More than a few great research universities in Asia began as undergraduate institutions focused on good teaching and gradually managed in a few decades to establish themselves as world ranked universities. Some newly established colleges and universities have become catalysts for curriculum change. The best have become performance oriented with mechanisms for external review of the three dimensions of scholarship: teaching, research, and knowledge exchange, both domestic and international.

4   Imagining High Quality Research Universities

Imagine what a tripling of the number of high quality research universities would mean for Asia's future and its contribution to the global common good. Asia's future hinges heavily on its research universities to upgrade the ethics and execution of basic, applied, and development research in science and technology while organizationally becoming more socially embedded to enable equitable access to higher order thinking skills for graduate employment and the healthier lives of its people.

The best universities in Asia have established sustainable cooperation with industry. Their progress is marked by increasing amounts of autonomy from government and a pattern of shared governance within their institutions. All have figured out how to anchor economic globalization for national development, while retaining the fundamental values that unify their societies.

High quality research universities across Asia confront several challenges: (1) Maintain and improve quality in research, teaching, and knowledge exchange;

(2) Improve the relevance of curriculum, including Science, Technology, Engineering, and Mathematics (STEM) and technical skills; (3) Build interdisciplinary teaching and research programmes; (4) Balance expanded access with greater affordability; (5) Establish partnerships with industry, regional counterparts, and the private sector; (6) Take advantage of technological disruptions to improve organizational responsiveness; (7) Become better attuned to the challenges of urbanization, health care, climate change; and (8) Promote a culture of innovation and entrepreneurship.

5   Positioning Asia's Research Universities

The time when Asia was a place with only a few traditional colonial universities focused on elite undergraduate education is long gone. Since the turn of the century, Asian universities have stunned the academic world. In 2019, five of the top 50 universities ranked by the Times Higher Education World University Rankings are Asian (Times Higher Education, 2018a). Ten percent of the world's top 200 universities are Asian universities. At this pace, a fifth of the world's best universities could be Asian by 2025 (excluding Australian universities, which some consider as being within the Asian block). The salience of the global rankings of universities began in the late 1990s, when Japan's universities were already well-established, and PRC and ROK were racking up impressive GDP figures. As PRC followed ROK's path towards mass higher education, the entire region became committed to building high quality research universities to drive global competitiveness. Of Asia's top 25, 12 are in PRC, five of which are in Hong Kong, China. Seven are in ROK, two in both Japan (Tokyo and Kyoto) and Singapore (National University of Singapore and Nanyang University), and one each in Israel (Tel Aviv University) and Saudi Arabia (King Abdulaziz University) (Times Higher Education, 2018b).

Asia's research universities have put to rest any hint of an abbreviated rise. Southeast Asian universities have studied counterparts in the Northeast neighborhood as much as in the West. Malaysia is determined to ensure that its leading universities will join the global elite, as do its Southeast Asian neighbours. The same is true in Central Asia (Nazarbayev University) and South Asia, where India's Institutes of Science and Technology (Indian Institute of Technology, Indian Institute of Science and Jawaharlal Nehru University) are on the rise.

Where Asian economies can move rapidly ahead is by accelerating ICT infrastructure investment at the same time that they increase their investment in high quality research universities. Several of Asia developing economies are investing heavily in high quality research universities, including PRC in East

Asia; Indonesia, Malaysia, the Philippines, Thailand, and Viet Nam in Southeast Asia; Bangladesh, India, Pakistan, and Sri Lanka in South Asia; and Mongolia, Kazakhstan and Uzbekistan in Central Asia. There are useful comparisons research universities in Asia's developed economies such as Hong Kong, China; Japan; ROK; Singapore; Taipei, China; and the United States.

6 Leading Research Universities: The Republic of Korea, Singapore, and Hong Kong, China

To climb the development ladder away from low-wage, low-skill intensive industry to high-income and innovative industries that reflects the acceleration of technological change and global interdependency, middle-income countries must rely more heavily on their higher education systems, and especially their high quality universities, in order to make the transition to a high-income society. Further growth hinges on upgrading the human capital for high skill-intensive industries.

6.1 *The Republic of Korea*

The Republic of Korea (ROK) did this as early as the 1970s by establishing the Korea Advanced Institute of Science and Technology (KAIST) to support basic and applied research. This placed them in a better position to invest in the ICT industry and eventually to move ahead in terms of telecom infrastructure and usage. In order to build the human capital base it needed, ROK instituted educational reforms that connected their higher education system with employer-based training. As ROK becomes successful, it engineered a gradual shift from wholly government investment in research universities to public-private shared investment to advance as a knowledge economy. An excellent example is the privately funded Pohang University of Science and Technology (POSTECH) that was able to achieve world-class ranking. Both KAIST and POSTECH are an integral part of ROK's sprawling system of colleges and universities.

6.2 *Singapore*

As a city state, Singapore also holds key lessons. Its growth experiences a common set of stages but on a smaller scale, including labour-intensive growth in the 1960s, skill-intensive growth in the 1970s, capital-intensive growth in the 1980s, technology-intensive growth in the 1990s, and knowledge and innovation-based economic growth from 2000 onwards (ADB, 2014). Its investment in skills, STEM, R&D, and universities with carefully differentiated missions promoted high-tech industries. Its two flagships, National Univeristy of Singapore (NUS) and Nanyang, are both ranked among Asia's top-five universities. The NUS has instituted a world renowned liberal arts programme with Yale University that drives its students to be creative with a more global and increasingly innovative mindset. Nanyang Technological University has struck a record number of tie-ups with big industrial players, such as Alibaba, BMW Group, Rolls-Royce, Delta Electronics, ST Engineering, SMRT, SingTel and Surbana Jurong. Singapore ensured it future with places like the Singapore University Design and Technology, 2009. Singapore invested heavily in upgrading technical education and subsidized multinational corporations to do training and raise the skill levels of its workforce. Partnerships with world-leading educational institutions enhanced the availability of talent pools.

6.3   *Hong Kong, China*

Hong Kong, China has become a key driver of the country's Greater Bay – an initiative to make South China the world's leading centre of innovation and technology. With a mere 0.7% of GDP investment for R&D, Hong Kong, China manages to have more world-class universities than any other city in the world. What is lacks in manufacturing it makes up for in quality higher education. The central government in Beijing has been strategic in identifying Hong Kong, China as a global knowledge hub that can provide high quality scientific and technological talent for a region of PRC that includes Shenzhen, Guangzhou, Macao, and the seven cities of the Pearl River delta. Beginning in the 1990s, Hong Kong, China's two universities that largely focused on undergraduate degrees were transformed into research universities. At the same time, Hong Kong, China established a new University of Science and Technology, upgraded five colleges to university status, founded an open university, opened the doors to many associate degree awarding self-funded community colleges, and announced the establishment of its first two private universities. To ensure its contribution to the Greater Bay Initiative, the SAR government will double the proportion of GDP for R&D.

7   Making the Best of Excellence Initiatives: the People's Republic of China, Japan, and the Republic of Korea

Several governments have invested in excellence initiatives to propel competition among their flagship and newly established universities. The number of governments making such an investment has increased year by year. These include the People's Republic of China (PRC), Denmark, France, Germany, Japan, Russia, the Republic of Korea (ROK), and Spain. They have injected additional funding to boost performance across their university sectors. These initiatives have impacted the participating universities and their higher education systems in a significant way. Among the most well-known in the Asian region are Brain [the Republic of] Korea; Japan's 21st Century Centre of Excellence; and PRC's 211 Project, 985 Project, and the Double World-Class Project.

These initiatives have propelled a new generation of universities forward. The most successful upgrading and transformation of universities has been based on bold vision. More importantly, their success hinged on the leadership's ability to change the mentality, conviction, and outlook of the academic community in the pursuit of academic excellence.

The Government of PRC has been the primary force behind the major excellence initiatives (Huang et al., 2014; Postiglione, 2015b). In 1995, the government introduced the 211 Project, an initiative that provided extra resources to those universities that could show promise in attaining high standards in academic and scientific disciplines. As the economy continued to grow, the PRC has seized the opportunity to launch an even more far-reaching excellence initiative. Known as the 985 Project, it selected universities and disciplines that would become first-class centres of excellence within ten to twenty years (Postiglione, 2014; Luo, 2013; Rhodes et al., 2014). The 985 Project's main principles were to institute personnel reforms, improve internal management, combine talent training with scientific research, and build academic platforms through disciplinary strengthening. From 1999 to 2007, the government selected 39 universities that received nearly RMB30 billion ($4.5 billion). In late 2017, PRC launched what has become known as the Double World-Class (DWC) Project that aims to create world-class universities and first-class disciplines at a global level. It will enable 42 world-class universities and approximately 456 world-class disciplines in 95 universities by the middle of the century.

For Asia, it is crucial to consider how to draw lessons from these excellence initiatives. In most cases, it involved internationalization as a way to attract academic talent to strengthen research capacity. In all cases, it meant reducing or eliminating "inbreeding", hiring their own graduates.

While it is not always easy to assess the precise results of the investment in excellence initiatives, when strategically planned and executed, the results can be impressive. PRC managed to add 24 universities to the world's top 500. Australia, Saudi Arabia and Taipei, China were also able to add additional universities. Japan and the United States, which already dominated the list, experienced a decrease over the decade in the number of world ranked universities. Some universities have not only moved forward but rocketed upward, including Shanghai Jiao Tong University and Fudan University in PRC, the Indian Institute of Technology in Bombay, King Saud University in Saudi Arabia, the

University of Aix-Marseille in France, and the Technion-Israel Institute of Technology in Israel.

In all cases, a key innovation has been the establishment of interdisciplinary centres of research excellence. An OECD review of excellence initiatives found this to be one of the greatest benefits. These centres are generously funded to conduct high-impact/high-risk basic research, usually in cooperation with noted scientists at name-brand international universities.

8 The Gold Standard: Vision, Talent, Resources, Governance

8.1 *Vision*

As a basis for setting objectives, both short and longer term, and strategic planning, a high quality university needs a vision anchored in national and local development, and committed to by all stakeholders. That vision should be one that is clear, achievable, and purposeful for defining the design, objectives, and balance of the mission of colleges and universities in the nation, region, and global spheres.

For a new college and university, the vision should express how to situate the new institution among the others. It is of paramount importance that the vision of the new institution has to differentiate itself from the rest of the rest of the pack. Yet, it should ensure that it does so without assaulting other institutions in the higher education system.

For new colleges and universities, the vision is the basis for the project. Upgrading existing institutions is a double edged sword. In some cases, government-university relations can be quite restrictive and make it difficult for a university to break free in order to institute and carry out reforms necessary to ensure quality. In other cases, internationalization can open up opportunities for injecting ideas, motivations, and resources into reform efforts. Even if government does not directly participate in the formation of a vision and project outline, it will always be the elephant in the room and should not be relegated to the periphery of the developmental (new institutions) or evolutionary (existing institutions) process.

8.2 *Talent*

The academic profession is the heart of college and university. Attracting talent will depend upon the terms offered in comparison to competitors. It is not always necessary to offer high salaries because talented scholars and scientists will often trade higher salary for better working conditions. These working conditions can include tangible benefits like laboratories and computers, as well as intangible, ones like academic freedom and merit based promotion. The best start is with a true scholarly commitment among academics and students.

In the case of a new college and university, accepting an appointment will hinge greatly on the academic reputation of the president and of the leading appointment in each academic department. The president is also hired for their social and intellectual capital networks and they may have to do leg work to convince the first tier of academic appointments to leave their current posts. That means making offers that can match not only salary and health care but also academic infrastructure.

In recruiting college and university leaders, headhunter firms and search committees should be as transparent as possible. The individual selected must be able to earn the respect of the academic community, not only the basis of his or her leadership experience, but also on the basis of that individual's academic reputation in a particular area of research.

In the case of a new institution, it is important to hire a president who can operate in an environment of known unknowns as well as unknown unknowns. A new institution needs a president that has survival skills in a rapidly changing environment. In short, the skills to work in an environment of uncertainties are essential, as well as the skills to make decisions on the fly about new organizational structures that will have long-term implications.

In the case of new colleges and universities, it is advantageous to have a vision that supports a break with traditional academic barriers, to establish a niche with an interdisciplinary approach to science and technology, and to set out a partnership design to propel collaborations with industry.

8.3   *Governance*

Shared governance and professional management go hand in hand. The latter is essential but should be subservient to the former. There is a need for regulations that are not overly onerous but ensure strict accountability and protect the college and university from political interference. This means academic and managerial autonomy and a degree of relative independence from government. This makes it possible for the competitive spirit to thrive in every aspect of academic and scientific work. Academic endeavours, the product of which can be useful to society, must have full sway. The critical thinking and innovative potential of academic staff, scholars, and scientists must be uninhibited. Autonomy means flexibility, and an exemption from weighty bureaucracy, and externally imposed standards. There is agility in good governance that makes it respond quickly to economic and social demands.

The only motivation of external pressure is control, and that is anathema to institutional quality. Diverse stakeholders are a resource if the institutional governance is inclusive enough to keep them engaged in the college and university community. It is up to cogent and astute college and university leaders to ensure that stakeholders drive the institution without stifling its functioning in a rapidly accelerating economy. A high quality college and university has its own regulatory framework that can create and ensure political support and build its reputation for impact. This can be done through an expert network of reviewers who are external to the university. This is especially important in newly established universities. A network of experts can help ensure that the new institution does not deviate far from its original vision and design, while providing it with competent steering.

8.4   *Resources and Sustainable Funding*

Resources and sustainable funding are essential in Asia where the leading universities have been fortunate to receive generous government funding. No institutions of higher education should expect funding to fall from the governmental sky. Government support is a key feature and it is vital, but it can be unhelpful if it becomes a crutch. The Asian situation contrasts with many top state universities in the United States, which has moved from a majority reliance on government finance to reduced state funding for annual recurrent expenditures (as little as 10% to 20% for some states). This has made them virtually private in operation but still state universities in name.

Asia's institutions of higher education will be expected to become more efficient, entrepreneurial, and innovative in finance. Building a sound financial base means being competitive rather than at the mercy of government. Endowments, grants, donations, service contracts, public-private partnerships and innovative initiatives are part of an increasingly competitive financial environment. Funding for resources must be sustainable to carry out future planning. Economic downturns, whether national or global, should be anticipated. In an environment of multiple sources of funding, colleges and universities must ensure a high standard of accountability through legitimate audits, especially where corruption has been a problem.

As colleges and universities become more oriented to the private sector, it is important to ensure that this does not disadvantage students from poor areas of the country. In some countries, there is a tendency among some leading colleges and universities to open access more widely to families who provide endowments or donations. Legacy admissions once begun are difficult to halt.

There are drivers, challenges, and risks, but these four (vision, talent, governance, resources) have to be aligned so that they are mutually complimentary rather than mutually averse to one another. They apply in one way or another to all institutions of higher education. The four are all part of an ecosystem that includes a favorable macro-environment, strong leadership at national level, a rigorous regulatory and quality assurance framework, and a structure of incentives for financial sustainability. The location of a college and university also matters along with digital telecommunication capacity that gives it national outreach. But in the final analysis, to maintain momentum, the most crucial pillars are funding, autonomy, accountability, and attracting the best talent possible.

9   Employability Ranking and the Problem of Misalignments

Times Higher Education annually releases the Global University Employability Ranking that lists the top 150 institutions for employability based on a survey of 7,000 major employers from over 22 countries or places. In 2018, Hong Kong, China has four universities in the annual ranking: HKUST ranked 16th, dropping four places from 12th last year, and is third in Asia, after the University of Tokyo (9th) and the National University of Singapore (10th). HKU climbed to 63rd, up from last year's 71st. CUHK slipped six places to 88th. PolyU is among the top 150 institutions for the first time and ranked 137th. The report said that universities in Hong Kong, China and Taipei,China have improved in general, while ROK made the biggest progress among Asian countries, and has six universities among top 20 from only one in 2011 (Times Higher Education, 2018).

Universities that are highly ranked in the employability of their graduates provide higher-level skills. Evidence from OECD countries shows an increasing proportion of graduates who are employed in knowledge-intensive industries. Such graduates will receive higher rates of financial and social return on their educational investment. Unemployment in OECD countries is lower among those with a higher education. Asia is only a little over half the average score of the OECD in average education and skill subindex score. Not only is the mean level of education lower in Asia, but there is a lower quality of higher education and a looser connection with labour markets.

To close the gap with advanced economies, Asian countries must increase education attainment levels, as well as the proportion of scientists and engineers in their populations. Asia has a long road and much ground to cover. The best way to begin is to raise the bar on the quality of higher education. In addition to increasing enrollments, there is a need to focus on improving quality, relevance, and skills development (Sharma, 2014).

The approach to quality improvement needs to change – development of new curricula and courses needs to be: (1) adaptable to modularization (2) offered through multiple channels and (3) amenable to life-long learning. For students who major in the STEM fields, a greater emphasis on soft skills will help trigger innovative and entrepreneurial abilities. Educational credentials need to be diversified so as to raise the status of Technical and Vocational education and training.

Diversifying higher education not only means establishing high quality research universities. It also means rethinking the extreme prominence of degree programmes. High quality universities can also offer associate degrees out of their Schools of Professional and Continuing Education. This may include technical qualifications that align with national and international standard qualifications framework.

The contemporary situation in many countries requires providing students with flexible offerings, including credit transfer arrangements, and multiple channels for engaging in educational programmes. Community colleges that offer associate degrees and skill-based lifelong learning will strengthen the status of higher technical and vocational education and training (TVET), as has been the case in Viet Nam, Singapore and ROK.

In short, a high quality university is one that is inclusive and can provide diverse qualifications and competencies that can meet the market of different demands in the rapidly changing workplace. The acceleration of technological change and the deepening of global inter-dependencies has made it more possible today than at any time in the past.

New universities with world standard research centres and smartly designed campuses can serve a variety of needs with the agility to provide requisite talent for specific sectors of the economy. This can be done by establishing new institutions from scratch, by upgrading existing institutions, by partnering with cross-border institutions or mergers. These can help jump-start research and development programmes that are benchmarked to global standards and best practices. A greater focus on STEM disciplines at all levels of education is needed to augment talent for innovation.

Most striking is the fact that many countries still underestimated and under-emphasized the potential of industry–university collaboration. Such collaboration is the basis for commercial incubation of innovation and technology. Places like Hong Kong and Shenzhen have set up plans to position their high-quality universities with technology parks that straddle their two locations. The DJI Drone Company in Shenzhen Special Economic Zone's science park was based on drone innovation in a university of Hong Kong, China. Universities can become more attuned to knowing the kinds of knowledge and skills that can drive innovation, attract venture investors, create new products, and support student entrepreneurship.

10 Regional Partnerships

Among the challenges for Asian region in the years to come is to forge mutually beneficial cross-border partnerships and programmes of high quality teaching and research (ADB, 2012). Those countries with well-established and regionally recognized research universities can form beneficial partnerships with emerging universities in other countries through educational and academic exchanges, as well as cooperation on research and teaching programmes. As competition for funding among colleges and universities becomes fiercer, partnerships become strategic. Evidence shows that colleges and universities are most effective when they participate in collaborative projects, nationally or internationally. College and university leaders in Asia have their own consortia to focus on issues of mutual benefit, such as academic exchanges and student mobility. These bring about unexpected synergies. High quality colleges and universities choose the best, regardless of nationality, and find ways to retain them, integrate them into the university community, and provide them with the technological resources to maximize their effectiveness in teaching and research.

Intra-Asian collaboration in higher education is still in its embryonic stage. The acceleration of technological change and regional inter-dependencies can help research universities to be better embedded in cooperative knowledge networks.

High quality research universities have the capacity to anchor economic globalization for local and national development. The process by which this occurs needs the engagement of a wide variety of stakeholders who are committed to building high quality research universities to support and propel economic development. Among those stakeholders are amphibious entrepreneurs who can build bridges across countries to attract resources and deepen meaningful cooperation. This includes forging closer intra-regional academic and institutional alliances, and learning from Asian neighbours, while moderating the overwhelming reliance on Western universities.

Disclaimer

Views expressed by the author do not reflect the views of the Asian Development Bank.

References

Antonio, A., Astin, H., & Cress, C. (2000). Community service in higher education: A look at the nation's faculty. *Review of Higher Education, 23*(4), 373–398.

Asian Development Bank. (2012). Regional cooperation and cross-border collaboration in higher education in Asia ensuring that everyone wins. Retrieved August 20, 2020, from https://www.adb.org/sites/default/files/publication/29931/regional-cooperation-higher-education-asia.pdf

Asian Development Bank. (2014). *Innovative Asia: Advancing the knowledge based economy: The next policy agenda.* Asian Development Bank.

Asian Development Bank. (2017). *Key indicators: Asia and the Pacific.* Retrieved May 28, 2020, from https://www.adb.org/publications/key-indicators-asia-and-pacific-2017

Huang, F., Finkelstein, M., & Rostan, M. (Eds.). (2014). *The internationalization of the academy.* Springer Press.

Luo, Y. (2013). Building world-class universities in [the People's Republic of] China. In J. C. Shin & B. M. Kehm (Eds.), *Institutionalisation of world-class university in global competition* (pp. 165–183). Springer.

McKinsey and Company. (2015). *The forces reshaping Asia.* Retrieved May 28, 2020, from https://www.mckinsey.com/featured-insights/asia-pacific/no-ordinary-disruption-the-forces-reshaping-asia

McKinsey and Company. (2017). *Artificial Intellgence and Southeast Asia's future.* Retrieved May 28, 2020, from https://www.mckinsey.com/industries/social-sector/our-insights/how-higher-education-institutions-can-transform-themselves-using-advanced-analytics

McKinsey and Company. (2018). *How higher education institutions can transform themselves using advanced analytics.* Retrieved May 28, 2020, from https://www.mckinsey.com/industries/social-sector/our-insights/how-higher-education-institutions-can-transform-themselves-using-advanced-analytics#

Microsoft. (2018). *Digital transformation to contribute more than US$1 trillion to Asia Pacific GDP by 2021.* Retrieved May 28, 2020, from https://news.microsoft.com/apac/2018/02/21/digital-transformation-to-contribute-more-than-us1-trillion-to-asia-pacific-gdp-by-2021-ai-is-primary-catalyst-for-further-growth/

Postiglione, G. A. (2014). What matters in global outreach? In Y. Cheng, Q. Wang, & N. C. Liu (Eds.), *How world-class universities affect global higher education.* Sense Publishers.

Postiglione, G. A. (2015). Research universities for national rejuvenation and global influence: [The People's Republic of] China's search for a balanced model. *Higher Education, 70*(2), 235–250.

Powell, W. W., & Grodal, S. (2005). *Networks of innovation. Handbook of innovation.* Oxford University Press.

Sharma, Y. (2014, September 12). Can Asia lead the future global knowledge economy? *University World News.* Retrieved August 20, 2020, from https://www.universityworldnews.com/post.php?story=2014091210432117

Times Higher Education. (2018a). *Best universities for graduate jobs: Global university employability ranking 2019.* Retrieved May 28, 2020, from https://www.timeshighereducation.com/student/best-universities/best-universities-graduate-jobs-global-university-employability-ranking

Times Higher Education. (2018b). *Asia university rankings 2018*. Retrieved May 28, 2020, from https://www.timeshighereducation.com/world-university-rankings/2018/regional-ranking#!/page/0/length/25/sort_by/rank/sort_order/asc/cols/stats

United Nations. (2019). *World population prospects: Highlights*. Retrieved May 28, 2020, from https://www.un.org/development/desa/publications/world-population-prospects-2019-highlights.html

United Nations Population Fund. (2000) *State of world population 2000: Living together, worlds apart: Men and women in a time of change.* Retrieved May 20, 2020, from https://www.unfpa.org/publications/state-world-population-2000

CHAPTER 7

World-Class University Policies and Rankings in Transition

A Comparative Study of the People's Republic of China and Japan

Akiyoshi Yonezawa and Futao Huang

Abstract

Two leading countries in East Asia, the People's Republic of China and Japan, have focused their attention on developing world-class university policies while the approaches are sometimes almost opposite. The authors examine the background ideas and processes guiding the development of these national policies to foster world-class universities, as well as the reactions of the leading universities toward these national policies. The contrasting ideas contained within the policies for universities, science, and technology in the two countries are also discussed.

Keywords

world-class universities – Japan – the People's Republic of China – multi-discipline – university strategy

1   Introduction

Policies to support the development of world-class universities are highly prominent in East Asia. Both governments and universities are now publicizing their strategies for achieving better positions in international university rankings (Hazelkorn, 2016; Yudkevich et al., 2016). Notwithstanding this, it is fair to say that they are not claiming that the ranking positions themselves are their final goals. Nevertheless, in achieving high recognition from international communities, these universities expect to attract global talent and resources that will enable them to fulfil their own missions, such as the investigation of academic frontiers, contributions to society and industry through knowledge creation and transfer, and fostering next-generation leaders in various fields (Stensaker et al., 2019).

In particular, the governments of nation states rely on advanced science and technologies to drive socio-economic development and are cognizant of the role of universities in enhancing innovation through knowledge creation and university-industry collaboration. Considering the highly complex nature of universities' activities and their organizational structures, external stakeholders such as governments and industry are constantly seeking convenient tools to understand the performance of universities and the value of investing in them. University rankings are frequently referred to because they provide easily accessible and concise information. University rankings also adept in response to demands for information to facilitate funding and partnerships with universities. Recent rankings have specified a wide variety of indicators related to the performance and impact of universities in research, collaboration with industry, and innovation.

Given these circumstances, two leading countries in East Asia, the People's Republic of China and Japan, have focused their attention on developing world-class university policies. In this chapter, we examine the background ideas and processes guiding the development of these national policies to foster world-class universities, as well as the reactions of the leading universities toward these national policies. We also analyse and discuss the contrasting ideas contained within the policies for universities, science, and technology in the two countries.

2   The Development of World-Class University Policies

2.1   *The People's Republic of China*

The Chinese government initiated the 211 Project in 1995 and the 985 Project in 1999, which was the earliest explicit policies intended to foster world-class universities. The former aimed to raise the educational quality of about 100 universities and hundreds of disciplines in the early 21st century, while the primary goal of the latter was to select nearly 40 universities from those included in the 211 Project and transform them into research-intensive universities with an international impact. Considerable progress has been made in accomplishing the objectives of the two projects. Notably, the implementation of the 985 Project has led to a significant improvement in the international reputation of several Chinese universities in recent years.

With the rapid expansion of China's higher education system and the massification of its higher education enrolment since the late 1990s, as well as its increased global competitiveness in higher education and research, the Chinese government launched the Double World-Class Project in September 2017.

Aside from the inclusion of only very few new universities, all the 985 Project universities have been included in the new project along with three former 211 Project universities. It is expected that the 42 universities will endeavour to become world-class universities (Huang, 2015).

Largely different from the previous two projects, the new project not only aims to build world-class universities but also to create around 100 world-class disciplines. Essentially, the main objectives of the new project indicate that efforts will be made to increase the prestige of Chinese universities worldwide with a focus on their global competitiveness in research, and also to improve the quality of the educational activities in Chinese universities. Generally speaking, the new project attempts to place similar emphasis on both research and teaching activities in Chinese academia. More importantly, the primary goal of the project is to improve the overall level of Chinese higher education, making China a centre of learning worldwide and boosting China's higher education power. Through all these efforts, China's soft power is expected to be boosted by the year 2050.

That said, as in the past, both the universities and the disciplines listed in the project are determined and accredited by the central government. The outcome of the selection process reflects the strong and clear political will and orientation of the central government. Under this condition, no radical changes have occurred in the regional distribution of the universities taking part.

However, some differences from the previous two projects can also be pointed out. First, the new project has a more ambitious goal of boosting China's soft power. Second, a much clearer road map has been created. For example, three main steps will be taken to achieve the goals. There is also a very strong emphasis on Chinese characteristics and the Chinese national context. For example, the basic principle of implementing the new project is that the universities and disciplines involved are rooted in China (solving Chinese problems and producing graduates dedicated to socialist construction). In addition, the selection of numerous disciplines related to Marxism, ideology, Chinese medicine and culture, and some strong disciplines with a long history in China, is remarkable.

2.2   *Japan*

Similar to China, the history of the development of world-class university policies in Japan has also spanned almost two decades. However, this has been achieved through a combination of various types of segmented funding projects. The first visible policy implementation started with projects to support research units (i.e., 21st Century Centres of Excellence, which started in 2002, and Global Centres of Excellence, initiated in 2007), with further selective support for a very limited number of research institutes under a programme of supporting cutting-edge research institutes, World Premier Initiatives (WPIS), which commenced in 2007. Alternatively, a series of funding for projects to support "globally competitive" universities, such as the Global 30 project, which was started in 2009, and the Top Global University project, which has been in operation since 2014, is focused on enhancing the international profiles of selected universities rather than providing direct support for their research activities. In addition, the Programme for Promoting the Enhancement of Research Universities initiated in 2013 aims to strengthen the management capacity of research universities (Yonezawa and Shimmi, 2016).

It is only quite recently that the national government started to identify official institutional categories for the purpose of differentiating the functions of the respective national universities. In 2017, the government set up a distinguished category within the national university sector called Designated National University (DNU) (Yonezawa, 2018). So far, seven universities – namely, the University of Tokyo, Kyoto University, Tohoku University, Tokyo Institute of Technology, Nagoya University, Osaka University, and Hitotsubashi University – have been approved as DNUs. Three more universities are under investigation as potential candidates of DNUS.

Different from the various funding projects that cover partial aspects of world-class universities, the DNU scheme bestows a distinguished legal status on the selected national universities. After World War II, all the national universities in Japan operated under an equal legal status regardless of their historical origins, such as "imperial universities" or "polytechnics". The awarding of this distinguished status was itself recognized as a significant policy change. The selected seven DNUS among the 86 national universities are expected to take an institution-wide approach by strategizing their policies to enhance international competitiveness, mainly through an active commitment to collaboration with industry to foster knowledge creation for innovation. At this moment, however, only small amounts of "start-up" funding are being provided, and the DNUS are expected to generate further income from non-governmental sources.

A further difference is that the DNU scheme was initiated as a cabinet-wide project. In addition to the Ministry of Education, Culture, Sports, Science, and Technology (MEXT), the Council for Science, Technology, and Innovation (CSTI) that deals with science, technology, and innovation policy under the Cabinet Office is heavily involved in the policy making concerning DNUS (Yonezawa, 2019).

At the DNUS, deregulation in relation to the university administration and management is pursued for capacity building to enhance the institutional autonomy of DNUs to compete globally. The selection of the candidate DNUs itself is based on the quantitative performance indicators mostly related with research excellence. However, the examination for approval by the expert committee (including international panel members) focuses more on the institutional capacity to set up a strategic approach to be a globally competitive university. The direct financial incentives to be selected as a DNU are rather limited, including only start-up funding. The scheme relies on the universities' own efforts for income generation.

Each university develops its own strategic plan to create the aptitude to be globally competitive in order to attain approval, focusing particularly on income generation capacity and contribution toward social development through innovation. The government closely monitors the progress of these strategic plans and road maps. The DNUs also submit their plans to improve ranking status, and these plans are also examined and monitored, with hardly visible financial support from the government to meet these challenges.

3 Case Studies

In this section, we examine the actual condition of two universities in these new "world-class university" schemes, Peking University in China and Tohoku University in Japan.

3.1 *China: Peking University*

Peking University was founded in 1898 and was the first national university in China. Originally, it was known as the Imperial University of Peking and also served as the highest institution for education at its founding. In 1912, it changed to its present name. Peking University is one of the top universities in China that was impacted by the ideas of German research universities in the early 20th century, as well as the U.S. patterns of educational philosophy by 1949, when the People's Republic of China was established. In the early 1950s, like other Chinese universities, it was restructured, modelled on the former Soviet Union. Since the late 1970s, when China adopted its policy of reforms and "open door", it has become one of the most representative of research and comprehensive universities. In 1994, Peking University was selected to be one of two universities (the other is Tsinghua University) that were included in the 211 Project. On its 100th anniversary, on 4 May, 1998, the then-President Jiang Zemin announced that China should improve the quality and international reputation of its higher education by building up several world-class universities by the 21st century. Based on his speech, the Chinese Government developed and implemented China's 985 Project. Peking University was in the first group universities to be listed in the 985 Project. It was later listed in the new national World-Class University and Discipline Project (Double World-Class Project, also referred as Double First-Class Project), launched by the Chinese Government in September 2017. Peking University has 41 disciplines which will be intensively supported and funded to become first-class disciplines worldwide. It has the largest number of disciplines than any other university in this regard. As mentioned, the purpose behind this project is to build numerous Chinese "first-class universities" and "first-class disciplines" in the world by the end of 2050. Like the other 41 universities, Peking University has created relevant strategies to achieve its goals and become a first-class university and produce first-class disciplines.

In the basic principles of the Plan of Building the World-Class University by Peking University, which was issued on December 28, 2017, among other specific points, five major tasks and requirements to be met in promoting the institution to be a first-class university were determined. The plan's basic principles emphasize two points. One is to designate the fostering of integrity and the promotion of the well-rounded development of people as the fundamental task of education. The other, in addition to promoting it as a first-class university, is to continue the emphasis on Peking University as an institution with Chinese characteristics. In terms of its specific goals, the plan suggests three steps to be taken in the next few years. The first is to, by 2020, make Peking University become first as a whole, and some disciplines to be ranked among the front row of world-class universities. It plans to intensively build 30 disciplines on the leading domestic level and world class. The second is, by 2030, to see that Peking University becomes listed among the top world-class universities as a whole and that a group of disciplines be ranked among those of the top world-class universities. Six inter-disciplinary groups will be intensively fostered – natural science, information and engineering, humanities, social sciences, economics and management, and medical science – and strategic, global, forward-looking, problem-focused research will be facilitated. The third is to, by 2048, have placed Peking University as the top world-class university and enable its mainstream disciplines to take the lead among world-class universities.

To achieve these goals, the plan makes the following recommendations: Firstly, strengthen the leadership of the Party and implement the general goals of the Party for the new era as determined in the 19th National People's Congress, building a collaborative system in which the Party takes a unified lead and forms a clear division of labour between the Party and administrative sectors (Huang, 2017a), and establishing a leading team and a committee of experts to develop Peking University as a world-class institution.

Secondly, to establish specifically designated organizations to stimulate and coordinate the process of making Peking University a world-class university at an institutional level. Thirdly, to strengthen performance-based evaluation systems. Fourthly, to create a campus culture in which all academics and administrative staff are making efforts to achieve this goal.

Further, the university has planned to take more particular measures in its teaching and research activities and to carry out effective reforms to realize its goals. For example, it will build an integrated and diverse education and training system by combining general studies with professional programmes and stimulate a university-wide free elective system, making it possible for all undergraduate students to freely change their specifications within their college. Also, it will promote the formation of two different models of doctoral education and training, one for professional education and another for academic research. In relation to recruiting and evaluating faculty members, the university will exercise a tenure-tracking system, attract world-class talents, improve the international competitiveness of faculty members, reform the evaluation systems of faculty members, and develop a system internationally competitive of salaries and award schemes. Other reforms include delegating more autonomy to individual departments or colleges in relation to budgetary allocation, educating and training students, and providing support for the development of applied and interdisciplinary areas, or programmes. More importantly, unlike other top universities of science and technology, it aims to construct a system of philosophy and social sciences based on socialist practice with Chinese characteristics. For example, it will take Marxism as a guide; uphold cultural self-confidence; strengthen China's leading role and its power of discourse in ideological areas; stimulate the excellence of Chinese culture to be further developed; construct the Chinese spirit, values, and strengths; strengthen the construction of the disciplines of Marxism theory; and make efforts to form a Chinese theory, and then to research, interpret, and solve Chinese problems with this theory.

3.2   *Japan: Tohoku University*

Tohoku University was found in 1907 as the third imperial university. Through its more than 110 year history, Tohoku University has maintained its position as one of the top universities in the country as well as in Asia. In its submission to become a DNU, the university carefully reflected its institutional context, such as its tradition of an open-door policy to a wide range of people, including women, international academics and students, and practice-oriented research. Tohoku University is also located at the epicentre of the Great East Japan Earthquake and Tsunami in 2011 and has led the knowledge-based contribution to disaster reduction and recovery as the flagship university in this area.

As an organizational structure, Tohoku University has a rather discipline-based academic tradition that covers all the major fields in the humanities, social sciences, natural sciences, engineering, and medical sciences. Adding to these schools and departments, Tohoku University has developed various research institutes, such as material science, electrical engineering, and disaster science. In particular, the Advanced Institute for Material Research (AIMR), established in 2007, developed a 100% English-based operation to attract global talents, and developed a multidisciplinary, cutting-edge research community. Within a tradition of interdisciplinary university-wide collaboration in research, Tohoku University proposed a three-layered system for research innovation and advanced studies, as shown in Figure 7.1. At the bottom, a cluster of basic departments is the foundation of academic activities. This implies the respect and utilization of department-based academic units mostly with a strong disciplinary-based academic tradition. In the middle, the layer of interdisciplinary research alliance advances cross-sectoral

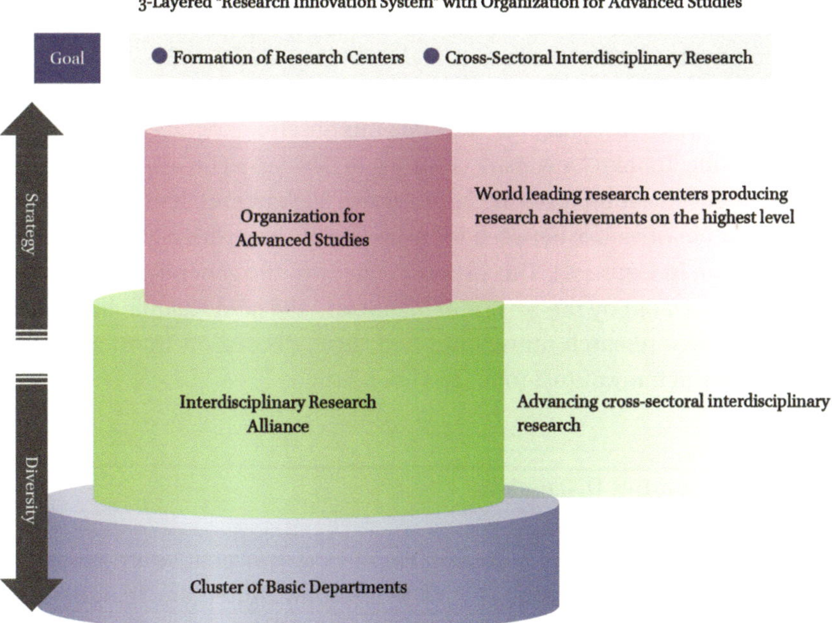

FIGURE 7.1   Strategic formation of research centres and system reform

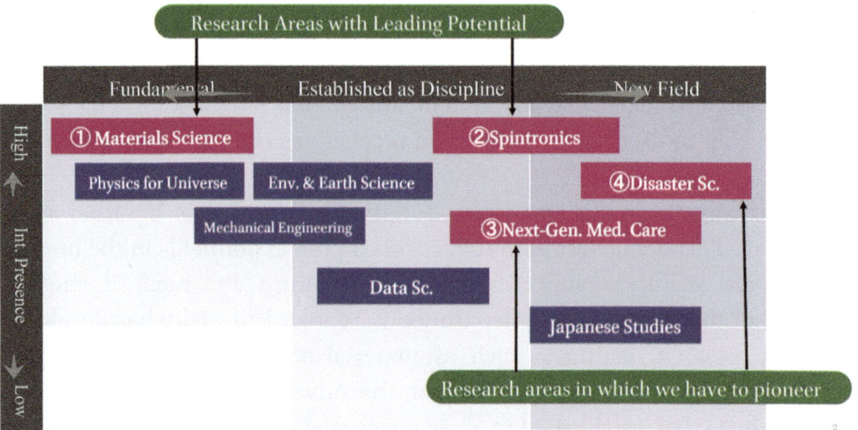

FIGURE 7.2   Prioritized areas for realizing world-leading research

interdisciplinary research. At the top layer, the world leading research centres produce research achievements at the highest level and are as the "star-players' organization" for advanced studies.

Also, Tohoku University undertook a comprehensive analysis across the academic fields and set the prioritized promotion of world-leading research centres in four research areas and international research clusters in nine fields with five other strong areas, as shown in Figure 7.2. Here, Tohoku University, which has a relatively strong international presence in fundamental fields, is trying to invest its resources in new and emerging fields, such as disaster sciences, next-generation medical care, data sciences, and Japanese studies.

Through these investments toward interdisciplinary, newly emerging research fields, Tohoku University is aiming to develop a constructive relationship between education fostering future global leaders, excellent research, and the co-creation of values between industry and society with a global perspective, as shown in Figure 7.3. This idea is in line with the general purpose of the DNU scheme set out by the government, namely, the co-development of globally competitive research universities and society based on frontier science, technology, and innovation (Yonezawa et al., 2019).

4   Comparative Discussion

The current approaches to fostering world-class universities in Japan and China are different, almost opposite, in terms of their direction. In its national policy, the Chinese government has emphasized discipline-based capacity building by identifying a list of departments as well as institutions to support

FIGURE 7.3   Tohoku University Vision 2030

becoming world-class, while the Japanese government is focused on an insti-tution-wide, cross-disciplinary approach to stimulate innovation through col-laboration with industry.

The dramatic increase in available resources in China and highly skilled tal-ent, together with the desire for international recognition, has motivated the drive for massive investment in discipline-based research, including the basic sciences. This approach has had a direct impact on improving the position of Chinese universities in the current global rankings as these stress research performance as determined by research publications and citations. The recent development of subject-based rankings is also encouraging as this supports the pursuit of discipline-based world-class university policies.

In contrast, in Japan, which has a mature society suffering from financial constraints and an ageing population, the government and universities can no longer expect a substantial increase in public funding for universities. Thus, close linkages and partnerships with industry and business through partici-pation in open innovation is a more realistic approach for attracting invest-ment in university activities. From the perspectives of government, industry, and taxpayers, the establishment of a virtuous cycle of mutual development between universities and industry through innovation based on knowledge creation is desirable and appealing. Here, the interdisciplinary approaches are favoured, and Japanese universities are in a relatively better position in the newly emerging rankings and indicators in relation to innovation.

Nevertheless, there are some similarities between the two countries. Both countries are strengthening their national, top-down commitment to the development of world-class university policies. This is perhaps one of the most important aspects that they have in common. It is also apparent that the universities were selected to realize a national ambition to increase the number of top-ranked universities. Furthermore, both countries have worked out clearly defined roadmaps or action plans for achieving their goals.

In China, three steps will be taken to achieve the goals of the Double World-Class Project. Namely, by 2020, several Chinese universities and some disciplines will be ranked as world-class, and several disciplines will be approaching the top end of those deemed to world-class. By 2030, even more universities and disciplines will be labelled world-class. Several of them will be at the top of the world-class universty rankings, while several disciplines will be at the top end of those considered to be world-class. Additionally, the overall quality of national higher education will have remarkably improved. By 2050, the number of Chinese world-class universities and disciplines will be massively increased, and those world-class universities and disciplines will be ranked at the top of the world-class rankings. China will also have a strong higher education system.

In Japan, Prime Minister Shinzo Abe's government developed a plan to have 10 Japanese universities ranked within the top 100 in the world by the mid-2020s. The DNU scheme is linked to this national goal, and the DNUs have been requested to clarify their plans and roadmaps to achieve high-ranking status. Here, however, the emphasis is more on institutional-level rankings and not necessarily subject-level rankings. That said, in the process of selection and monitoring, the universities have been required to identify their strong and weak fields, and to indicate how they are planning to develop balanced academic profiles as comprehensive research universities.

In China, both the universities and disciplines listed in the Double World-Class Project are accredited by the Ministry of Education. The outcome of the selection process reflects the strong and clear political will and orientation of the central government, which comprises a number of national strategies and needs, the current distribution of universities at a national level, and regional development.

In Japan, the selection of the DNUs was made through two steps: first, the shortlisting of candidate universities based on quantitative indicators in research performance and, second, the submission of strategic plans and interviews by the selection committee, which also included international members. In the first stage, only seven universities were shortlisted, three of which were subsequently selected, and the other four universities were approved later. The shortlisting was apparently decided in a top-down manner, and MEXT is substantially committed to the design of this selection scheme.

Adding to this, in China, there is a very strong emphasis on Chinese characteristics and the Chinese national context. In other words, the basic principle behind the implementation of the Double World-Class Project is that the involved universities and disciplines remain rooted in China (i.e., solving Chinese problems and producing graduates dedicated to socialism). While facilitating the advancement of new disciplines and especially the hard sciences, China anticipates that it may also support disciplines with Chinese characteristics, such as Chinese medicine and culture. In Japan, the stress is more on national competitiveness in science, technology, and innovation, so research universities are considered key tools in this economic drive. At the same time, the universities are requested to clarify their ideas on how to strengthen their humanities and social sciences education and research (Huang, 2017b).

5   Implications for Policy and Practice

Finally, here the authors provide the policy implications for broadening these policy options to foster world-class universities in both China and Japan to a wider, international audience.

5.1   *From the Perspective of China*

The main implications from the case study of China are summarized below. Firstly, as building world-class universities and disciplines is concerned with various stakeholders and requires a huge amount of financial investment and strong support from local authorities and different areas of society, it is highly important to create strong partnerships and collaboration between the central government, local authorities, universities, and industry and business, as well as with other stakeholders.

Secondly, different from the 211 and 985 Projects, building world-class disciplines constitutes a new goal of the Chinese Double World-Class Project of 2017, and, in addition to research activities, improving the quality and international competitiveness of key disciplines is also key to the accomplishment of these goals. Thirdly, a "grass roots" approach is important in the aim to create first universities and disciplines, because none of these national or institutional goals can be realized unless individual academics and administrative staff are highly motivated and making efforts in the same direction. Fourthly, institutional leadership matters, too, as building world-class universities and disciplines will not be successful unless individual universities, especially their institutional leaders, have clear and realistic goals, as well as competent leadership, and can create generally accepted evaluation systems and governance arrangements that reflect campus cultures. Finally, nothing is more important than fostering top graduates and yielding internationally recognized research outcomes.

5.2   *From the Perspective of Japan*

What the Japanese Government and leading universities are trying to do is to develop a virtuous cycle for the development of social ecosystem between the universities and society through both human resource development and knowledge creation. Here, the governance and management reforms of the universities are key. World-class universities in the contemporary context are requested to develop their capacities in regard to leadership and management to meet the needs of society and attract public and private resources. Public funding for the higher education system overall is unlikely to increase under the severe constraints of the national budget. Thus, to be world-class, the concentration of higher education funding to the top university is the only option in order to maintain or increase the level of funding for top universities. To designate a distinguished status is the first step. However, the actual process of realizing the expected virtuous cycle for the development the society as a whole is not yet clear except for an emphasis on the spirit of nationwide collaboration. That said, it is true that the Cabinet Office is facilitating dialogues between the top leaders of the universities, government, and industry.

References

Hazelkorn, E. (Ed.). (2016). *Global rankings and the geopolitics of higher education: Understanding the influence and impact of rankings on higher education, policy and society*. Routledge.

Huang, F. (2015). Building the world-class research universities: A case study of China. *Higher Education, 70*(2), 203–215. https://doi.org/10.1007/s10734-015-9876-8

Huang, F. (2017a). Who leads China's leading universities? *Studies in Higher Education, 42*(1), 79–96. https://doi.org/10.1080/03075079.2015.1034265.

Huang, F. (2017b, September 29). Double world-class project has more ambitious aims. *University World News*, p. 476. Retrieved March 25, 2020, from https://www.universityworldnews.com/post.php?story=2017092913334471

Stensaker, B., et al. (2019). Stratified university strategies: The shaping of institutional legitimacy in a global perspective. *The Journal of Higher Education, 90*, 539–562. https://doi.org/10.1080/00221546.2018.1513306

Yonezawa, A. (2018). Japan: World-class universities for social innovation. *International Higher Education, 96*, 21–23. https://doi.org/10.6017/ihe.2019.96.10779

Yonezawa, A. (2019). National university reforms introduced by the Japanese government. In C. D. Wan, M. N. N. Lee, & H. Y. Loke (Eds.), *The governance and management of universities in Asia: Global influences and local responses* (pp. 81–93). Routledge.

Yonezawa, A., Hammond, C. D., Brotherhood, T., Kitamura, M., & Kitagawa, F. (2019). Evolutions in knowledge production policy and practice in Japan: A case study of an interdisciplinary research institute for disaster science. *Journal of Higher Education Policy and Management, 42*(2), 230–244. https://doi.org/10.1080/1360080X.2019.1701850

Yonezawa, A., & Shimmi, Y. (2016). Transformation of university governance through internationalization. In N. C. Liu, Y. Cheng, & Q. Wang (Eds.), *Matching visibility and performance* (pp. 103–118). Sense Publishers.

Yudkevich, M., Altbach, P. G., & Rumbley, L. E. (Eds.). (2016). *The global academic rankings game: Changing institutional policy, practice, and academic life*. Routledge.

PART 2

Institutional Models

∵

CHAPTER 8

The Future of Chinese Universities

Pathways and Strategies

Zhongqin Lin

Abstract

Shanghai Jiao Tong University (SJTU) is one of the rapidly developing universities in the People's Republic of China in the past 20 years. SJTU adheres to scientific planning and carries out strategic planning every five years to steadily build itself into a world-class university. During the twenty years from the 10th Five-Year Plan to the 13th Five-Year Plan, it has carried out strategic planning based on different themes. Though SJTU has made remarkable progress in recent years, it is still far from being one of the world's leading universities. Considering the future challenges, SJTU is formulating the 14th Five-Year Plan and strives to fulfill the task of "comprehensively promoting the overall ability of the university and achieving world-class status".

Keywords

rapid developments – future challenges – strategic planning

1 Introduction

Chinese higher education has made remarkable progress in the past 40 years thanks to the government's attention and support as well as the Chinese universities' persistent efforts. Shanghai Jiao Tong University (SJTU), one of the rapidly developing universities in the People's Republic of China, can be viewed as the epitome of the rapid development of Chinese higher education. Now and into the foreseeable future, on the basis of maintaining the current development trend, Chinese universities need to set out their future ambitions.

2   The Rapid Development of Chinese Higher Education

Since China's reform and opening up, the development of Chinese higher education can be divided into three phases. The first phase is marked by the restoration of Chinese higher education in 1977 when the Chinese leader Deng Xiaoping put forward the development principle of respecting knowledge and talent, with the main task of gearing education to the needs of modernization, the world and the future. During this period, China resumed the higher education entrance examination in the winter of 1977, held the National Science Congress and the National Education Work Conference in 1978, and issued *The Decision on the Reform of the Education System* in 1985 that involved reorganizing and updating the faculty structure of higher education institutions (HEIs), publishing a catalogue of specialties, improving the conditions of teaching in HEIs, building an educational system with bachelor, master and doctoral programmes, and initiating international educational exchanges.

The second stage is marked by the building of high-level universities and key disciplines after 1995, when the Chinese leader Jiang Zemin proposed the development aim of rejuvenating the country through science and education", with the main task of "leveraging education for national revival, and constantly promoting educational innovation". During this period, the 211 and 985 Projects were launched in 1995 and 1999 respectively, after the issue of *The Overall Construction Plan of Project 211* (1995) and *The Action Plan for Revitalizing Education for the 21st Century* (1999), involving strengthening the scientific research function of universities, reforming the personnel system of HEIs, merging universities, expanding the enrollment in higher education, and promoting the internationalization of higher education.

The third stage is marked by the further promotion and development of world-class universities and world-class disciplines after 2015, when the Chinese leader Xi Jinping put forward the development aim of cultivating people with moral integrity, with the main task of being oriented towards the frontiers of global science and technology, being geared to the needs of the national economy and the whole country. During this period, *The Overall Plan for Promoting the Construction of World-class Universities and Disciplines* was published in 2015 and the *Achieving Decisive Victory to Build a Well-Off Society* report was issued in the 19th National Congress in 2017, which clearly set out the goals of Chinese higher education development, speeding up the construction of world-class universities and world-class disciplines, and bringing out the full potential of higher education. By the middle of this century, the number and strength of world-class universities and world-class disciplines in China will be in the forefront of the world, and China will become a powerful country in higher education.

2.1   *The Perspective of Rapid Development*

China has established the largest higher education system in the world. Higher education in China is rapidly shifting from massification to popularization, and innovation, international influence, and the reputation of Chinese HEIs have significantly improved.

Recent years have seen the rapid growth of the number of Chinese HEIs, the gross enrollment rate (GER) of higher education, the number of enrolled students in HEIs, and the number of enrolled graduate students, etc., among which, the GER has increased from 1.6% in 1978 to 48.1% in 2018 (MOE, 2019b). The population who has access to higher education is rapidly becoming a major competitive labour force, instead of the cheap labour force of earlier years. China's influence on the world higher education landscape is increasing. With the expansion of higher education, the total number of Chinese students studying abroad has exceeded five million, and China has become the world's largest source of international students (MOE, 2017). The number of students studying abroad each year has increased from 1,000 in 1978 to more than 660,000 in 2018. While the number of outbound students continues to grow, China has also become the fourth largest destination country in the world after the United States, Australia, and Canada.

The innovation of Chinese universities has improved rapidly. The number of scientific papers indexed by Web of Science has increased by 20 times, and the proportion of the total number of global papers has increased by 10 times, with the number of indexed papers ranking second globally in the past decade (Zhang, 2019). After the number of papers reached the second in the world, improving the quality of the papers has become the main task for Chinese HEIs. According to the Category Normalized Citation Impact (CNCI) based on the InCites database, most of Chinese HEIs' CNCI are lower than the global benchmark; however, in the last decade, the nine leading Chinese universities (the C9 universities)[1] have surpassed the global benchmark, and the 211 Project universities have also surpassed the benchmark. In general, a total of 189 HEIs in China have surpassed the global benchmark, which is a six-fold increase from 30 years ago (ARWU, 2019a).

With the improvement of innovation capability, the international influence and reputation of Chinese HEIs are constantly improving. The global ranking of Chinese HEIs has been rising rapidly in the past 15 years. Taking ARWU (the first multi-indicator global university ranking in the world, which started from 2003) as an example, the number of Chinese HEIs in the world's top 200 list has increased from 0 in 2003 to 20 in 2019, and the number of HEIs in the top 500 list is growing in parallel, with 66 HEIs in 2019, ranking the second in the world (the United States leads with 137 HEIs) (ARWU, 2019b). In addition to Tsinghua University and Peking University, Shanghai Jiao Tong University, Fudan University, Zhejiang University, and the University of Science and Technology of China have also been listed among the top 100 in various global rankings, including ARWU, QS, THE and U.S. News. In terms of the international influence of disciplines, Chinese HEIS demonstrate a strong performance in engineering and sciences.

2.2   *The Drives for Rapid Development*

One of the core factors for Chinese higher education to achieve rapid development is the strategic support from the government. At the level of national planning, China regards education as part of an overall national strategy, and includes strategies to develop the country through science and education, to advance the country through developing talent, to encourage innovation-driven development, and to prioritize education. At the national policy level, the Chinese government has put forward a series of significant long-term plans and initiatives to build a number of key universities, such as the Project 211, the Project 985, and the Double World-Class Project; advanced a wide range of major scientific research programmes, such as the 863 Programme, the 973 Programme, the National Key Research and Development Programme, the National Science and Technology Major Project, and the National Natural Science Funds; and it has promoted a number of major platforms, such as the National Key Scientific Facilities, State Key Laboratories and Provincial and Ministerial Key Laboratories. After entering the 21st century, apart from the strategic emphasis and policy support, the Chinese government's investment in higher education and scientific research has increased by more than 10 times. National fiscal funding for higher education has increased from billion C¥56.4 billion in 2000 to C¥1346.4 billion in 2019 (MOE, 2019a). Science and technology funding for HEIS has increased from C¥7.6 billion in 2000 to billion C¥145.7 billion in 2018 (State Council, 2018).

Another core factor in the rapid development of Chinese higher education is the greater public attention to education. Chinese people generally believe that education can change the fate of ordinary people and help families out of poverty. A number of surveys (for example, CCTV-2's annual "Economic Survey of China") have shown that Chinese people's willingness to spend money on education has been continuously on the rise. With increasing levels of consumption, education consumption is now higher than housing and health care, and it has become the most popular item for Chinese people to invest in. Chinese people give more weight to education and believe it is a bridge to a civilized society. This cultural tradition is an important force driving the rapid development of both Chinese education and higher education.

3 The Strategic Plans and Developments of sJTU in the Past 20 Years

3.1 *A Brief Profile of sJTU*

Shanghai Jiao Tong University (sJTU), is one of the HEIs which enjoys a long history and a world-renowned reputation. Since its establishment, sJTU has cultivated a large number of outstanding alumni, including former Chinese President of China Jiang Zemin, world renown scholars including Qian Xuesen, Wu Wenjun, Xu Guangxian, and patriotic hero such as Wang Zhengyi, etc. The university now has nearly 40,000 students, including about 16,000 undergraduates, 16,000 Masters' students, and 8,000 doctoral students. It has about 3,000 full-time faculty members. In 2019, its fiscal revenue was C¥13.8 billion, of which C¥6.2 billion was invested in education and C¥4.2 billion in scientific research. Now it has developed into a comprehensive university with 10 schools in engineering, five schools in sciences, four schools in life sciences, and 12 schools in humanities and social sciences. There are 67 undergraduate disciplines awarding bachelor degrees, 56 disciplines awarding Master's degrees, and 45 disciplines awarding doctoral degrees. The university has made great achievements in many disciplines. For example, in terms of the Essential Science Indicators (ESI), the university has six disciplines in the top 0.1%, one in the top 0.01%, and 19 in the top 1%. Also, five disciplines were listed as A+, 10 as A and A– respectively, at the Fourth National Discipline Evaluation in 2017.

sJTU carries out strategic planning every five years to substantially promote academic excellence and build itself into a world-class university. During the twenty years from the 10th Five-Year Plan to the 13th Five-Year Plan, it carried out strategic planning with different themes. The focus of the 10th Five-Year Plan was to "fill gaps on a resources-driven basis", the 11th Five-Year Plan was to "increase quantity on an indicators-driven basis", the 12th Five-Year Plan was to "attach equal importance to quantity and quality on a targets-driven basis", and the 13th Five-Year Plan was to "prioritize quality on a mission-driven basis" (see 4.3 for further discussion) (sJTU, 2020). Centred on the principle of "comprehensive academic structure, research-orientation and internationalization", sJTU firmly promotes a strategy of strengthening the university with talent and a strategy of internationalization, and it carries out a wide range of major initiatives, including promoting the implementation of strategic plans, constantly raising academic standards and requirements, strengthening key performance incentives, vigorously building scientific research bases, and exploring and practicing special educational zones. Consequently, it has obtained remarkable achievements in the following six aspects: talent cultivation, faculty upgrading, discipline construction, scientific research, internationalized operation, and university governance.

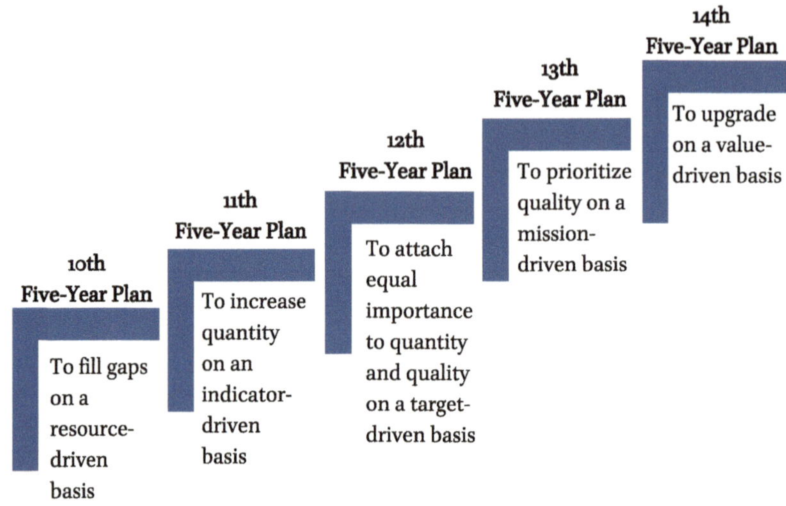

FIGURE 8.1   Focus of STJU's strategic plans in the past 20 years

3.2   *The Development of SJTU over the Past Two Decades under the Guidance of Strategic Planning*

3.2.1   Talent Cultivation

During the 10th Five-Year Plan period, with a focus on adjusting the talent cultivation structure, SJTU mainly optimized the proportion of graduate students and undergraduate students. During the 11th Five-Year Plan period, with a focus on improving the quality of talent cultivation, SJTU improved the quality of graduate students, and the excellence of doctoral theses. During the 12th Five-Year Plan period, with a focus on improving the internationalization of talent cultivation, SJTU increased overseas study programmes and the number of international inward students. During the 13th Five-Year Plan period, with a focus on "cultivating people with moral integrity" and implementing the "Four in One" education concept which emphasized "value guidance, knowledge exploration, capacity building and personality development", SJTU improved career guidance for students and the quality of international students (SJTU, 2020). After two decades of development, the structure and quality of students in SJTU have been optimized. For example, the ratio of graduate students to undergraduate students in 2019 was three times that of 2001, and the number of international students in 2019 was five times that of 2001. Also, the talent cultivation model keeps updating in SJTU to make sure that Chinese students can enjoy world-class higher education experience without having to go abroad. Specifically, SJTU has successfully implemented a variety of initiatives related to talent cultivation, including Zhiyuan College, Zhiyuan Honours Programme, ACM Pilot Class, IEEE Pilot Class and Qian Xuesen Class, etc.

3.2.2   Faculty and Staff

During the 10th Five-Year Plan period, with a focus on improving the academic degree structure and professional title structure of full-time teachers, SJTU improved the proportion of teachers with doctorates and with senior professional titles. During the 11th Five-Year Plan period, with a focus on improving the international level of full-time teachers, SJTU constructed a talent pyramid system to introduce and cultivate academic talents. During the 12th Five-Year Plan period, with a focus on building a high-level faculty, SJTU mainly implemented a plan to introduce high-caliber overseas talents. During the 13th Five-Year Plan period, with a focus on comprehensively improving the faculty, SJTU facilitated the honorary and tenure-track recruitment of high-level talents. After two decades of development, the structure of the faculty has been continuously optimized. The proportion of full-time faculty with doctorates in 2019 was nearly three times that of 2001, and the proportion of full-time faculty with overseas doctoral degrees in 2019 was nearly five times that of 2001. Meanwhile, the tenure faculty system has been built, and the number of high-level talents has multiplied. Specifically, there are over a thousand faculty members in the tenured system, and likewise over a thousand post-doctoral researchers, which serves as a talent pool for the tenure system. Also, SJTU has increasingly enhanced the system to nurture multi-dimensional talent. It takes systematic measures to improve the structure of faculty and staff, to develop a diversified evaluation system to help form a talent system of five categories, i.e. faculty members, research scientists, supporting staff, administrative staff, and counselors and tutors.

3.2.3   Discipline Development

During the 10th Five-Year Plan, with a focus on strengthening the comprehensive structure of disciplines, SJTU improved the structure of liberal arts and medical disciplines. During the 11th Five-Year Plan, with a focus on strengthening the construction of main disciplines, SJTU optimized the layout of disciplines. During the 12th Five-Year Plan, with a focus on realizing the balanced development of disciplines, SJTU improved the ranking of first-level disciplines. During the 13th Five-Year Plan, with a focus on promoting inter-disciplines and building an ecosystem of discipline development, SJTU increased the number of disciplines and the proportion of quality disciplines in ESI (1/1000). After two decades of development, the layout and structure of disciplines in SJTU have been optimized, with 56 first-level disciplines covering major areas of science, engineering, medicine, and humanities and social sciences, and 47 doctoral programmes. Among which, 17 disciplines have been selected as Double World-Class disciplines. In SJTU, a number of disciplines enjoy international reputation.

3.2.4   Scientific Research

During the 10th Five-Year Plan, with a focus on expanding the scale of scientific research, SJTU increased the number of papers published in international journals. During the 11th Five-Year Plan, with a focus on boosting the scientific research competitiveness, SJTU increased the total number of citations and the number of projects funded by the National Natural Science Foundation of China (NNSF projects). During the 12th Five-Year Plan, with a focus on improving the level and quality of scientific research, SJTU increased the number of citations per paper and major scientific research projects. During the 13th Five-Year Plan, with a focus on promoting the impact of scientific research, SJTU increased the number of papers published in top journals and the number of highly-cited papers. Scientific research projects in SJTU in the last two decades have grown steadily. Since 2010, the number of NNSF projects has ranked first in China for 10 consecutive years, and the number of research projects funded by National Social Science Fund (NSSF) has been growing continuously. Also, the number of high-level papers has significantly increased. The annual number of papers published in Nature, Science, Cell and other leading journals has increased from a couple in 2001 to about ten in recent years. From 2001 to 2019, the number of papers published on LANCET and PNAS ranked second and third in China respectively. Moreover, SJTU has achieved major progress regarding the national awards, winning a total of 93 National Science and Technology Awards and 72 Outstanding Achievements Awards in Humanities and Social Sciences.

3.2.5   International Partnerships

During the 10th Five-Year Plan, with a focus on actively developing international cooperation, SJTU implemented the policy of "going out" and "bringing in". During the 11th and 12th Five-Year Plans, which focused on improving the level and quality of international cooperation in education, SJTU promoted cooperation with top global universities. During the 13th Five-Year Plan, with a focus on expanding globally and building overseas centres, SJTU enhanced its international reputation and influence. After two decades of development, international cooperative education at SJTU has been continuously expanded. It cooperated with the University of Michigan in 2000, and successfully established the Joint Institute with the University of Michigan at SJTU in 2006, which has become a model of internationalized education. In 2012, SJTU cooperated with ParisTech to establish the SJTU-ParisTech Elite Institute of Technology (SPEIT), which was awarded as the Excellent Cooperation Project between Chinese and French Universities by both governments in 2016. In 2017, SJTU cooperated with the Moscow Aviation Institute to build the Sino-Russian Joint Research Institute. Apart from these, international cooperation at SJTU is carried out in various fields, involving joint doctoral degree programmes, cooperative double degree programmes, international scientific research cooperation, and international co-authored theses.

Over the past 20 years, SJTU has drawn up the "Three Steps" strategy, continuously and substantially improving its core competitiveness, academic capability, and international influence, gradually becoming a world-class university, and successfully completing the first two strategic objectives of the "three Steps" strategy, laying a solid foundation for the third step of "comprehensively promoting the overall ability and achieving the world-class status". SJTU has strengthened the core position of "cultivating people with moral integrity", and it has formed a distinctive training system for top innovative talents. SJTU has gathered a group of high-caliber faculty members of international standard, built a number of world-class disciplines, produced various influential original research, built an internationalized educational system with its own distinctive characteristics, and explored the governance pattern of a world-class university with Chinese characteristics.

4   Key Strategic Planning for the Future

4.1   The Current Socio-Economic Contexts for Developing Academic Excellence

With the global economy slowing down, and downward risks in the economy continuing to increase, educational funding from governments is negatively affected. Also, increased trade barriers and the geopolitical conflicts have multiplied the difficulties in international exchanges and cooperation. Against this backdrop, it is necessary to seek a new pathway for development in the process of globalization. Mastering core technologies is an important component of comprehensive national strength; thus, it is urgent to conduct major basic research and achieve technological breakthroughs. At the same time, new information technology and AI- and digital-based economy bring about more industries, and a new round of scientific and technological revolutions and industrial transformation are reshaping the global innovation landscape. The integrated development of digitalization, networking and intelligentization is profoundly changing the way that people work, study and live, and China must accelerate its new infrastructure development and usher in new drivers for further development.

4.2   Building WCU as Responsibility and Mission for Chinese HEIs

China's development in various fields has entered a new era. The principal contradiction facing Chinese society has been transformed into one between unbalanced and inadequate development and the people's growing need for a better life. China is shifting from a major economy to an economic power; its economy is shifting from a stage of high-speed growth to a stage of high-quality development; and its science and technology aims to realize innovation as the primary driving force for development and promote the strategic upgrading of China's overall scientific and technological level. In this context, it is urgent for China to make major breakthroughs in key fields and key technologies. Universities should better serve the country and the world through science, technology and education, and integrate moral values into all aspects and fields of education. They should also deepen reform in science and technology, stimulate innovation, and improve the efficiency of the innovation system. Furthermore, they should serve economic and social development. Building world-class universities is the unshakable responsibility and mission for Chinese HEIs, which conforms to the development trend. Centred on talent cultivation, the top Chinese universities will speed up the construction of global universities with Chinese characteristics in the next 30 years, being equipped with a global vision and commitment to solve national problems.

4.3 Future Challenges for SJTU

Though SJTU has made remarkable progress in the past twenty years, it is still far from being one of the world's leading universities. First, there is a large number of published papers, but the quality of these papers still needs to be improved. Though it is not uncommon for researchers in SJTU to publish high impact papers, the quantity still lags behind. Second, the number of high-quality disciplines needs to be increased; top disciplines in SJTU pale into comparison with world-class universities. Third, there are large number of titled faculty, but relatively low proportion of them are leading talents of international standard. Fourth, the size of student body is large, but there are only a small number of outstanding alumni. Fifth, interdisciplinary research needs to be promoted with major initiatives and policies. Therefore, in order to build the university into a world-class university, the university, colleges and departments need to pay close attention to the fundamental factors causing these problems, develop effective solutions and take transformative measures when formulating the 14th Five-Year Plan.

4.4 The "Three-Step" Strategy of SJTU

The development of SJTU has always been accompanied by the development of the country, and SJTU is actively building world-class university with Chinese characteristics. The vision of SJTU is to provide world-class universities with excellent faculty and students; to accelerate the construction and formation of academic discipline clusters with world-class influence; to build a community to attract global talents; to make more contributions to the world and the country; and to become a desirable destination for students world-wide.

Under the guidance of this vision, SJTU adheres to the goal of pursuing excellence, making efforts to develop the comprehensive capability of the university through long-term layout and step-by-step construction. Since 1996, the university has established a "Three-Step" strategy. The first step covered 1996 to 2010, during which the main task of SJTU was to improve the layout and consolidate the foundation of the university, aiming to build a comprehensive research-oriented university with a high level of internationalization and quality, and which laid a solid foundation to building SJTU into a world-class university. The second step was from 2011 to 2020, during which the main task of SJTU was to make breakthroughs and highlight the strengths of the university, aiming to be ranked among (or close to) the world's top 100 universities. The third step is planned from 2021 to 2050, during which the main task of SJTU is to comprehensively promote the overall ability of the university and achieve world-class status, aiming to fully realize its goal to become a world-class university (SJTU, 2020).

Currently, the third step is divided into two stages. The first stage is from 2021 to 2035. SJTU's goal in this period is to achieve domestic and global recognition on its talent cultivation, scientific research, social service and cultural leadership, and to be ranked among world-class universities in terms of key academic indicators and overall capability. The second stage is from 2035 to 2050. SJTU's goal in this period is to become a top world-class university enjoying a global reputation in terms of the outcomes of talent cultivation, the quality of scientific research, and the governance system, as well as educational ideas.

5   Conclusion

Since the reform and opening up, coupled with the influence of government's strategies and people's belief, Chinese higher education has witnessed significant improvements in talent cultivation and knowledge creation, as well as its international influence, rapidly moving from a stage of restoration to a stage of building world-class university and disciplines. As one of the landmark universities with rapid development in China, SJTU, under the influence of the current world landscape and the mission of the times, will adhere to the idea of "harmony in diversity and all flowers blooming together", cooperate with universities all over the world, conduct in-depth communications and exchanges, and make concerted efforts for progress and the development of the whole world.

Note

1 C9 universities are Tsinghua University, Peking University, Fudan University, Shanghai Jiao Tong University, Nanjing University, Zhejiang University, University of Science and Technology of China, Harbin Institute of Technology, and Xi'an Jiao Tong University.

References

Academic Ranking for World Universities. (2019a). *Methodology for ShanghaiRanking's global ranking of academic subjects 2019*. Retrieved July 22, 2019, from http://www.shanghairanking.com/shanghairanking-subject-rankings/Methodology-for-ShanghaiRanking-Global-Ranking-of-Academic-Subjects-2019.html

Academic Ranking for World Universities. (2019b). *Academic ranking of world universities 2019*. Retrieved July 22, 2019, from http://shanghairanking.com/ARWU2019.html

Ministry of Education. (2017). *Zhong guo cheng wei shi jie zui da de liu xue shu chu guo he ya zhou zui da liu xue mu di guo* [*China has become the world's largest country of students studying abroad and the largest destination of students in Asia*].
Retrieved July 22, 2020, from http://www.moe.gov.cn/s78/A20/moe_863/201703/t20170309_298739.html

Ministry of Education. (2019a). *2019 nian quan guo jiao yu jing fei zhi xing qing kuang tong ji kuai bao* [*Statistics on national education expenditure in 2019*]. Retrieved July 22, 2020, from http://www.moe.gov.cn/jyb_xwfb/gzdt_gzdt/s5987/202006/t20200612_465295.html

Ministy of Education. (2019b). *Jiao yu bu: Quan guo pu tong gao xiao 2663 suo gao deng jiao yu mao ru xue lv 48.1%* [*MOE: The gross enrollment rate of the 2 663 institutions of higher learning nationwide was 48.1 percent*]. Retrieved July 22, 2019, from http://edu.sina.com.cn/gaokao/2019-07-24/doc-ihytcerm5876983.shtml

Shanghai Jiao Tong University. (2020). *The working paper of 14th five-year plan*. Internal report: Unpublished.

State Council. (2018). *2018 nian quan guo ke ji jing fei tou ru tong ji gong bao* [*Report on national investment in science in 2018*]. Retrieved July 22, 2020, from http://www.gov.cn/xinwen/2019-08/30/content_5425835.htm

Zhang, Zh. H. (2019). *China now No 2 in cited scientific papers*. Retrieved July 22, 2019, from https://global.chinadaily.com.cn/a/201911/20/WS5dd4930fa310cf3e355788ff.html

CHAPTER 9

Providing Access to Excellence

A Roadmap for World-Class Universities

Kim A. Wilcox and Christine A. Victorino

Abstract

As we envision the future of higher education in America and around the globe, institutions that embrace faculty excellence and student success will be better equipped to tackle the world's greatest challenges. Greater access and success among lower income, "first-generation", and under-represented minority students, in particular, will become central to creating the next generation of research, as well as a defining characteristic for world-class universities. This institutional case study will describe the recent transformations at the University of California, Riverside, and its emergence as a world-class institution committed to access, inclusion, and excellence.

Keywords

faculty excellence – student success – access – world-class universities

1   Introduction

Beginning with the rise of the research university in Germany in the 19th century, the term "world-class university" has become synonymous with "outstanding research university". That clarity of definition has made the task of assessing and comparing universities relatively easy, in that there was only one primary dimension to the assessment scale: research prominence. Generally speaking, those schools with a large investment in research and a history of important research discoveries, have been seen as world-class. It is worth remembering, however, that the word university is derived from the Latin for universitas magistrorum et scholarium, or "community of teachers and scholars". From that, it follows that a world-class university could be conceived as a collection of world-class teachers and scholars regardless of their research output. In other words, it is the composition of the people who make up the university that determines its value and quality.

For most observers, the connection between a pre-eminent research environment and the presence of outstanding teachers and students is self-evident. You simply cannot create a world-class research enterprise or a history of outstanding research achievements with a mediocre faculty and student body; so the distinction is unimportant. But that analysis again assumes there is only one dimension of assessment: research productivity. Moreover, if most universities are comprised of largely the same types of people, then there is no means of knowing what the research prowess would be of a different-looking faculty or student body. Increasingly, universities are recognizing the limitations of a unidimensional perspective on quality and are now looking to other activities as they assess their effectiveness and success.

One good example of a dimension to assess success in higher education is community engagement. Whether the engagement involves growing a regional economy, improving local health care, or assisting community social programmes; universities have come to recognize that they have a responsibility to engage with the broader society. As a result, the breadth and success of community engagement efforts is now part of what many consider when assessing world-class universities. The Carnegie Foundation (based in the United States) acknowledges the community engagement efforts of universities by inviting them to apply for a prestigious Carnegie classification in community engagement (Driscoll, 2015). More recently, there has been an initiative to include university engagement as a possible indicator for world university rankings (Grant, Douglas and Wells, 2019).

In this chapter, we argue for the consideration of another dimension of assessment for world-class status – the composition of the student body and the faculty themselves. In our opinion, a university cannot truly be considered world-class unless it includes a diverse faculty and student body that reflects the population of its state or nation, in terms of wealth, gender, race, and ethnicity.

Universities have always enjoyed great freedom in selecting students and faculty that fit their goals and values. The question before us in the 21st century is what, if anything, the current criteria for selection of students and faculty say about an institution's values, its contribution to society, and its right to be considered world-class. Although universities have traditionally been measured for their research output, taking our university, the University of California, Riverside (UCR), as a case study, we contend that access and diversity measures should also be considered as important indicators of world-class status.

2   Importance of Access to Higher Education

One of the world's greatest challenges is growing social inequality. In 2019, North America and Europe controlled 57% of the world's wealth, though they contain only 17% of the world's adult population (Shorrocks et al., 2019). The People's Republic of China, by contrast, with 18.5% of the global population had a more reasonable 17.7% of global wealth – a percentage, however, that is growing very quickly. At the same time, half of the adults in the world held less than 1% of global wealth.

Wealth is not only distributed unevenly between countries, but within countries, as well. For example, China and the United States, two nations with very different histories and political structures, share this same internal problem. In the United States, the top 1% of the population earns 20% of the national income, while in China the top 1% earns 13% of the national income (Alvaredo et al., 2017), with similar patterns in most countries around the globe.

Arguably, the best tool for any nation to reverse this trend is education. Education holds the promise to advance an individual in society regardless of where their family conditions placed them at birth. But, in countries both rich and poor, access to education is also unevenly distributed, effectively blocking the road to success for millions of individuals, and helping to ensure that the rich continue to get richer, while the poor get poorer. In the United States, children with parents in the top quartile of parental income are 4.8 times more likely to attain a bachelor's degree by age 24 than those from the bottom quartile (Pell Institute, 2019).

In many countries, wealth and minority status are also inextricably linked. In the United States, the median White family household has 20–40 times more wealth than the median Latino or African American family (Collins et al., 2019). Given these stark differences in household income, it is therefore unsurprising that university enrolment and graduation rates also differ by race and ethnicity. To illustrate, only 36% of African American children enrol in college compared to 64.7% of Asian and 41.1% of White students (National Centre for Education Statistics [NCES], 2017). The effect of this inequity is compounded by the fact that graduation rates are also lower for students from under-represented groups. So, if a student is an African American high school student in the United States and among the mere 36% of Black students nationally to get into college, the student's chance of then graduating is still just 40%, and only 34% if you are Black and male.

In the United Kingdom, Black students are more likely to attend university than their White peers, but are substantially under-represented at elite institutions. Black students make up about 8% of the population, but represent just 4% of students enrolled in the Russell Group of universities – a collection of prestigious research universities across the United Kingdom – and less than 2% at Oxford and Cambridge Universities (Swerling, 2019). So, despite the greater likelihood of Black students of attending a university in the United Kingdom, there appears to be systematic barriers to attending top-tier research universities.

This systemic injustice has many consequences beyond just the inequitable distribution of college degrees. It also means that countries around the world are failing to take advantage of the total talent pool of their nation, and as a result, they and the rest of the world are being deprived of an untold number of ideas and discoveries that could improve life for us all. Bell et al. (2018) have suggested the term "Lost Einsteins" for this phenomenon. How many possible "Einsteins" were never given a chance to hone their talents and provide all of humanity with their insights, simply because they were born into the wrong family, or the wrong region, or the wrong country.

Using Nobel recipients as one indicator of the impact of this bias, consider that since its beginning in 1901, 597 people have received the Nobel Prize, but only 53 have been women and only 19 of those women received their prize in the fields of science and medicine (The Nobel Prize, 2019).[1] Similarly, there have been just 15 Black recipients in the history of the prize, and none in science and medicine. This is not a reflection of different abilities, but different opportunities. The effects of education take decades to be felt, given that schooling through to graduate school generally takes at least 20 years and then more time is needed for the graduate to develop their career and realize their potential. So it is urgent that we move now to diversify our campuses, so that observers in 2120 are not still bemoaning the host of lost opportunities across the globe.

3 University of California, Riverside's Roadmap from 2010 to 2020

The University of California, Riverside (UCR) provides an institutional case study for achieving research excellence, while demonstrating success in faculty diversity and student success. Established in 1954, UCR was among a cohort of new campuses that included the Santa Barbara, Davis, and San Diego campuses during the 1950s and early 1960s. At its founding, the Riverside campus aimed to distinguish itself from its University of California peers, as a smaller, more student- and undergraduate-focused institution. Specifically, then-Provost Gordon Watkins sought to build the "Swarthmore of the West", referencing the elite, private liberal arts college near Philadelphia.

By the 1980s, however, UCR needed to expand, or else risk the campus's closure or merger with another university. With decreasing state investment in public higher education, combined with the faculty's desire to bolster the institution's research capacity (akin to their University of California peers), the campus began a long and sustained period of student enrollment growth and accompanying tuition revenue. Additionally, through the 1990s, Chancellor Ray Orbach worked deliberately to attract students who reflected California's broad racial and ethnic diversity.

By the 2010s, UCR was firmly established as an "R1" research university (Carnegie classification: very high research activity), as well as a Hispanic-Serving Institution. The campus student population included nearly 29% Latino students and 36% under-represented minority (URM: Latino/Hispanic, African American, and Native American) students. More than half of students were first-generation college students (52%) or from low-income backgrounds (55% federal Pell Grant recipients).

Notwithstanding these major institutional shifts, California Governor Jerry Brown publicly chided UCR for its low graduation rates, compared to its sister campuses in Berkeley, Los Angeles, and elsewhere (Gordon, 2013). Later that fall, U.S. News and World Report announced its annual university rankings, where UCR's position was on a downward trajectory. Over a period of five years, the university dropped 27 places in the rankings. In the Washington Post in 2015, Chancellor Kim Wilcox scoffed at the rankings criteria, "Whatever this system values is inconsistent with what public universities provide" (Anderson, 2015). He believed that the U.S. News formula emphasized exclusion, wealth, and prestige, instead of recognizing the public mission of institutions, like UCR, that more effectively serve and graduate the nation's low-income and under-represented minority students, while maintaining the highest levels of research productivity and excellence.

Facing external pressure from the state and declining confidence due to the rankings, UCR immediately focused on implementation of its strategic plan, UCR 2020: The Path to Preeminence. The primary aspiration of the strategic plan was to achieve the profile of an institution in the Association of American Universities (AAU), an invitational-only group of 65 distinguished research universities from across North America. The strategic plan detailed a range of targeted efforts related to elevating academic excellence, increasing student access and diversity, and promoting greater engagement locally, nationally, and globally (University of California, Riverside [UCR], 2010).

One of the first operational issues to address, however, was the mismatch between UCR's student enrolment and institutional capacity. Total enrolment was 8,746 in 1993 and had grown to 21,285 over a 20-year period; but faculty numbers had not kept pace, resulting in one of the highest student-faculty ratios in the University of California system. In addition, administrative processes that worked well for a campus of fewer than 10,000 students were inadequate for a campus of nearly 25,000 students. UCR's culture of centralized authority resulted in a bottleneck of decisions in the Chancellor's and Provost's offices, a perceived lack of transparency, and unnecessary distance between decision-makers and the individuals responsible for implementing those decisions.

Campus leaders further recognized that positioning UCR for the future would require both transforming the institutional culture and shifting the broader narrative about the role of higher education. Internally, that meant distributing decision-making authority, providing greater budget transparency, hiring more faculty and staff, and engaging in robust dialogue among internal and external campus stakeholders. Outside the university, the campus's senior leaders engaged more broadly to augment the nation's understanding of what constitutes a great university in the 21st century.

While the strategic plan focused on multiple areas for improvement, this chapter will focus on two primary and concurrent efforts: growing faculty excellence and improving student success.

4   Growing Faculty Excellence

UCR set an ambitious goal to grow the faculty by approximately 300 – a priority outlined in the strategic plan and consistent with the campus's aspiration to achieve the profile of an AAU institution (Gordon, 2014). The faculty expansion provided an opportunity for the campus to invest strategically in emerging fields of scholarship, foster cross-disciplinary work, and further diversify the faculty. In 2013, the campus employed 660 full-time instructional and clinical faculty members. That number grew to 904, which represents a 37% increase (see Figure 9.1). This growth touched every part of the academic enterprise, with every department having made at least one successful faculty hire.

A significant portion of the faculty expansion involved a cluster hiring initiative, which helped stimulate faculty collaboration in interdisciplinary and emerging areas of scholarship. Notably, UCR hired a variety of innovative clusters, ranging from Indigenous Studies to Translational Plant Sciences to Autonomous and Intelligent Systems. At the same time, the campus hired two Nobel Laureates in Physics and Chemistry, and increased the number of National Academies Members to 22. In terms of research expenditures (Higher Education Research and Development [HERD] Survey, 2018), UCR grew from $130.3 million in 2010 to $167.8 million in 2018 (representing a 29% increase),

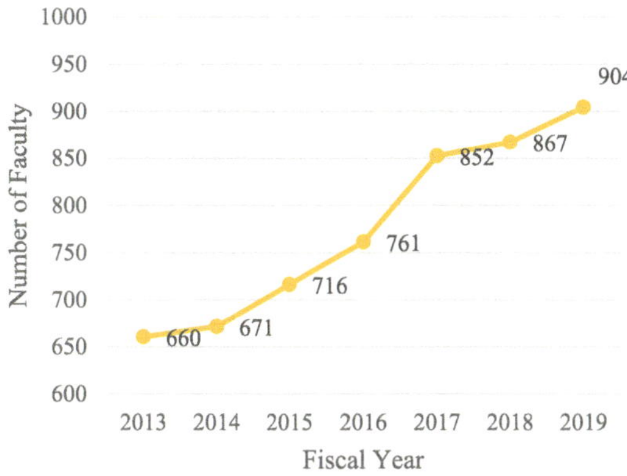

FIGURE 9.1
Full-time ladder-rank and clinical faculty

with continuing gains expected as recently hired, junior faculty develop and strengthen their research activities.

Perhaps more significant, the campus also improved faculty diversity. Prior to 2013, UCR's incoming faculty cohorts averaged 36% women and 10% under-represented minority (URM: Hispanic/Latinx, African American and Native American) faculty members over a 15-year period. To help increase faculty diversity, the campus reshaped hiring practices by broadening recruitment efforts, asking all candidates to provide diversity statements, and mandating diversity training for search committees (Flaherty, 2017). The campus immediately observed dramatic progress in the 2015–16 cohort, which included 22% URM faculty, the largest percentage of any cohort. In 2016–17, UCR reproduced this outcome with 22% URM faculty in the incoming cohort, along with 47% women, the second largest percentage since 1984.

5   Improving Student Success

In 2016, UCR enrolled the most diverse incoming class in its history, with 62.5% first-generation and 51.2% under-represented minority undergraduate students. At the same time, UCR students' academic credentials have steadily risen, with average incoming high school GPAs increasing from 3.43 to 3.80 over ten years (on a 4.0 scale).

To improve student success, the campus convened a Graduation Rate Task Force and implemented the majority of its recommendations. These included introducing new technology tools for course and degree planning, developing academic interventions to improve mastery of course content and grades, prioritizing the availability of courses and sections necessary for students to graduate, and high impact practices to enhance the quality of the undergraduate experience. Consequently, the campus significantly improved in various metrics, such as the number of units enrolled per quarter and first-year retention rates. In addition, UCR improved four-year graduation rates by more than 20 percentage points, and six-year graduation rates by nearly nine percentage points (see Figures 9.2 and 9.3). At the same time, UCR achieved near-parity in graduation rates across racial/ethnic and income groups. In fact, UCR graduates more low-income students (i.e., federal Pell Grant recipients) than the entire Ivy League combined (Hebel and Smallwood, 2019). Moreover, the Education Trust, a non-profit think tank, named UCR among the best in the United States for graduation rates among African American (Nichols and Evans-Bell, 2017) and Latino students (Nichols, 2017).

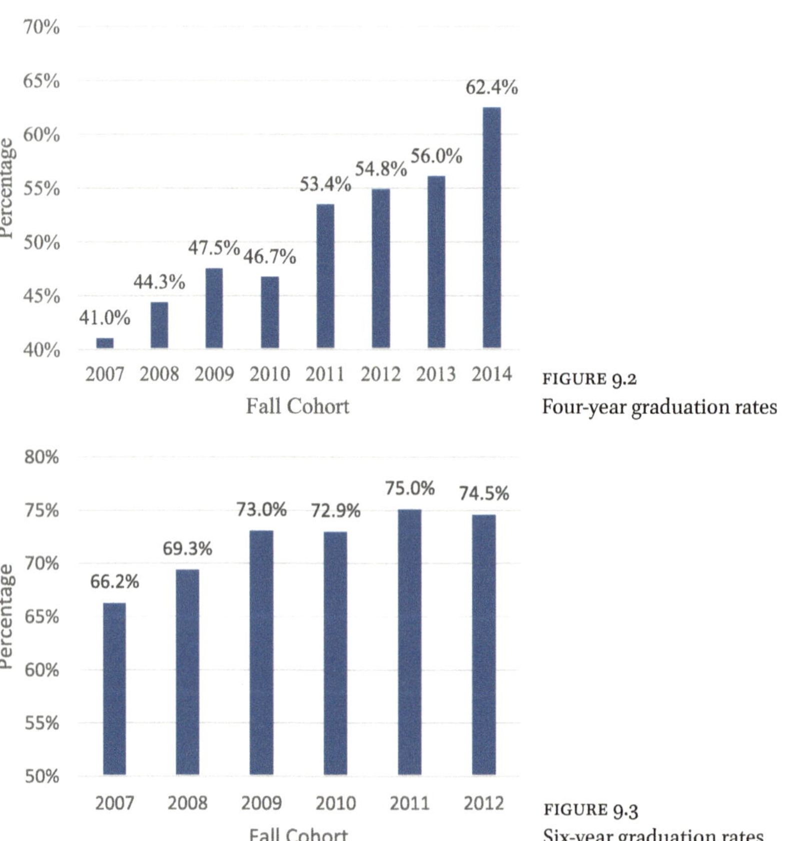

FIGURE 9.2
Four-year graduation rates

FIGURE 9.3
Six-year graduation rates

As a result of these efforts, UCR has become recognized as a leader in student success among research-intensive universities, and has joined with other institutions committed to this work. UCR is a member of the American Talent Initiative (ATI) and the University Innovation Alliance (UIA). ATI membership places UCR among a group of "elite" institutions that have achieved relatively high graduation rates. The UIA, a collection of 11 large public research universities from across America, is dedicated to developing and disseminating best practices to increase access and success among low-income students across the nation.

Following these efforts focused on student success, California Governor Gavin Newsom publicly congratulated UCR for ranking first for social mobility in the U.S. News and World Report (2019). This represented a sea change in the state's recognition of UCR's distinct mission and value to the state. Moreover, this represented a continuing shift in how university rankings measure institutional quality. Specifically, in 2018, the U.S. News and World Report eliminated admissions rates and added Pell-recipient graduation rates to its rankings criteria. As a consequence, UCR improved by 39 places in the rankings in one year – the highest one-year increase among all ranked institutions. Similarly, UCR moved up 80 spots in Forbes' "Best Value Colleges" and 83 spots in the *Wall Street Journal/Times Higher Education* university rankings, both in just two years. By 2020, UCR held the distinction of America's fastest-rising university.

6 The "Secret Sauce" of Success

Unfortunately, UCR's story is a rarity in higher education, both in the United States and around the globe, in that few universities have achieved both research success and diversity among its faculty and student body. But UCR's story makes it clear that such dual success is not only achievable, but attainable simultaneously.

Many people ask how we have made such progress in these two missions, what is our "secret sauce"? The answer is that it took an untold number of specific actions and decisions by the thousands of people for us to achieve all that we have. Upon reflection, however, UCR success in diversity was driven by three things – culture, people, and programmes. From its beginnings, UCR has been more deeply committed to ensuring the quality of our students' experience than most large universities. Chancellor Orbach recognized the value of this student-focused culture and the key role it could play in helping traditionally marginalized students succeed at UCR, when they might not have succeeded elsewhere. He was correct; students from under-represented backgrounds began to enrol and thrive at UCR.

Chancellor Orbach's efforts to diversify the student body not only improved the lives of the students that he recruited, but their presence on the campus helped to reify the culture itself. That culture then started to replicate itself in the people who chose to join the university. Faculty, staff, and administrators were increasingly drawn to UCR because they wanted to be a part of this culture. Many of these recruits had been first-generation or low-income students, themselves; many were also members of traditionally under-represented groups. As academics, many faculty members understood the importance of the research and scholarship that was underway at the university; but because of their personal experiences, they also understood the importance of including a diversity of students in the research process.

The programmes institutionalized at UCR have also been significant, from learning communities to undergraduate research programes and extensive peer mentoring networks in both student and academic affairs, to name just a few. Many universities in the United States have programmes like these, aimed at increasing the participation and educational success of low-income students and of under-represented faculty, staff, and students. While these programmes are well-intentioned and often effective, collectively they have had a limited impact on shifting demographic representation at universities across the nation. Our belief is that such programmes are necessary but not sufficient for achieving success. They can only be truly effective when built on a base of culture and people who support the values motivating those programmes.

7   The Road Forward

The notion of world-class is malleable. It, of course, varies by subject and domain, and has changed markedly over the centuries as the world and its peoples have changed. The question of world-class status became more salient for universities in the late 20th century when a host of publishers and organizations found the monetary value of rankings. Those rankings have driven a variety of institutional behaviours as well as conversations among higher education leaders about how best to measure institutional success across the globe. That conversation is still in its infancy and will evolve significantly in the coming years. To date, discussions about rankings have largely focused on measurement issues, such as how best to assess research prowess (funding level, Nobel Laureates, patents, etc), or whether to account for inherent differences in national support and culture, etc.

We believe there is a more fundamental issue at hand that has to do with what we, as a society of scholars, want from our universities and what we want them to become. The current competition among schools is really a competition to become more like those at the top, whose leadership positions were solidified in the early and mid-20th century. It is not a competition to become something different and more aspirational as a body. Our hope is that universities around the globe can collectively describe the optimal university for the 21st century and then identify markers that would lead us all toward that archetype. We must look to the future, not continue to reinforce the past.

Getting ranking systems to include a wider array of institutional markers is a key step forward, but we should not stop there. We should start now to describe the important characteristics of scholarly activity, student body demographics, faculty cohort, societal impact, etc., that we believe should define a truly world-class university for today and for the future.

Acknowledgement

The authors wish to recognize Elizabeth Claassen Thrush for her helpful comments and editorial assistance during preparation of this chapter.

Note

1   Marie Curie won the prize twice, once in 1903 and once in 1911, so there have been 54 prizes awarded to women with 20 in science and medicine, but only 53 and 19 recipients, respectively.

References

Alvaredo, F., Chancel, L., Piketty, T., Saez, E., & Zucman, G. (2017). Global inequality dynamics: New findings from WID world. *American Economic Review, 107*(5), 404–409.

Anderson, N. (2015, September 9). UC-riverside vs. U.S. news: A university leader scoffs at the rankings. *The Washington Post.* Retrieved February 7 2020, from https://www.washingtonpost.com/news/grade-point/wp/2015/09/09/uc-riverside-vs-u-s-news-a-university-leader-scoffs-at-the-rankings/

Bell, A., Chetty, R., Jaravel, X., Petkova, N., & Van Reenen, J. (2018). Lost Einsteins: Who becomes an inventor in America? *CentrePiece – The Magazine for Economic Performance*, No. 522. Centre for Economic Performance, LSE.

Collins, C., Asante-Muhammed, D., Hoxie, J., & Terry, S. (2019). *Dreams deferred: How enriching the 1% widens the racial wealth divide.* Institute for Policy Studies. Retrieved February 7, 2020, from https://inequality.org/wp-content/uploads/2019/01/IPS_RWD-Report_FINAL-1.15.19.pdf

Driscoll, A. (2015). Analysis of the Carnegie classification of community engagement: Patterns and impact on institutions. In D. G. Terkla & L. S. O'Leary (Eds.), *Assessing civic engagement: New directions for institutional research* (pp. 3–16). Jossey-Bass.

Flaherty, C. (2017, September 28). Making diversity happen. *Inside Higher Ed.* Retrieved February 7, 2020, from https://www.insidehighered.com/news/2017/09/28/how-two-institutions-diversified-their-faculties-without-spending-big-or-setting

Gordon, L. (2013, May 15). Jerry Brown urges UC to stress graduating students in 4 years. *Los Angeles Times.* Retrieved February 7, 2020, from https://www.latimes.com/local/la-xpm-2013-may-15-la-me-uc-regents-20130516-story.html

Gordon, L. (2014, April 24). At inauguration, UC riverside chancellor calls for campus growth. *Los Angeles Times.* Retrieved February 7, 2020, from https://www.latimes.com/local/lanow/la-xpm-2014-apr-24-la-me-ln-uc-riverside-20140424-story.html

Grant, J., Douglas, D. R. B., & Wells, J. (2019, October). *A global initiative to measure university engagement.* Paper presented at the 8th International Conference on World-Class Universities, Shanghai, China.

Hebel, S., & Smallwood, S. (2017, September 20). This one university enrolls more Pell students than the whole Ivy League. *Open Campus.* Retrieved February 7, 2020, from https://www.opencampusmedia.org/2019/09/20/this-one-university-enrolls-more-pell-students-than-the-whole-ivy-league/

Higher Education Research and Development Survey. (2020, January 6). National Science Foundation. Retrieved February 7, 2020, from https://www.nsf.gov/statistics/srvyherd/#tabs-2

National Centre for Education Statistics. (2019). *The condition of education.* Retrieved February 7, 2020, from https://nces.ed.gov/programs/coe/pdf/coe_cpb.pdf

Nichols, A. (2017, December 14). A look at Latino student success. *The Education Trust.* Retrieved February 7, 2020, from https://edtrust.org/resource/look-latino-student-success/

Nichols, A., & Evans-Bell, D. (2017, March 1). *A look at Black student success: Identifying top- and bottom-performing institutions.* The Education Trust. Retrieved February 7, 2020, from https://edtrust.org/resource/blackstudentsuccess/

Pell Institute. (2019). *Indicators of higher education equity in the United States.* Retrieved February 7, 2020, from http://pellinstitute.org/indicators/reports_2019.shtml

Shorrocks, A., Davies, J., & Lluberas, R. (2019). *Global wealth 2019: The year in review.* Retrieved February 7, 2020, from https://www.credit-suisse.com/media/assets/corporate/docs/about-us/research/publications/global-wealth-report-2019-en.pdf

Swerling, G. (2019, March 29). Black and Asian students more than twice as likely to go to university than White students, new data reveals. *The Telegraph.* Retrieved February 7, 2020, from https://www.telegraph.co.uk/news/2019/03/29/black-asian-students-twice-likely-go-university-white-students/

The Nobel Prize. (October, 2019). *Women who changed the world*. Retrieved February 7, 2020, from https://www.nobelprize.org/women-who-changed-the-world/

University of California, Riverside. (2010). *UCR 2020: The path to preeminence*. Retrieved February 7, 2020, from https://strategicplan.ucr.edu/sites/g/files/rcwecm2701/files/2019-03/ucr_2020_-_final.pdf

U.S. News and World Report. (2019). Top performers on social mobility. *U.S. News and World Report*. Retrieved February 7, 2020, from https://www.usnews.com/best-colleges/rankings/national-universities/social-mobility

CHAPTER 10

Global, Innovative, and Open for Business

The American Research University

Eric W. Kaler

Abstract

Economic and business development and progress depends on the generation of new ideas and technologies, and American research universities have been at the forefront of creating new knowledge for many decades. Here I describe the impact and workings of large, land-grant public universities in the United States, including how faculty can work with companies and create intellectual property. The general results are highlighted with specific examples from the University of Minnesota.

Keywords

research university – intellectual property – research funding – technology commercialization – sustainable research

1 Introduction and Historical Perspective

Large American research universities have an enormous role in innovation, in the creation of new businesses, and in the application of knowledge to society's great challenges. I will use my institution, the University of Minnesota, Twin Cities, as an example; however, every university in the United States is structured somewhat differently. Most universities with a research focus in the United States provide undergraduate education and both graduate and professional education across a comprehensive range of subjects. Nearly all are focused on the simultaneous education of students and the creation of new knowledge. How they blend those two central missions to create economic growth and prosperity can vary dramatically from institution to institution. A comprehensive review of the history and impact of American universities is given by Cole (2009).

© KONINKLIJKE BRILL NV, LEIDEN, 2021 | DOI: 10.1163/9789004463165_010

In the United States there are many kinds and sizes of universities and colleges. There are many relatively small liberal arts colleges that have limited graduate education and research capacities. Two kinds of larger universities that focus on both undergraduate and graduate education and research can be distinguished by the way they are governed. In the first case, private universities are self-governing, with a governing board that is independent, self-perpetuating, and autonomous. The revenue to run these institutions comes primarily from endowments, tuition income, research support, and, in some cases, income from clinical work in medical schools or hospitals.

In the second case, public universities are governed by boards that, one way or another, are selected by the citizens of the state in which they are located. The method of selection ranges from direct election by the voters to an appointment by the governor that is ratified by a legislative body, with many ways in between. There are no public national universities in the United States, but instead they all depend on the support of one of the fifty states, in addition to the endowment and other revenue sources available to private schools. As a consequence, tuition charges, particularly for undergraduate students, are lower at public universities and public universities are usually larger in size than private ones. There are also universities that operate to generate a profit; they do not generally have research activities. Finally, there are institutions devoted to job training in a variety of fields, and they offer degrees or certificates in vocational areas after a variable period of study. They also generally have no research activities.

Some public universities have what is called a "land grant" mission. That term arises from legislation passed in 1862 and signed by the 16th president of the United States, Abraham Lincoln. It is remarkable that during the darkest period of American history, so far, and in the middle of a Civil War, our leaders were able to focus on the need for more education, and the legislation Lincoln signed was called the Morrill Act. Named after its author, Representative Justin Morrill from Vermont, the act called for the federal government to grant to states land that could be used or sold to create new Universities. At the time, higher education was limited to wealthy individuals, mostly men, who could afford to attend private institutions primarily in the eastern part of the United States. These land grant institutions mostly evolved into large state universities, but there are a few private land-grant universities, such as Cornell University in New York (Cole, 2009).

As a consequence of the Morrill Act, education could be made available to many more people across the country. In the language of the Act, those universities were "... [T]o teach such branches of learning as are related to agriculture

and the mechanic arts … in order to promote the liberal and practical education of the industrial classes in the several pursuits and professions in life". It
is fair to say that the Morrill Act fundamentally changed the nature of higher
education in the United States and helped unlock the intellectual power that
led to U.S. industrial strength in the 20th century. The Act also laid out a commitment to agriculture, engineering and a liberal education. That has evolved
until today land-grant institutions have the mission to teach, conduct research
and engage with our communities to solve problems. There is always a focus
on excellence, of course, and there are many highly-ranked public universities
in the United States, but there is also always the underlying emphasis of the
need to make higher education accessible for all qualified students.

Over the 150 years since the Morrill Act, U.S. universities have evolved in
significant ways. The first step was the investment of federal research funds in
agricultural research and development, and the creation of agricultural exper-
imental stations, which were enabled by the 1887 Hatch Act. Closely related
outreach to users of that research was funded in the Smith-Lever Act of 1914.
The outreach was delivered by generations of so-called extension agents who
travelled rural America to teach best practices in agriculture.

The engagement of the federal government in the funding of research of all
kinds grew rapidly in the years following World War II. This led to a remarkably
innovative economy in the United States, with many inventions and products
coming from this funding. Two principal avenues for funding are the National
Institutes of Health, whose National Institutes of Health Grants Office was
established in 1946, and the National Science Foundation (NSF), which was
established in 1950. Today, they combine to provide close to $50 billion in
research support annually, primarily to universities. Significant university
research support also comes from other parts of the federal government, notably the Departments of Energy, Defence, and Agriculture.

The genesis and growth of the NSF has been particularly important to the
flourishing of research in the natural sciences and engineering in the United
States. Its form, and particularly its connection to the national political conversation, evolved in the late 1940s. The vision that prevailed was championed by
Vannevar Bush in his 1945 document "Science – The Endless Frontier". Bush saw
an organization that would fund the best basic research based on peer-reviewed
of proposals. The research was not to be militarily classified or confidential,
and the goal was to publish results in the open literature. The connection to
government and political forces was provided by the presidential appointment
of both the NSF director and the members of the National Science Board, who
are advisory directors (National Science Foundation, 1994).

Prior to 1980, patent rights to inventions made with federal grant funding belonged to the federal government, not the inventor or the university. The lack of direct benefit to the inventor discouraged the hard work of product development and eventual commercialization. In order to unlock the commercial value of university inventions, in 1980 Congress passed the Bayh-Dole act, named after the two Senators who sponsored it. That enabled universities, as well as the individual inventors personally, to patent and license discoveries, and to share in royalty income. This unleashed a flood of commercial activity that continues to this day. Most universities thereafter were, to a greater or lesser degree, in the idea development and commercialization business, not just the research and education business.

Like most healthy businesses, a research university has many sources of funds. The University of Minnesota is a typical example (Figure 10.1). Because of substantial research activity in human health and medicine, the National Institutes of Health is the largest funder. Next is state and local government, including through a novel economic development programme called the Minnesota Discovery Research and Innovation Economy that is described below. This level of support reflects the deep connections between a land-grant institution and the state that it serves. Examples of that research range from studies of transportation challenges to environmental work to protect water supplies, and from public health programmes to agricultural and outreach approaches, supported in partnership with federal programmes. The National Science Foundation, with its focus on science and engineering research is next, followed by sources within the university, and then by business and industry. All in all, about 65% of the funds awarded are ultimately from the Federal government. This is typical for most research universities in the United States. These amounts reflect the funds awarded to the institution in the 2018 financial year. Because many grants run for several years this is not a reflection of the annual expenditures, which are shown further below.

2 The Role of Business and Industry

The support of research at the University of Minnesota by business and industry is significant, and research universities in the United States interact with businesses in several ways. The usual forms of support of university research are grants or contracts. In the case of a grant, funds are given with the expectation that the faculty member or other researcher will use them to support research in an agreed upon area, but recognizes that the early results and

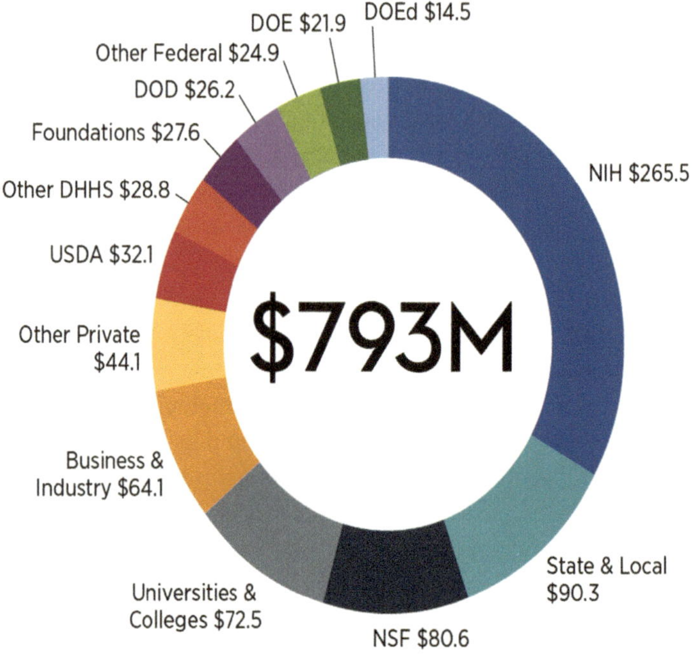

Federal agencies: DHHS: Dept. of Health and Human Services • DOEd: Department of Education • DOE: Dept. of Energy • NIH: National Institutes of Health • NSF: National Science Foundation • USDA: US Department of Agriculture
Dollar amounts shown in millions

FIGURE 10.1   Research awards to the University of Minnesota for fiscal year 2018 shown by the source of funds (from https://regents.umn.edu/sites/regents.umn.edu/files/2019-08/docket-board_of_regents-feb2019.pdf)

intellectual curiosity may lead to work in different directions than were perhaps originally anticipated. A contract, on the other hand, usually describes a list of research or development results that are expected to be delivered in a timely way. In both cases, there is concern on the part of the company and the university that the ownership and use of any potential intellectual property (IP) be accounted for carefully. An exception to the worry about allocation of intellectual property occurs when the support from a company, or an individual, is classified as a gift. A gift comes without obligations to spend the funds in a specific way, or indeed to even report in detail how the funds were used. The donor thus has no input to how the money was spent, but gifts to universities in many cases can be tax-deductible.

It turns out that for most grants and contracts with industry the creation of valuable intellectual property is quite rare, and at the University of Minnesota we view a focus on intellectual property ownership as short-sighted. To be clear, most industrially-funded research begins as a conversation between a faculty member and a researcher at a company. In the traditional way, university lawyers and company lawyers worried a great deal about the ownership of intellectual property that might emerge from the work. In other words, there was a great deal of effort spent on the possibility that the research might yield an invention that might be patentable, that it might go into a product that might go on sale, and might make a profit. And there was a lot of anxiety about how that hypothetical future profit would be shared.

At the University of Minnesota, we have dramatically streamlined the way we partner with industry. Called Minnesota Innovation Partnerships or MN-IP, this programme provides several options for structuring intellectual property ownership and licensing. These options range from a modest up-front prepaid fee for all of the intellectual property, with royalties only becoming due after annual sales exceed $20 million, to an agreement for a non-exclusive licence with the right to subsequently negotiate an exclusive royalty-bearing licence. Sponsors may also negotiate a licence after the intellectual property has been developed. We now view our work as a partnership, not as a transactional quid pro quo. As a result, our funding from these sources has grown by nearly a factor of five (see Table 10.1). For further details see OVPR (2020a).

TABLE 10.1   Results of the Office of Technology Commercialization

	2014	2015	2016	2017	2018
New licenses	154	268	194	213	230
Current revenue generating agreements	429	544	528	545	575
Gross revenues	$27.4	$20.2	$46.9	$22.6	$16.1
Issued patents (U.S. and foreign)	104	136	168	147	186
MNoIP research agreements	51	69	81	72	86
Companies W/MN-IP research agreements	44	54	62	51	58
Sponsored research commitments	$4.3	$10.8	$12.2	$20.9	$21.3
Startup companies	15	16	17	18	13

SOURCE: HTTPS://RESEARCH.UMN.EDU/UNITS/TECHCOMM/ABOUT-US/STATISTICS

3   Managing the Research Enterprise

As mentioned above, the creation of the NIH and NSF mechanisms for funding university research in the late 1940s, and then the Bayh-Dole Act in the 1980s, created the need for universities to manage this research enterprise. Most research universities have an Office for Research, or one with a similar title, typically led by a Vice President or Vice Provost, who facilitates this work. The mission statement for the University of Minnesota's Office of the Vice President for Research (OVPR) is "The OVPR serves the University of Minnesota and the public by advocating for and facilitating the research and scholarly activities of its faculty, staff, and students. In fulfilment of this mission, we provide the specific expertise, systems, and services that support the University's goal of becoming a top public research university".

In terms of day-to-day operations, the staff in OVPR focuses mainly on helping faculty write and win research contracts from a variety of sources including the NIH and NSF. Once a grant is awarded, the OVPR provides a framework for the budgeting and management of the funds, as well as help in providing the required periodic progress reports to the funding agency. The office also pays careful attention to ensure researchers are following all of the relevant federal, state, and local rules, regulations, and laws, both financially and in the conduct of research.

At the University of Minnesota, the unit that supports faculty in seeking, acquiring, and managing externally sponsored funding for research, training, and public service has 49 people. The Human Research Protection Programme employs 20 people who are working to ensure the safety, rights, and well-being of human research subjects. They review and monitor the use of human subjects and the use of potentially hazardous biological agents in research. Animals may also be used in research and the 11 people staffing the Office of Animal Welfare provide administrative support, inspection, and compliance functions for the Institutional Animal Care and Use Committee (IACUC).

Research activities of similar size are spread across the United States. The top public universities in terms of research spending are shown in Table 10.2. The University of Michigan leads public research universities with over $1.5 billion spent annually. Michigan has the second largest expenditures in the country. The top private university in terms of research expenditures is Johns Hopkins, which spends over $2.5 billion annually. Other private universities with over $1 billion in spending are the University of Pennsylvania, Duke University, Harvard University, Stanford University, Cornell University, Massachusetts Institute of Technology, and Yale University.

TABLE 10.2   Annual research spending by the top ten public universities

University		Expenditure	ARUW (2018)		
			World	U.S.	U.S. Public
Michigan	1	$1,530,139	27	20	6
UC San Francisco	2	$1,409,398	21	17	5
Washington	3	$1,348,220	14	12	3
Wisconsin	4	$1,193,413	28	21	7
UC San Diego	5	$1,133,454	15	13	4
North Carolina	6	$1,102,063	30	22	8
UCLA	7	$1,076,917	11	9	2
Pittsburgh	8	$939,706	90	42	22
Minnesota (TC)	9	$921,681	37	25	9
Texas A&M	10	$905,474	151–200	59–69	28+

SOURCE: NSF/HERD DATABASE (HTTPS://WWW.NSF.GOV/STATISTICS/SRVYHERD/)

4   Technology Commercialization

Another important aspect of the activity of the OVPR is the commercial-iza-tion of the inventions of our faculty and staff. There are 45 people engaged in that work in the Office of Technology Commercialization. The mission of the office is to protect and license University-developed technologies. Substantial work is also aimed at evaluating and nurturing University technologies with the potential to enable a start-up company.

The activity has grown steadily (Table 10.1), with the most recent year show-ing 230 licences of university technology to companies and 13 new companies created. The start-up companies formed based on university research can be classified into six broad areas (Table 10.3).

Software and information technology make up the largest sector, followed by biology-related companies and those centred on pharmaceuticals. The medical device area is third, and the relatively large effort in that area correlates with the large commercial biomedical device industry based in Minnesota. Earl Bakken was a University of Minnesota employee when he invented the wearable pace-maker in 1957. He had earlier founded Medtronic, which last year had almost $30 billion in revenue. Medtronic and its competitors, Boston Scientific and St.

TABLE 10.3   Distribution of start-up companies by industry sector

Startups by sector	FY18	FY06 – FY18
Bio/Pharma	2	32
Engineering and PhySci	0	16
Software/IT	4	36
Med Device	4	26
Energy and Env	2	16
Food/Agriculture	1	6
Minnesota	8	102
Outside Minnesota	5	30
Total	13	132

Jude, maintain large research and business operations in Minnesota, and they make Minnesota the "Silicon Valley" of the medical device industry.

An example of a smaller medical-related company that developed from research at the University of Minnesota is Miromatrix. Their business is based on developing a way to grow organs from an individual's own cells for eventual implantation. Miromatrix's technology allows the removal of cells from an organ but preserves the environments required for the introduction of organ-specific cells that can grow into a new organ. They also maintain the vascular network in the organ so it can be reconnected to the patient's blood supply and preserve the outer capsule of the organ. The resulting organs can be transplanted utilizing the same techniques as current organ transplantation. (See https://www.miromatrix.com/ for more details.)

5   Innovative Partnerships

States may also support targeted research, and in Minnesota we have created an initiative called the Minnesota Discovery Research and Innovation Economy or MnDRIVE programme (see https://mndrive.umn.edu/). This programme is supported by the state government at the level of $18 million annually to target specific research relevant to the state, but of course applicable around the world. The areas of targeted investment are robotics, sensors and advanced manufacturing; food; water and the environment; and in the medical areas of brain and central nervous system conditions, and a cancer clinical trial network.

As more fully described at https://mndrive.umn.edu/, the MnDRIVE initiative on robotics, sensors, and advanced manufacturing envisions the University of Minnesota playing a vital role in bolstering Minnesota's positions of leadership in sensors, robotics and automation, and as a contributor to the renaissance of domestic manufacturing, particularly additive manufacturing. Its unifying theme recognizes that robotics, autonomous systems, and modern manufacturing systems are fundamentally structured on the integration of sensing, feedback and controls, and actuation. Applications range from 3-D printing of parts on demand to autonomous vehicle technology.

Given that the world's population is expected to grow to more than 9 billion people during the next 40 years, we will require a 70% increase in food supply. Despite today's abundance, nearly one billion people around the world are undernourished, and even in Minnesota, more than 10% of our residents lack sufficient food. The economic and human toll of hunger and malnutrition not only affects countries that have inadequate food and nutrition, but also affects the global economy. Food-borne illness and obesity caused by non-nutritious food drives chronic diseases and adds to health care costs. The three focus areas in this food initiative are precision agriculture, the application of bioinformatics and other large data methods to improve crop and animal health, and food safety innovations, including in both animals and humans.

The overall goal of the water and environmental initiative is to support and stimulate research and development of environmental remediation by using microorganisms, plants, enzymes, or chemicals, either by themselves or in combination, to remove pollutants from the environment. In this work, university researchers partner with state industries and government agencies to bring the results of research from the lab to field practice. This work connects directly to the University's land grand mission and to the role of the extension agents a century ago. The work should lead to both improved water and environmental quality across all watersheds. In turn this will enable greater employment and commerce both in agriculture and tourism.

The brain and central nervous system disease research recognizes that the social and economic impacts of brain conditions are devastating, with estimates of annual health care and lost productivity costs in the United States to be at nearly $500 billion. Brain conditions, including Parkinson's disease, stroke, epilepsy and mental illness, are chronic afflictions that diminish a person's quality of life. These conditions affect one in five Americans. Through high-impact research and discovery in the field of neuromodulation, MnDRIVE trains the next generation of scientists and clinicians, and brings new and improved therapies to Minnesotans suffering from brain conditions. The initiative will expand university partnerships with industries to bring neuromodulation innovations to market. Both patients and state's economy will benefit.

Cancer is a leading health challenge in the United States and around the world. Nearly half of all Minnesotans will be diagnosed with a potentially life-threatening cancer during their lifetimes, and cancer is the leading cause of death in Minnesota. To make progress and allow patients access to the best care, healthcare providers need equitable knowledge of cutting-edge cancer research as well as access to the full menu of options for patient care. Development of a multi-site cancer clinical trials network will provide greater access to trials in prevention and treatment across the entire state of Minnesota.

The MnDrive initiative has produced great results for the University of Minnesota. After five years of work, 1,200 researchers have been supported, more than \$360 million has been generated in external funding for their research, and 303 inventions have been disclosed. This kind of programme can be a model for a productive partnership between a university and state government (OVPR, 2020b).

6 Sustainable Research

Much research today is focused on addressing challenges with solutions that are sustainable from an environmental and business point of view. This research should lead to processes and products that minimize environmental and societal impacts. An interesting example is the use of wind energy to drive a small-scale ammonia synthesis plant that can provide both energy storage and nitrogen for agriculture. Researchers at the University of Minnesota have built such a small-scale pilot facility near a wind turbine in western Minnesota with support from the Department of Energy, a Federal agency.

Ammonia is an essential element of fertilizers and is also a carbon-neutral liquid fuel. Ammonia is produced commercially using the Haber-Bosch (HB) process. This process requires very large capital investments for reactors to operate at high pressure and temperature, large amounts of power (the HB process uses 1–2% of the energy produced world-wide), and distribution infrastructure to ship the ammonia. Technology enabling the small- and medium-scale synthesis of ammonia can move production closer to the consumer, and, if renewable energy sources are used, ammonia can be produced without producing carbon dioxide. The U.S. Department of Energy has focused on this problem, and note: "However, significant technical challenges remain in either adapting the HB process for smaller scale use or developing alternative electrochemical processes for fuel development" (Advanced Research Projects

Agency-Energy [ARPAE], 2017). New methods involving lower pressures and absorption methods have created a process suitable for small-scale applications which is more compatible with intermittent energy sources (see ARPAE, 2017). The proof-of-concept work by University researchers is essential to the ultimate success and utility of this method (Palys et al., 2019).

7 Research Consortia

The final example of technology development also highlights the University of Minnesota's deep connection to the People's Republic of China and its engagement in tackling its environmental challenges. The first Chinese students came to the University of Minnesota in 1914. In 1979, the University of Minnesota was one of the first American universities to send a delegation to China when U.S.-Chinese relations were re-opened. The university welcomes thousands of Chinese students each year, and large research universities continue to be an important link between the two countries.

The following example also shows another way a university can interact with industry, which is through a university-industry consortium. In a such a consortium, many companies interested in a technology come together and combine forces with the university to develop science and engineering at a level that is more fundamental than the product generation they would engage in for profit. Consortia are characterized by members having access to early-stage pre-competitive research, and access to students and faculty expertise. Companies generally pay an annual membership fee.

The University of Minnesota's Centre for Filtration Research is such a consortium (see http://www.me.umn.edu/cfr/). Fourteen companies are investing in ideas about filtration, which is a central industrial process. The director of the centre, Dr. David Pui, is addressing one of the main challenges to the environment in China, namely poor air quality due to a high concentration of particles sized 2.5 microns or less – so called PM2.5. These particles are a significant health hazard. Dr. Pui and his colleagues have developed the Solar Assisted Large Scale Cleaning System (SALSCS) (see Figure 10.2). They estimate that by placing eight giant SALSCS's outside of Beijing's 6-ring highway, they can reduce PM2.5 by 15% in 30 hours (Cao et al., 2015 and 2018).

Xi'an was the first city to build a pilot scale SALSCS with dimensions of 60 m x 43 m x 60 m high (Figure 10.3). On two sides, there are U.S. filter systems from the 3M company and the Donaldson company. On the third side is a Chinese domestic filter system. Money Magazine named the Xi'an SALSCS as one of the 28 Incredible Made-in-China Innovations that are changing the

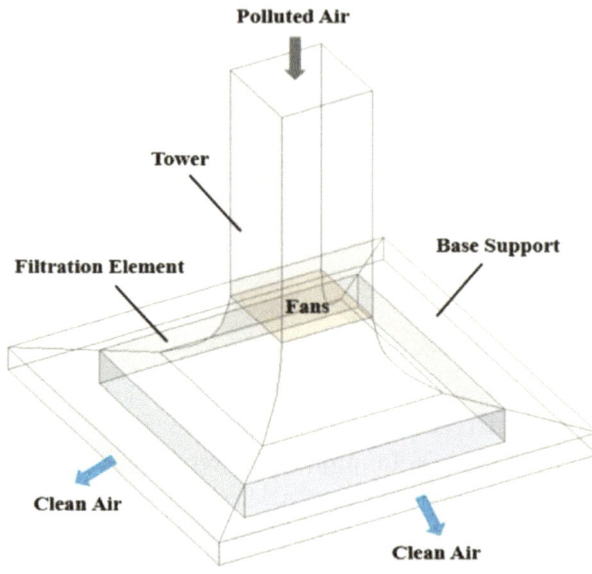

FIGURE 10.2
A schematic diagram of the Solar Assisted Large Scale Cleaning System (SALSCS) (by David Pui, University of Minnesota)

FIGURE 10.3
A photograph of the SALSCS built in Xi'an, China (by David Pui, University of Minnesota)

world. A second generation SALSCS was built in Yancheng Science Park in Jiangsu Province. Measurements show that the area surrounding the SALSCS on the downstream side has a 12% reduction in the concentration of PM2.5 when the SALSCS is turned on. Improvements in air quality can have many positive effects; for example, a survey of housing prices in the clean air affected-area found a 4.5% increase in price compared to an equivalent home in an untreated area (Lan et al., 2020).

8   Conclusion

Large American public research universities have played a central role in the discovery and development of many scientific and medical breakthroughs. Much of the work of research universities is also in service to society as they tackle problems related to health, societal, environmental, and sustainability challenges. Research universities today also play a key role in establishing start-up companies that can be the engine of economic growth. These universities have also educated generations of students from around the world and enabled progress towards a better quality of life for all.

References

Advanced Research Projects Agency-Energy (ARPAE). (2017). *Solid-state Alkaline Electrolyzer Ammonia Synthesis*. Retrieved June 23, 2020, from https://arpa-e.energy.gov/?q=slick-sheet-project%2Fsolid-state-alkaline-electrolyzer-ammonia-synthesis

Cao, Q., Pui, D. Y. H., & Lipiński, W. (2015). A concept of a novel Solar-Assisted Large-Scale Cleaning System (SALSCS) for Urban Air Remediation. *Aerosol Air Quality Research, 15*(1), 1–10. https://doi.org/10.4209/aaqr.2014.10.0246

Cao, Q., Shen, L., Chen, S.-C., & Pui, D. Y. H. (2018). WRF modeling of PM2.5 remediation by SALSCS and its clean air flow over Beijing terrain. *Science of the Total Environment, 626*(1), 134–146. https://doi.org/10.1016/j.scitotenv.2018.01.062

Cole, J. R. (2009). *The great American university*. PublicAffairs.

Lan, F., Lv, J., Chen, J., Zhang, X., & Pui, D. Y. H. (2020). Willingness to pay for staying away from haze: Evidence from a quasi-natural experiment in Xi'an. *Journal of Environmental Management, 262*. https://doi.org/10.1016/j.jenvman.2020.110301

National Science Foundation. (1994). *The National Science Foundation: A brief history*. Retrieved May 10, 2020, from https://www.nsf.gov/about/history/nsf50/nsf8816.jsp

Office of the Vice President for Research (OVPR). (2020a). Retrieved May 1, 2020, from https://research.umn.edu/units/techcomm/sponsoring-research-mn-ip

Office of the Vice President for Research. (2020b). Retrieved May 1, 2020, from
    https://mndrive.umn.edu/about/mndrive-5
Palys, M. J., Kuznetsov, A., Tallaksen, J., Reese, M., & Daoutidis, P. (2019). A novel system
    for ammonia-based sustainable energy and agriculture: Concept and design opti-
    mization. *Chemical Engineering and Processing – Process Intensification, 140,* 11–21.
    https://doi.org/10.1016/j.cep.2019.04.005

CHAPTER 11

A New Model for Graduate and Professional Education

The McDonnell International Scholars Academy

Mark S. Wrighton

Abstract

The McDonnell International Scholars Academy was founded in 2005 by Washington University in St. Louis. The McDonnell Academy is a global partnership among premier academic institutions that involves graduate and professional education to prepare global leaders in academia, government, business, and non-governmental organizations. There are 34 academic partners associated with the McDonnell Academy, with at least one partner university on every populated continent. Outstanding alumni of these 34 partners represent most (at least 75%) of the students selected to be a McDonnell Scholar. McDonnell Scholars are degree candidates at the masters or doctoral level in any area offered by Washington University, and receive full tuition and a generous living stipend for up to five years to support their degree experience. The Scholars also receive a travel award to go to St. Louis and to return home once a year. A unique feature associated with being a McDonnell Scholar is that the Scholars have intellectual, cultural, and social experiences with other Scholars who are diverse in terms of their backgrounds and in terms of their degree programmes. Traditional graduate and professional degree programmes have students only interacting with other students in the same degree programme. McDonnell Scholars are encouraged to remain networked with each other following completion of their degree requirements, representing a global network of leaders in many areas of intellectual activity and professional pursuits.

Keywords

graduate education – professional education – international collaboration – international education – academic partnerships – international partnerships

© KONINKLIJKE BRILL NV, LEIDEN, 2021 | DOI: 10.1163/9789004463165_011

1   Introduction and Background

Washington University in St. Louis was founded in 1853 at a time when St. Louis, Missouri, was arguably the most important city in North America. St. Louis was the "staging" area for the westward expansion of the United States, and it became known as the "gateway city". Designed by artist and architect Eero Saarinen in 1948, an iconic 192 m (630 ft) tall Gateway Arch was completed in 1965 and is the symbol of St. Louis. Washington University was founded as a private university to serve the growing needs of a flourishing city. Today, Washington University remains a private research university and is widely regarded as one of the great research universities of the United States with exceptional research strength in life sciences. The operating income for the fiscal year that concluded on June 30, 2019, was about $3.5 billion, including over $500 million for research. The student body totals about 15,000 with about half in graduate and professional degree programmes leading to masters or doctoral degrees. The undergraduate students have exceptional academic indicators and are competitive with other students attending America's most outstanding colleges and universities. Twenty-four people associated with Washington University as faculty or alumni have won the Nobel Prize in chemistry, physics, economics, or medicine.

Though Washington University has recruited students from countries around the world for more than a century, it was decided in 1995 that a strategic initiative should be launched to strengthen ties with other parts of the world. Part of the objective was to enhance the education mission and the quality and impact of research programmes. The purpose of the initiative included enhancing opportunities to recruit talented graduate and professional students, to develop partnerships for collaborative research, and to strengthen relationships with alumni and potential employers of alumni outside the United States. Indeed, Washington University has long valued the importance of international students and faculty, and in 2020 about 30% of the faculty were born in a country other than the United States. The 1995 international initiative was started with a focus on Asia and the rationale for this focus was several-fold: (1) Asia represents a large fraction of the world's population; (2) economic growth in Asia was significant and predicted to continue to be so; (3) a large number of United States-headquartered companies had aspirations to strengthen their activities in Asia, especially in China; (4) students from Asia were interested in American higher education; and (5) a significant fraction of Washington University's international alumni live and work in Asia. In 1996, Washington University founded its International Advisory Council for Asia, including members of the Board of

Trustees, alumni living and working in Asia, parents of current or former students, and friends of the University. The purpose of the Council was to advise the University on priorities for engagement in Asia and to assist the University's leaders to better understand governments, businesses, and universities in Asia.

The Council was chaired by a member of the Board of Trustees, and it met every 18–24 months in a major city of Asia or in St. Louis, where Washington University is located. Most meetings were in Asia, and the participation at each meeting included the Chancellor, the deans of the seven schools of the University, the Provost, Dean of the Graduate School, Vice Chancellor for Alumni and Development Programmes, Vice Chancellor for Public Affairs, and other distinguished leaders in the administration. Meetings in Asia typically also included distinguished members of the faculty who made presentations of their work to the Council and at premier universities in the cities visited. Every meeting of the Council was attended by 20–25 senior leaders from the University based in St. Louis. The approximately 30 Council members included a few from St. Louis, but most were living and working in Asia. Council members from Beijing, Delhi, Hong Kong, Jakarta, Manila, Mumbai, Seoul, Shanghai, Singapore, and Tokyo, were regular attendees and active participants in the meetings. Each meeting included opportunities to engage alumni in the city being visited and to learn directly about and from leaders in academia, business, and government.

The meetings of the Council typically lasted two or three days and included opportunities for members and for the University leaders to learn about the local history, culture, economy and political issues. The small number of meetings held in St. Louis were intended to make sure that Council members from Asia were all up to date on knowledge about the programmes and priorities of the University. The first meeting of the Council was held in the fall of 1996 in Taipei. The culminating meeting with respect to the founding of the McDonnell International Scholars Academy was in 2004 in Seoul. In between, the Council met in Hong Kong, St. Louis, Tokyo, Singapore, Delhi, Shanghai, and Beijing. During the period 1996–2004, Washington University's quality and visibility rose significantly, with a dramatic increase in the number of undergraduate applications and a significant rise in the academic indicators (SAT, rank in class, quality of high school curriculum) of the matriculating students. An evolving goal of the Asia initiative was to attract undergraduate applicants from Asia who would be commensurate in quality with those being recruited from the United States. The work of the International Advisory Council for Asia laid the foundation for a much stronger international engagement, especially, of course, in Asia.

2   Launch of the McDonnell International Scholars Academy

The proposal to establish the programme that became the McDonnell International Scholars Academy was made in Seoul, the Republic of Korea, at the 2004 meeting of the International Advisory Council for Asia. The University proposed a programme based on partnerships with premier international universities. Though focused initially on potential partners based in Asia, the proposed programme was envisioned to expand to the rest of the world. The vision was to create a partnership with research universities that would engage the partners, bilaterally and multi-laterally, in collaborative education and research programmes. A major aspiration was to build the infrastructure to facilitate faculty and students to collaborate in addressing major global problems, such as climate change, that cannot be solved by any single university, indeed, not solvable by any single country. The new model for graduate and professional education stemming from the proposed McDonnell Academy was foreseen to engage talented masters and doctoral students attracted to Washington University as graduates of the partner universities in the McDonnell Academy.

Of course, the McDonnell International Scholars Academy is not the only premier educational opportunity for international students at outstanding universities around the world. Perhaps the most well-known programme is the Rhodes Scholar Programme founded early in the 20th century (Pietsch, 2011), a programme of Oxford University. More recently, and after the founding the McDonnell International Scholars Academy, the Schwarzman Scholars programme based at Tsinghua University was founded (Osnos, 2013), and Stanford University launched its Hennessy-Knight Scholars Programme in 2016 (Gioia, 2016). These important programmes offer excellent opportunities for those selected for the programmes. The McDonnell Academy has a unique and significant component, namely partnerships with premier universities around the world. The partnerships bring more faculty and students into collaborative education and research programmes.

2.1   *McDonnell Academy Partners*

Washington University sought to identify top universities from around the world to become strategic partners. Of course, like many major research universities in the United States, Washington University already had a very large number of partnerships with other international universities. Typically, these partnerships were formalized with a "memorandum of understanding" and often involved a single faculty member desiring to do collaborative research with a single faculty member at another university. The proposal to establish the McDonnell Academy was to focus on a relatively small number of university partners that would become strategic partners. These would become "preferred" but not "exclusive" partners, leaving open the opportunity for individual faculty members to establish more traditional collaborative arrangements.

Partner universities were to be ones regarded as among the best in their region. The aspiration was to partner with universities receptive to engaging in collaborative education and research programmes. Fudan University in Shanghai, the People's Republic of China, had already become partnered in 2002 with Washington University in connection with a joint venture to offer an Executive MBA degree programme in Shanghai, and it was an example of a premier university thought to be a potential partner. Fudan University, like other prospective partners, already had a significant number of their graduates in graduate and professional programmes at Washington University. It was felt that such universities could be approached about becoming founding members of the McDonnell International Scholars Academy.

An important criterion in selecting partners would be the research interests and strengths of the partner. An objective, of course, was to provide opportunities for faculty to work together on major global problems that would be of interest to faculty and students of all partners. The meetings of the International Advisory Council for Asia over the course of about eight years provided excellent background in connection with selecting university partners based in Asia.

2.2   *McDonnell Scholars*

The core educational programme of the Academy was proposed to involve the education of McDonnell Scholars, an intellectually diverse group of graduate and professional students. The objective was to work to recruit a small number of exceptionally talented graduate and professional students to become McDonnell Scholars. Prospective Scholars would apply to Washington University for a masters or doctoral degree in an area of their choosing, and they would also apply to become McDonnell Scholars. Washington University would evaluate all candidates and offer admission to the very best. The Scholars would be alumni of the partner universities. Ultimately, the Scholars recruited would become alumni of both Washington University and one of the partner universities. Thus, the Scholars would become an important part of the linkage between Washington University and the strategic partner universities. In addition to academic criteria, the Scholars selected were to be interested in becoming "global leaders", individuals who would have the potential to emerge as leaders in academia, the professions, government and not-for-profit organizations. McDonnell Scholars would receive support for full tuition, a living stipend, and a travel award to go to St. Louis and to return home once a year. The financial commitment was to be for up to five years, providing for completion of the degree programme of the Scholar. While such support is commonplace for PhD students in the United States, such generous financial support for students in professional degree programmes (law, medicine, social work, business, art, architecture) is rare.

The unique aspect of the McDonnell Scholars programme is that the Scholars would spend time together on intellectual, cultural and social programmes, and would participate together in formal preparation for leadership. Generally, students involved in graduate and professional education in the United States only interact with students in their own degree programme. For example, PhD students in chemistry interact with other PhD students in chemistry, and art students engage with other art students. The McDonnell Academy would provide all Scholars engagement with the other Scholars, and each Scholar would come to know and appreciate the academic aspirations of the other Scholars and build enduring relationships among a culturally and intellectually diverse group of future global leaders.

The proposal to establish the McDonnell International Scholars Academy was not intended to be the path to recruit all international graduate and professional students. Washington University had about 6500 graduate and professional students at the time the Academy was conceived. But the Academy was envisioned to be small, approximately 100 McDonnell Scholars from around the world. Thus, the Academy was to become a special experience for the students selected to be a McDonnell Scholar. It is true, however, that the universities proposed as potential partners in the McDonnell Academy are ones from which Washington University had already recruited excellent students for masters or doctoral degrees.

2.3 *McDonnell Academy Ambassadors*

In order to significantly engage with partner universities of the McDonnell Academy and to assist in identifying strong candidates to be McDonnell Scholars, Washington University would appoint an outstanding member of the faculty to become the "Ambassador" to each partner university. The role of the Ambassador was envisioned to be an individual who would work to build "academic commerce" between Washington University and the partner university being served by the Ambassador. Academic commerce means faculty and student exchange programmes, collaborative education programmes, and collaborative research programmes engaging students and faculty. Such academic commerce was envisioned to engage more students and faculty than those drawn in as McDonnell Scholars and Ambassadors. Drawing in participation of leading faculty as Ambassadors also assures "buy in" by key academic leaders of Washington University. Ambassadors were envisioned to be special advisors to the McDonnell Scholars recruited from the university they serve.

McDonnell Academy Ambassadors would have the special role of being a key liaison between Washington University and a partner, and also an important link to the broader Washington University community. Distinguished members of the Washington University faculty included individuals who were graduates of prospective partners, and it was felt that such individuals would be among the best ambassadors. Such Ambassadors would provide another important link to nurture a strong relationship with prospective partners. Washington University alumni also hold faculty positions at some of the prospective universities, another potential contribution to a strategic partnership between Washington University and a partner.

2.4 *Funding for the McDonnell Academy*

It was realized from the outset that new support for the McDonnell Academy would be needed. Providing full tuition, a living stipend and travel awards to McDonnell Scholars is expensive, approaching $100,000 per year. In addition, there are expenses to support the travel and activities of the Ambassadors, special programmatic elements for the McDonnell Scholars and, of course, to support collaborative research projects. The initial funding objective was to achieve an endowment of $1 million for each McDonnell Scholar, and to secure funding for research through grant and contract proposals to foundations, governments and corporations.

3 Development of the McDonnell International Scholars Academy

After discussion and further refinement of the proposed programme with input from key members of the International Advisory Council for Asia, Washington University set out to develop the McDonnell International Scholars Academy in 2005. Professor James V. Wertsch was appointed founding Director. Much effort was expended to engage potential university partners, to secure philanthropic support, and to recruit leading faculty to serve as Ambassadors.

3.1 *McDonnell Academy Partners*

Washington University soon received commitments from a significant number of Asia-based universities to join the partnership. The invitation to join the McDonnell Academy was well-received, and there was great interest in having distinguished graduates of the partners become McDonnell Scholars. Within a few months, 15 university partners were committed to join Washington University's initiative. As of 2019, there were 34 partners in the McDonnell Academy with at least one partner on every populated continent. The number of partners was originally envisioned to be 30 to 35, with the aim of having about 100 McDonnell Scholars in residence at steady state. Table 11.1 lists the partners as of 2019.

In addition to the prospect of having graduates become McDonnell Scholars, the partners were deeply interested in collaborative education and research programmes that would potentially engage faculty and students who would work with Washington University faculty and students, and with peers from other partners. Research problems envisioned included ones related to energy, the environment and sustainability, public health, and other major global challenges that cannot be fully addressed by a single institution.

3.2   *Faculty Ambassadors*

Recruitment of leading Washington University faculty to serve as Ambassadors occurred easily and quickly. Faculty interested in international collaboration opportunities, and often with an interest in a particular university partner, were invited to become Ambassadors. Ambassadors receive a modest honorarium and a stipend for travel to visit the university they serve. The Ambassadors in place in 2019, as shown in Table 11.1, represent intellectual diversity, as envisioned for the Academy. Several of the Ambassadors are alumni of the university they serve, and this further enhances the opportunity for strengthening the engagement with the partners in the Academy.

3.3   *Philanthropic Support*

Washington University approached a number of United States-headquartered multinational corporations to seek support for McDonnell Scholars. Of course, multinational corporations need talented people in many areas of their organizations, and initial funding for support of McDonnell Scholars was seen as an opportunity for the corporations to learn about talented graduate and professional students and to learn about important research universities outside of the United States. The corporations understood from the outset that McDonnell Scholars would not be bound to join any of the sponsoring corporations. Indeed, it was decided that McDonnell Scholars after graduation from Washington University would be free to return to their home country, or seek to remain in the United States, or go to a third country, for their initial employment. This is the same policy for all graduate and professional students at Washington University. Within a few months, 10 corporations committed to supporting McDonnell Scholars, including corporations headquartered in St.

TABLE 11.1   McDonnell International Scholars Academy partner universities as of 2019

Continent	Country/Region	Universities
Asia	Hong Kong, China	The Chinese University of Hong Kong
		Hong Kong University of Science and Technology;
		University of Hong Kong
	India	Indian Institute of Technology Bombay
		Indian Institute of Technology Delhi
		Jawaharlal Nehru University
		Tata Institute of Social Sciences
	Indonesia	University of Indonesia
	Japan	Keio University
		University of Tokyo
	The People's Republic of China	China Agricultural University
		Fudan University
		Peking University
		Tsinghua University
		Xi'an Jiao Tong University
	Singapore	National University of Singapore
	The Republic of Korea	Korea University
		Seoul National University
		Yonsei University
	Taipei,China	National Chiao Tung University
		National Taiwan University
	Thailand	Chulalongkorn University
	Turkey	Boğaziçi University
		Middle East Technical University
Europe	Hungry	Budapest University of Technology and Economics
	Israel	Interdisciplinary Centre Herzliya
		Technion – Israel Institute of Technology
	The Netherlands	Utrecht University
South America	Brazil	State University of Campinas
	Chile	University of Chile
	Mexico	Tecnológico y de Estudios Superiores de Monterrey
Oceana	Australia	University of Melbourne
		University of Queensland
Africa	Ghana	University of Ghana

Louis like Emerson and Monsanto (now Bayer), and some headquartered in other places, including Corning, Inc. and the Boeing Company. All of the corporate sponsors had an interest in becoming knowledgeable about the partner universities in the Academy and potentially engaging the exceptionally talented McDonnell Scholars through internships and possible employment relations.

In addition to corporate sponsors, John F. McDonnell, a member of the Board of Trustees and of the International Advisory Council for Asia, made a $10 million endowment commitment in 2005 to support the Academy, and the Academy was named in his honour to recognize his important support and his contribution to the vision of the Academy. Mr. McDonnell made an additional $20 million endowment commitment in 2017, recognizing the success of the Academy and the need for additional endowment support for the growing McDonnell Academy. Other gift commitments to Washington University have brought the endowment commitment to about $75 million. In addition, corporations and foundations have continued to provide current support for the Academy and its programmes.

3.4   *McDonnell Scholars*

The McDonnell International Scholars Academy was publicly announced in New York City in October of 2005, and the first 12 McDonnell Scholars were recruited to join Washington University in the fall of 2006. The number of McDonnell Scholars in residence at Washington University as of 2020 is 87, approaching the goal envisioned at the outset, about 100 McDonnell Scholars, and as of 2020 there are about 130 McDonnell Scholars that have completed their degrees and are employed in different parts of the world, mainly in academia and corporations. As the Academy grew in attractiveness, it was decided that United States citizens should be eligible to become McDonnell Scholars and up to 25% of the Scholars can be from the United States. A part of the commitment of the "U.S. Scholars" is that a portion of their masters or doctoral programme takes place at one of the international partner universities. After graduation from Washington University, McDonnell Scholars are encouraged to remain connected with each other and with Washington University, and proactive efforts to facilitate networking have been launched.

All schools of Washington University have enjoyed the benefit of having McDonnell Scholars as students. The Scholars are outstanding and do extremely well at Washington University, and all Scholars have successfully completed a masters or doctoral degree at Washington University. Working to assure that all academic units of the University benefit from the Academy is important, in order to sustain internal University support for the McDonnell Academy.

As of 2020, McDonnell Scholars who have graduated with their masters or doctoral degree are still early in their independent careers. However, importantly, a significant number of them are now engaged in academic careers at universities that are partners in the McDonnell Academy. Such faculty members will strengthen the partnership activities between Washington University and the partner universities. Also, such faculty will be able to assist in identifying talented candidates to become McDonnell Scholars. Table 11.2 sets out information for McDonnell Scholar alumni and the nature and location of their employment. As had been hoped, McDonnell Scholars span a wide range of intellectual areas and have developing careers in many areas, contributing the development of a network of global leaders.

3.5 *Unique Experiences of McDonnell Scholars*

McDonnell Scholars meet together for intellectual, cultural, and social activities on the campus of Washington University. For example, the Scholars might attend a concert by the St. Louis Symphony and then have a session with the musical director for both a social and intellectual engagement. The Scholars also are engaged in formal leadership education. Through these programmes, the Scholars come to know each other and develop meaningful relationships that continue beyond their Washington University experience. These interactions build trust among the Scholars, and the Founding Director of the

TABLE 11.2   Career paths of McDonnell Scholar alumni[a]

Career type[b]	Region of the world
Aacademia – 38%	Africa – 1%
Corporate – 25%	Asia – 29%
Entrepreneurship/NGO – 6%	Europe – 5%
Professions – 31%	Middle East – 3%
	North America – 56%
	Oceania – 4%
	South America – 2%

a As of April, 2020 these are data for 129 McDonnell Scholar Alumni.
b Nearly 40 different employers including 8 universities that are partners in the McDonnell International Scholars Academy.

McDonnell Academy, Professor James V. Wertsch, says that the Academy provides a "safe place to discuss unsafe subjects". The Scholars have intellectual engagement with each other and discuss presentations made by Scholars on subjects that can be controversial. With the trust developed among the Scholars, open discussion of difficult subjects can be undertaken.

The McDonnell Scholars typically do two cohort trips, one to Washington, DC, and one to New York City, over two years. These trips are intended to build an understanding of the United States government, business, politics, culture and history. The cohort trips include a number of activities including meetings with leaders, like the Secretary General of the United Nations, members of Congress, media, and business leaders, enrich the experience of the Scholars. There is time for social engagement, too, typically including a Broadway theatre performance when in New York City, for example, and time to interact with successful alumni of Washington University. These experiences together build camaraderie among the Scholars and deepen friendships, while also enriching appreciation for the differing interests and aspirations of the Scholars.

3.6   *McDonnell Academy Partners Meetings*

Approximately every two years, the McDonnell Academy convenes a meeting of the partners, aiming to bring together academic leaders and students to hear about pressing global challenges and approaches to solving the associated problems. These symposia are intended to strengthen collaborative education and research programmes involving more faculty and students than just the McDonnell Scholars and the Ambassadors. Typically, the partners meetings includes attendance of presidents, other academic leaders, faculty and students of the partners, with total attendance of about 300 people, including the McDonnell Scholars and Ambassadors. Two meetings have been held in St. Louis, and others have been held in cities co-hosted by a partner: Hong Kong, Mumbai, Brisbane, and Beijing. Workshops have been held on many topics including: energy; environment; sustainability; public health; issues around the supply of nutritious food and clean water; and the ageing of the global population. Travel to these meetings by the McDonnell Scholars is another unique experience for them during their masters or doctoral degree programme. By including all Scholars as active participants in the partners meetings, the Academy provides another unique cohort experience. An international trip together, especially, is a good way to provide a common experience for the McDonnell Scholars that strengthens their preparation for leadership roles.

From the work at the partners meetings and the initiatives of the Ambassadors, a number of research projects and collaborative education projects have been undertaken among the McDonnell Academy partners. These include the continuation of the joint venture with Fudan University to offer the Executive MBA degree, but new projects include dual degree programmes with Xi'an Jiaotong University in social policy and with Yonsei University in finance. Research collaboration on energy and the environment have been significant and involve many of the partners through the McDonnell Global Energy and Environment Partnership. Programmes for collaborative research have attracted financial support from governments and corporations, including a major effort involving several partners to address the challenges associated with the combustion of coal.

4   Challenges for the Future

The McDonnell International Scholars Academy is a unique undertaking, and the educational programme for the McDonnell Scholars represents a new model for graduate and professional education. Much progress has been made, but the McDonnell Academy is still early in its development and some challenges have emerged as the Academy has matured.

One challenge is the cost of the Academy. Each Scholar requires significant support. Though the experience is unique, high quality, and innovative, the "new model" will be difficult to apply to the entire population of about 7000 graduate and professional students at Washington University. However, there are relatively low cost ways to implement some elements of the Academy to benefit all graduate and professional students. A high priority in this regard would be to provide opportunities of students from differing degree programmes to have intellectual, cultural and social experiences together and in relatively small groups, about 100, the size of the group of McDonnell Scholars.

A second challenge for the McDonnell Academy is the uneven level of engagement among the university partners. All partners have engaged at some level, but some much more than others. The vibrancy of the Academy depends on having partners who are committed to be engaged in collaborative education and research, and who are encouraging students to become McDonnell Scholars. With the aspiration to recruit only about 100 McDonnell Scholars at steady state, the recruitment of Scholars from any one partner will be limited. Thus, engagement with partners must include substantive "academic commerce" to involve faculty and students, not just the McDonnell Scholars. It is important to build more funding for collaborative education and research, in order to build such programmes. The preponderance of the funding, including the research, has come from private support, especially major philanthropic commitments to build the endowment at Washington University. But the spendable income from endowment is devoted largely to support the Scholars. Research support from corporations, governments, and foundations is needed to provide meaningful funding in response to the strong collaborative research proposals from Academy partners.

The McDonnell Scholars understand that there is an expectation that they remain connected with each other and with Washington University. They are designated as McDonnell Scholars for life with the obligation to work collaboratively with each other when a need arises and to help strengthen the ties between Washington University and the partner university from which they graduated earlier. How does Washington University engage all of the McDonnell Scholars in a way that will be meaningful to the Scholars? Including them in the meetings of the McDonnell Academy partners is one way, but support for their travel and participation is an associated problem.

A fourth challenge relates to recruiting Ambassadors who will devote time, energy, and creativity to their work. A strong Ambassador can greatly influence the strength of the partnership with the university they serve. But how long should an Ambassador serve? As Ambassadors retire, renewal will be important. The Academy has very successfully gone through a major leadership transition with Professor Kurt Dirks becoming Director of the McDonnell International Scholars Academy in 2019. Professor Dirks succeeded the Founding Director, Professor James V. Wertsch who served 14 years as Director. Doubtless new leadership will bring additional innovations and opportunities for greater impact. The strong endowment will assure a sustained McDonnell International Scholars Academy, and new global challenges will stimulate new approaches to the best educational experiences for the Scholars and spawn new collaborative education and research programmes to engage the partners.

Acknowledgements

The author served as Chancellor of Washington University from 1995 until 2019 and is deeply grateful to Mr. John F. McDonnell, former Chairman of the Washington University Board of Trustees, who provided wise advice and generous financial support to the Washington University community and especially to the Academy. Professor James V. Wertsch and his wife, Mary Wertsch, made enormous contributions in leading the McDonnell Academy from its founding in 2005 until 2019. Finally, the author is grateful to Professor Kurt Dirks for taking the leadership reins for the Academy to build upon the work of Professor Wertsch.

References

Gioia, M. (2016, February 24). Stanford launching the Knight-Hennessy scholarship to attract top graduates. *Stanford Daily*. Retrieved June 22, 2020, from https://www.stanforddaily.com/2016/02/24/stanford-launching-knight-hennessy-scholarship-to-attract-top-graduates/

Osnos, E. (2013, April 26). Rhodes east: Why is the Schwartzman scholarship in China? *New Yorker*. Retrieved June 22, 2020, from https://www.newyorker.com/news/evan-osnos/rhodes-est-why-is-the-schwartzman-scholarship-in-china

Pietsch, T. (2011). Many Rhodes: Travelling scholarships and imperial citizenship in the British academic world, 1880–1940. *History of Education, 40*(6), 723–739. https://doi.org/10.1080/0046760X.2011.594096

CHAPTER 12

Recreating French Excellence

Sorbonne University, the University of Paris and the French Ecosystem of Higher Education and Research

Christine Clerici, Jean Chambaz and Sebastian Stride

Abstract

The French system of higher education and research has long been structured around a tripartite system in which the most prestigious institutions for education and research were specialised schools on the one hand and national research organizations on the other.

Over the last fifteen years, the pressure of globalization has led the French state to question this model and to launch a process of reforms, which encourages the emergence of world-class research-intensive universities by integrating and/or merging existing institutions. This has led to the creation of four world-class universities in Paris: Sorbonne University, Université de Paris, Université Paris Sciences et Lettres and Université Paris Saclay.

This article briefly recounts the history of the French system of higher education and research, the reasons for which it was not competitive and the way in which it has evolved over the last 15 years.

Keywords

merger – higher education and research system – France – rankings – bibliometry – history of universities – world-class universities – excellence initiatives

1 The Idiosyncrasies of the French Higher Education and Research System

The old University of Paris, often known as the Sorbonne,[1] was one of the great medieval universities, alongside Bologna, Oxford, and Salamanca. However, unlike these universities, it lost its status and reputation (and for a century its very existence) after the French revolution.

For almost two centuries, the French higher education system was centrally organized and led by the French Ministry, whose administrative representative ruled the University of Paris whereas *La Sorbonne* was a building that housed his premises and various faculties and schools in central Paris.[2]

This explains why Sorbonne University and the University of Paris, which were created respectfully in 2018 and 2019, can claim to be universities with centuries of history.

Their (re)creation symbolizes the (re)emergence of French world-class universities and illustrates both the idiosyncrasies of the French system of higher education and research and the deep impact that international comparison has had in France over the last fifteen years.

1.1   *Historical Background*

Unlike in other European countries, universities, like other medieval corporations, were abolished in France in 1793 and were substituted by schools and faculties that specialized in different fields, themselves integrated into a single Imperial University or University of France in 1808 under Napoleon. For the following two centuries, universities lost both their prestige and independence.

Officially, the University of Paris was recreated in 1896, but it remained a purely administrative entity which regrouped the different faculties and schools of the Academy of Paris. In 1970, this University of Paris was once again divided into 13 independent universities, numbered from 1 to 13. These regained a modicum of autonomy but remained closely overseen by the French Ministry in charge of Higher Education that continued to own all buildings and directly employ all staff until 2007.

For the last 200 years, the French government has thus considered universities to be simply administrative entities distributed throughout the national territory. On the official maps of the French Ministry, individual universities were not even distinguished – there were no names, just the legal status of different buildings.[3]

As a result, the term *university* lost its value in the French language. Students and researchers did not identify themselves as belonging to a university but to a *school* or a *faculty*. In French, we still use the term "fac" (i.e. faculty) or "école" (i.e. school) to talk about our place of work rather than the term *université* (university).

This situation was exacerbated by the existence of two types of institutions that were not considered universities but elite institutions for higher education on the one hand and for research on the other: the *grandes écoles* and the national research organizations.

In France, high performing students from wealthy or intellectual families, trained at the right secondary schools, have traditionally been encouraged to spend a further two years in high school after their *baccalauréat* rather than going to university. During these two years they follow *classes préparatoires* (preparatory classes), which enable them to pass a competitive exam to enter a *grande école* in what would be the third year of undergraduate education elsewhere in the world. This formed a very efficient system to reproduce elites.

As a result, going to a university, is still often seen as a failure or as "second best": prestige in engineering is associated with *écoles d'ingénieur* (engineering schools) like École Polytechnique, in Business with *écoles* de commerce (business schools) like HEC, in the natural sciences and humanities to the *École Normale Supérieure*.[4] In France, high performing undergraduate students are thus taught within the high school system by high school teachers, who can be brilliant but have little link to research.

This paradoxical situation is reinforced by the existence of a parallel research system that remains independent from universities.

Historically, new institutions are sometimes necessary to open new fields of knowledge that are not yet accepted in existing institutions. The Collège de France was created in the 16th century to teach fields not yet allowed at university and many other examples exist in Paris, such as the French Academy of Sciences created in the 17th century, or the École Pratique des Hautes Études in the 19th century. In most countries many of these institutions would have aspired to become universities or been integrated into universities. In France, on the contrary, institutions linked to universities tried to become independent because prestige lay outside the university.

With the growing importance of research from the mid-20th century onwards, it is therefore unsurprising that the French state built a parallel system around national research organizations, such as the French National Research Centre for Scientific Research (CNRS), whose weight is far greater than in any other country in the world.[5]

A further element of complexity lies in the structure of research laboratories that are mostly joint ventures between national research organizations and universities. Today, half the researchers within the laboratories hosted by our universities are directly employed by our universities and another half by national research organizations who have their own research strategies. The French state allocates the responsibility for research strategy to these national research organizations whilst denying a similar responsibility to research universities.

This historical background explains how difficult it is to compare the French higher education system to that prevalent in most of the world. When the Academic Ranking for World Universities (ARWU) was first published in 2003, in France there was a sense of surprise that French universities were not better ranked (in 2003, only two were in the top 100: Pierre et Marie Curie

[Paris 6], 65th and Paris Sud [Paris 11], 72nd), but there was a deeper feeling of surprise that the institutions that were best ranked were universities and not the *grandes écoles* or national research organizations.[6]

Of course, the process of the internationalization of higher education and research has been underway for many years, but until recently, the French system was felt to be very high performing. It had evolved organically and had a strong coherence which came from the checks and balances added through the centuries.

This internal coherence broke down when the reference framework ceased to be national. It became unsustainable in a global environment once students and staff enlarged their perspective beyond national borders and comparisons were made using global parameters.

1.2   *Why Change Was Both Inevitable and Necessary*

International rankings are sometimes used to illustrate the difficulties of comparing French institutions with the rest of the world. However, if international rankings had been created in France, the leading institutions would probably have been French, as is the case in the "professional ranking of world universities" created by the École des Mines in 2007 and in which five of the top 20 institutions were French *grandes écoles*.[7]

The French system needed to change not because of rankings but because (1) students and academic staff increasingly consider their education and career at a global level rather than a national one and (2) the tripartite system (universities, *grandes écoles,* national research organizations) is structurally suboptimal for both education and research purposes. What the emergence of rankings did was to put this issue firmly on the French political agenda.

1.2.1   The Impact on Student and Staff Choices

The first difficulty for the French system is that the globalization of higher education and research as a sector is slowly but surely changing the way individual students and scholars make choices and this is leading to an alignment at a global level.

The clearest example is probably the system of *classes préparatoires*, which we mentioned above. Spending two more years in high school before passing a competitive exam and being accepted by one of the *grandes écoles* may make sense for someone who wishes to follow a career within France but is increasingly at odds with international trends: why spend two further years at high school to prepare for a highly competitive exam in order to be potentially accepted by a *grande école*, whose prestige is largely national, when your results at high school enable you to be immediately accepted for a Bachelor programme at a university that is more prestigious according to international rankings, and which will furthermore ensure that you are immediately in contact with cutting-edge research?

The same is true of researchers who no longer think about career possibilities in purely national terms but are open to job offers from around the world.

This is sometimes simplified as implying a purely economic academic market in which French institutions cannot compete because they are not able to offer the same salaries. However, studies prove that the key factors are linked neither to salary nor quality of life (although both are important) but to the quality and prestige of the research environment. The main factors that influence career choice are thus "peers among top-five worldwide" (for later stage researchers) and "tenure based on research performance only" (for early stage researchers) (Janger and Nowotny, 2013), whereas the key factors that influence a decision to work abroad include "opportunity to improve my future career prospects", "outstanding faculty, colleagues, or research team", and "excellence/prestige of the foreign institution in my area of research" (Franzoni, Scellato, and Stephan, 2015).

In other words, researchers are attracted to world-class institutions, which already host many excellent researchers in their field.

The power of prestige is nothing new in the academic field, however, it used to be country based. Once it becomes global, the playing field enlarges and local value systems are swept aside.

1.2.2 French Research Performance

To better understand the challenges facing the French system of higher education and research, the French League of Research Intensive Universities (CURIF) recently ordered an in-depth comparative study of research performance (SIRIS Academic, 2019).

The results of this study clearly show that, in Europe, both the French and the German systems underperform dramatically when compared to the countries such as Denmark, the Netherlands or Switzerland, all of which actually perform better than the United Kingdom or the United States.

The weak performance of France and Germany is true when looking at global performance indicators such as (1) share of production and citations and (2) research focused university rankings and particularly obvious in the case of more selective indicators (top 50% is better than top 10%; ranking in top 500 is better than ranking in top 100).

But it is even clearer when looking at more detailed indicators of excellence performance such as:
- general bibliometric data with field-weighted citation impact, proportion of citations in Top 1% and Top 10% and fine-grained performance across 251 fields;

- performance in cutting-edge fields such as biotechnology or fast evolving technological topics;
- indicators of individual performance such as highly-cited researchers and ERC awards.

The French performance is particularly weak in cutting-edge fields, at an institutional level (rather than a country level) and on very selective indicators.

This weakness is symbolized by our performance in the European Horizon 2020 framework programme where France and Germany both stand out with cumulative losses of well over €1 billion, whereas a country such as the Netherlands has gained close to €1 billion from over the same time period.

Such an apparent lack of competitiveness needs to be interpreted with care because one of the key reasons for it is linked to history and language.

English has only recently become the uncontested scientific lingua franca, with the proportion of publications in English passing well above 50% at a global level in the 1970s (Augusto and Ammon, 2007). Smaller countries, like Denmark or the Netherlands, and emerging scientific powerhouses like the People's Republic of China, have adapted because they had never built strong national research systems: the ultimate aim for an ambitious scholar has always been to become a professor in Berlin, Paris or Oxford.

In France and Germany (like in Japan and Russia), the transition was much harder and is still ongoing. Being accepted in a *classe préparatoire*, publishing an article in French for the Academy of Sciences or being awarded a national prize remain prestigious. Of course, each of these achievements is remarkable. The problem is that none can be compared at a global level and none are therefore taken into account when a French research performance is compared to that of other countries. This is important, because it determines the choices that students, researchers, and companies make when they decide where to study, where to pursue their career, and where to invest in innovation.

This said, the disappointing performance of the French research system is not only due to history. It is caused by:
- a clear lag in investment in research and development compared to other European and OECD countries;
- a strong negative impact of the structure of the research system, due in particular to the role assigned to national research organizations;
- a lack of control of universities over their human resources;
- the need for increased autonomy, accountability and improved models of governance.

This is the second reason for which the transition from a national to a global system of Higher Education and Research is so complex and so important.

1.2.3   Measuring French Research Performance

The relatively weak performance of the French research system is exacerbated by more prosaic difficulties caused by the way research performance is measured.

Indeed, the fact that over half the researchers working in laboratories of major research intensive universities are employed by national research organizations embedded in universities causes a first difficulty in terms of visibility, which ranking and bibliometric agencies have not been able to solve.

Up until this year, French national research organization employees who work full-time within universities were not counted as HiCi researchers of the universities where they work because they were expected to include their employee as primary affiliation in Clarivates HCR list.[8] This year, the French Ministry of Higher Education and Research finally required all national research organizations to communicate to their researchers that they should include the university where they carry out their research as primary affiliation, rather than the national research organization. As a result, in 2020, many French universities will improve their rankings substantially,[9] despite no actual change having occurred in the research actually taking place in our laboratories.

This positive change will, however, not affect many other similar issues such as the way the affiliation of authors in Nature and Science articles is counted[10] or the problem of joint affiliation of authors in articles referenced by Web of Science.[11] These problems are intrinsically linked to the structure of the French system of higher education and research and will only be solved through a better integration of research laboratories within French universities.[12]

The separation of the higher education system between national research organizations, *grandes écoles* and universities has an even greater impact on rankings that rely on reputational surveys, such as QS and THE.

These rankings were designed in the U.K. context where universities are both selective and clearly focused on different missions, with elite institutions (Russell Group) tending to be comparatively small and very research-intensive. As a result, these rankings are dominated by small universities, with a large proportion of graduate students, a very strong research focus, and a highly visible brand.[13]

In 2015, Paris Diderot University was the leading French University, according to the Times Higher Education citation indicator, with a score of 92.2, and a research performance that was clearly world-class. However, in this same Times Higher Education ranking, Paris Diderot was also one of the worst performing universities on research criteria with a score of 19.7.

The difference between the score on citation (which presumably should measure research impact) and the score on research is explained by the fact that THE relies largely on reputational surveys to measure research criteria. In other words, they depend on international scholars identifying "Paris 7 – Diderot" as one of the top 10 universities in their field. This did not happen because very few scholars at a global level are aware of the complexity of the French system of Higher Education and Research.

So, when they filled in the reputational survey in, they thought of their French colleagues and either assumed they worked at the University of Paris (which did not yet exist), or knew that they worked at CNRS (which THE does not take into account because it is not a university), and presumably ended up including a non-French institution once they realized that neither the University of Paris nor CNRS where considered valid answers by THE. In the French context, THE's "research criteria" thus did not measure "research" but a very different parameter, which could be called "degree of understanding of the French HE&R system".

2 Changing the French System of Higher Education and Research

Deep shifts in the reference framework of a higher education and research system such as the one we have just described, take decades. The switch to global points of references started in the 1970s[14] with a tipping point in the mid 2000s when newspapers started commenting on the performance of national universities in international rankings such as ARWU. This kick-started a global process of reforms and investment programmes often explicitly focused on creating "world-class universities".

In the French case, this shift implies a major transformation of the existing system that should end the distinction between *grandes écoles* and universities, better integrate national research organizations and better differentiate universities according to their strengths and strategies (for example, research intensive vs universities focused on the needs of their territories).

The end aim is clear: creating world-class universities that improve the performance of the French system of higher education and research, act as key hubs connecting global networks to local ones and are trusted by students, scholars and the general public alike.

This is the aim of Sorbonne University and the University of Paris.

2.1 *Legal Framework and Excellence Initiatives*

In France, the key reforms started in the mid 2000s with the creation of a National Funding Agency in 2005 (*Agence nationale de la recherche* [ANR]) and a National Evaluation Agency in 2006 (*Agence d'évaluation de la recherche et de l'enseignement supérieur* [AERES], today called *Haut Conseil de l'évaluation de la recherche et de l'enseignement supérieur* [HCERES]). Together these two agencies transformed the way French research operated by boosting a project-based approach at a national level (ANR) and systematically evaluating institutions, educational programmes and research laboratories (AERES).

These were followed in 2007 by a new law, the so-called *Loi relative aux libertés et responsabilités des universités* (LRU), which increased both the autonomy of universities and the decision-making capacity of the governing board and the president of the university. This law gave greater responsibilities to universities in managing their budget, their human resources (though their academic staff remain mostly civil servants) and the buildings in which they operate, amongst other aspects.[15]

The Plan Campus, launched in 2008, focused on renovating and/or building new campuses to "world-class standards". It was followed in 2010 by the PIA, a major investment programme, launched by the French government[16] whose flagship action (*initiative d'excellence* [IDEX]) was modelled on the excellence initiatives previously launched in countries like Germany and China. This aimed to enable the emergence of 5 to 10 world-class universities in France by providing long-term investment in the form of an endowment of between €500 million and €1 billion Euros to selected projects.

Further reforms followed, including a new law on higher education and research in 2013 and further legislation in 2019.

2.2   *University Systems or University Mergers?*

One of the main debates in France over the last ten years has been centred around the best way to enable a transformation of the system. Two visions existed: (1) create university systems, which would enable the different types of institutions to work together and progressively transform themselves; (2) merge institutions to create single universities.

The first model was initially favoured by the government, which created a specific legal entity called *pôles de recherche et d'enseignement supérieur* (cluster of research and higher education [PRES]) in 2007, based on the voluntary association of institutions, which were transformed in *communautés d'universités et établissements* (community of universities and institutions [ComUE]) with the law of 2013, based on a mandatory association of all institutions in an administrative district.

This model suffered from a deep misunderstanding of the difference between universities and university systems that led to major difficulties. Whereas university systems such as the University of London or the University of California can boost collaboration between institutions in a given territory or create common services such as libraries (Senate House in London is a classical example), they are rarely ranked by international ranking agencies and do not define common international strategies or ask researchers to include a single affiliation in their publications.

By contrast, in France, PRES first and ComUE later were imagined as university systems that would be taken into account by international rankings and would therefore be comparable to traditional universities despite not being a single legal entity and not having the necessary authority to implement a strong single strategy.

The second model, namely a full merger, was first defended by the presidents of the three universities of Strasbourg, University Strasbourg 1 (Louis Pasteur) specializing in Medicine and STEM, Strasbourg 2 (Marc Bloch) specializing in Humanities and Social Sciences, and Strasbourg 3 (Robert Schuman) specializing in Law, Political Sciences and Management.

The case of Strasbourg is particularly interesting because it underlines how the process of transformation that France is undergoing has been driven by universities themselves before being appropriated and supported by the state.

The University of Strasbourg has alternated between French and German periods throughout its history and benefited from massive state investment as one of two German imperial universities between 1870 and 1918. As a result, it has always retained a distinctive culture and played an important role in the history of French higher education and research (French research in chemistry, for example was boosted by Alsatian researchers who moved to Paris after the French defeat of 1870, and is the only public French university with a Faculty of Theology, because it was not part of France when the 1905 law on the separation of the churches and the state was passed)

The specific Franco-German history of Strasbourg, the shared feeling that the separation of the university into three disciplinary universities in 1970 had been a mistake imposed by the French state, the close collaboration between the three universities and exchanges within the European Confederation of Upper Rhine universities (EUCOR)[17] convinced the three universities to propose a possible merger in 2001. The process was thus launched before the impact of globalization on the French system had become clear and without any state support.[18] The merger was finalized on 1 January 2009, despite pressure from the ministry to follow a progressive path towards integration by first creating a PRES.

2.3   *Four World-Class Universities in the Paris Region*
The merger of three specialized universities to (re)create a comprehensive University of Strasbourg was followed by a series of comparable mergers, which gave rise to the universities of Aix-Marseille, Bordeaux, Clermont-Ferrand,

Grenoble-Alpes, Lille, Lorraine and Montpellier, all of which have happened in the last ten years.

However, in cities with denser ecosystems of higher education and research institutions, such as Lyon, Toulouse and especially Paris, the process was much harder because choices needed to be made and these choices were not self-evident.

In 2010, Greater Paris was thus home to 17 universities, most of which were not comprehensive, dozens of *grandes* écoles and, by far the largest concentration of research potential of national research organizations. Most of these institutions were members of PRES.

Paris was key because, as a result of the French tradition of "centralization", it concentrated all the French institutions, which could potentially be ranked within the world's top 50 in the different international rankings. In other words, it was clear from the beginning of the process that the leading French world-class universities would necessarily be situated in Paris but the perimeter of these universities was unknown.

In the first round of excellence initiatives (PIA 1), between 2010 and 2012, four Parisian consortia were selected: Paris Sciences et Lettres, Université Paris Saclay, Université Sorbonne Paris Cité and Sorbonne Université.

These four excellence initiatives were the kernel from which four world-class universities are now emerging.

2.3.1 (Re)creating Sorbonne University

The initial project was presented by six institutions of higher education and research and four national research organizations. Each of the six core institutions was highly specialized and the overlaps between them were limited in terms of disciplinary fields thus facilitating a process of integration. The aim was simple: to (re)create a world-class comprehensive university at the heart of Paris by merging institutions specialized in different fields.

The project faced two main challenges: first, the existing prestige of the six institutions in their respective fields and the diversity of legal statuses made a full merger complex[19] and, second, synergies between fields needed to be actively promoted because each institution was specialized and located on a different campus.

Sorbonne University was finally created on the 1st of January 2018 with the merger of Paris Sorbonne and Pierre et Marie Curie, two of the most prestigious universities in France in Humanities on the one hand and Sciences and Medicine on the other. Université Panthéon Assas chose to leave the project, whilst the other institutions remained associated alongside four national research organizations (CNRS, IRD, INRIA and INSERM) in the Sorbonne University Alliance.

Today Sorbonne University is one of the world's leading comprehensive universities with three faculties (Humanities, Medicine, and Science and Engineering), 55,000 students, and a prominent role in a wide range of fields.

One of our main focuses throughout the merger process has been to ensure that it enabled a true transformation in both education and research by boosting multidisciplinary approaches. This was particularly important, because the founding universities gave rise to a faculty (in the case of Paris Sorbonne) or two faculties (in the case of Pierre et Marie Curie.

This is why Sorbonne University launched two major initiatives. In education, the traditional undergraduate cycle was transformed by creating a Major/Minor system that enables students to graduate in two different fields, either within the same faculty or across faculties. In research multidisciplinary institutes in fields such as Artificial Intelligence, Data, Environment, Health Engineering, Heritage and Music promoted projects that integrated teams working in different fields.

2.3.2 (Re)creating the University of Paris

The University of Paris resembles Sorbonne University in structure with three faculties in Humanities and Social Sciences, Medicine, and Sciences, and an Institute of Earth and Planetary Science. But the story and challenges of creating the University of Paris were very different.

The initial project, called Sorbonne Paris Cité, was presented by eight institutions of higher education and research, four *universités* (Paris 13, Paris Descartes, Paris Diderot, and Sorbonne Nouvelle) and four other institutions (École des hautes études en santé publique, Institut national des langues et des civilizations orientales, Institut de physique du globe de Paris, and Sciences Po).

However, unlike in the case of Sorbonne University, the main universities were comprehensive and not all the institutions were research intensive to the same degree. As a result, not only was a full merger difficult to achieve but it could well have been counterproductive. The difficulties of moving beyond a simple university system resulted in a failure of the Excellence Initiative when it was reviewed by the international jury after four years. This led to a major crisis and an in-depth re-evaluation of the project.

Three institutions finally chose to move ahead with a full merger: the two main comprehensive universities, Paris Descartes and Paris Diderot, and the Institut de Physique du Globe de Paris. The project was selected as an excellence initiative in 2018 and the merger was formally finalized on the 1st of January 2020.

Currently the University of Paris is concentrated on building the three faculties each of which integrates departments and research groups from both universities. This makes the process more complex than in the case of Sorbonne University but strongly contributes to the emergence of a truly common identity in which the best practices of both universities can reinforce the university as a whole.

The University of Paris is a comprehensive university with specific strengths. In particular, it is the one of the leading universities in continental Europe in Health and Life Sciences with 15 university hospitals in Paris and amongst the best worldwide in fields such as Geosciences, Mathematics, Physics, Psychology or Linguistics.

2.3.3 Creating University Paris-Saclay and Paris Sciences et Lettres University

The final two world-class universities, Paris Sciences et Lettres and Paris Saclay, involve a process of integration that is more complex than that of Sorbonne University or the University of Paris but which is key to the long-term success of the French Higher Education system because it implies a merger not only of *universités* but also of *grandes écoles*.

Both passed a decisive milestone on 1 January 2020 when they became *établissement expérimentaux*, thanks to the new ordinances.[20] In the case of Université Paris Saclay, this step also involved the full merger of the former ComUE Paris Saclay and the Université Paris Sud. We expect that both will be taken into account by the major international rankings alongside Sorbonne University and the University of Paris from this year onwards.

3 Conclusions

Our article outlines the complex history of French Higher Education: from the medieval "universal" universities to a national vision with a division of French higher education and research into *grandes* écoles, universities and national research organizations, to the emerging global "World-Class Universities" of today. This history highlights the importance of institutional transformations over the last 10 years.

There are still many tasks ahead, both in terms of reforms of the legal framework, boosting higher education as a whole, and a deeper transformation of the way French research-intensive universities work.

At a national level, France is ranked among the higher education systems with least autonomy by the European University Association.[21] We still do not have control over our recruitment processes or the career paths of our staff, and half of the academic staff in our universities remain employed by National Research Organizations such as the CNRS. The French government is working to solve these issues and we trust that French universities will soon be able to take part on a level playing field on the global scene. We are actively preparing for such changes by improving our strategic capacity, building internal data systems and setting up strategic advisory boards.

Just as important, we need to move towards an open science model, based on the free diffusion of the data and results of research. Obstacles to this move are often systemic, and vested interests within the academic system itself prevent action. This is why large, visible research-intensive universities have a specific responsibility in taking the lead and initiating changes in the standard practices of research.

Indeed, beyond the question of open science, optimizing a system to produce "highly-performance research", measured by citations, prestigious awards, and highly cited researchers is clearly not the only mission that a research and higher education system should be aiming for. Developing socially relevant knowledge, producing research with a strong local impact, and educating students are all crucial objectives, where the results are not relevant only in comparison, but very much intrinsically: educating a student is an achievement in itself, whether or not you are trying to compare yourself to others. These are missions, which we share with all other institutions of higher education in France and which require a deep transformation of the higher education and research system as a whole.[22]

There are still many more changes to come, but the first key step is now behind us: France once again has world class comprehensive universities.

Notes

1   The University of Paris was initially a corporation of Masters and Students, of which Sorbonne was one of the Colleges.

2   The official page of the Chancellerie des Universités de Paris thus describes them as follows: "the Sorbonne has become the symbol of all French universities and academies", "the role of the Chancellerie des Universités de Paris is to supervise the legality and exert budgetary control over Parisian universities" (https://www.sorbonne.fr/en/, accessed April 26, 2020).

3   Atlas régional. Effectifs d'étudiants 2012–2013, Ministère de l'Éducation supérieur et de la recherche, 2014 (p. 168). The same Atlas also contains a map, which localizes individual universities on p. 174. However, even on that map the universities are all symbolized by a simple

green square with a number from 1 to 11 inside and no name or other identification. The latest Atlas published in 2019 retains the same format but includes the names of individual universities in caption.

4   The only fields where prestige has always remained linked to the university are Medicine and Law.

5   The fact that universities were so weak also increased the power of individual, more conservative, faculty professors and encouraged the State to develop a new research institution outside faculties.

6   This is highlighted by both French scientific analysis of rankings and by newspaper articles. For example Harfi and Mathieu (2006).

7   http://www.mines-paristech.eu/About-us/Rankings/professional-ranking/. The five in question were HEC Business School, École Nationale d'Administration (ENA), Sciences Po, École Polytechnique and École des Mines.

8   Clarivates list of Highly Cited Researchers (HCR) includes primary and secondary affiliations of all scholars. It is the key source for HiCi, one of the six indicators used by ARWU to calculate the global ranking of universities. To avoid large scale gaming, ARWU only includes primary affiliations to calculate the HiCi indicator (Bornmann and Bauer, 2015). As a result, at Sorbonne University a single researcher changing their affiliation from Sorbonne University to the CNRS in 2018 directly resulted in a drop from the 36th to the 44th position in the ARWU.

9   Preliminary calculations indicate that many will improve their ranking by over 25%, passing for example in the case of Sorbonne University from 44th to c. 32nd.

10   The Nature and Science indicator of ARWU uses fractional counting to attribute articles to institutions. The corresponding authors of articles are thus awarded the maximum of one point per article; however, if they have two affiliations indicated on two separate lines, then only the first affiliation is awarded the maximum number of points. Once again, because many of our researchers are employed by national research organizations, this has a strong negative impact on our scientific production, with a number of articles being awarded less points despite being produced in laboratories situated within our universities.

11   CWTS Leiden counts articles published by researchers in our universities with an affiliation to a national research organization and the university as co-publications. As a result, the total number of publications taken into account for France by CWTS Leiden is less than those taken into account for Italy, whereas in the Web of Science (which is used by CWTS Leiden), the total number is far more. In the case of leading French institutions, such as the École Normale Supérieure, this has led to them not being taken into account by CWTS Leiden in certain years (for example in 2013) despite being the institution with the best results on key indicators, such as the PP Top 10% (in 2019, they were ranked 19th in the world on this indicator). Today, it results in a deficit of visibility on the P criteria currently used by the French government as a key indicator to measure the impact of Excellence Initiatives in France: if researchers from national research organizations were considered as employees of universities and signed their scientific papers as such, French universities would immediately gain hundreds of places in CWTS Leiden.

12   Both Scopus and Web of Science have attempted to solve the problem by linking total research production of one laboratory to the institution to which it belongs. This is helpful when the laboratory is a joint venture between a university and a national research organization but when it is a multiple venture between various universities and various national research organizations it can result in aberrant results. Unlike previous examples, French universities benefit from this. For example, some of the Shanghai GRAS subject rankings include French institutions, which are not specialized in the field in question. This occurs because the organization enhanced tool of Web of Science links the total scientific production of all

the researchers in a laboratory to each individual institution, even if one of the individual institutions only employs a tiny percentage of the researchers.

13   Indicators such as proportion of graduate students or proportion of staff per student, obviously favour these universities over larger, non-selective universities with a majority of undergraduate students such as those in France.

14   This is when scholars in certain fields started thinking about publishing in journals like Nature and Science rather than national reviews, to take a classical example.

15   These examples give a good illustration of how little strategic capacity French universities used to have.

16   The three successive programmes d'investissement d'avenir (programmes of investment for the future) total €57 billion.

17   EUCOR was launched in 1989 (https://www.eucor-uni.org/en/about-us/history-of-cooperation/).

18   Representatives of the state only discovered the plan after Jean-Yves Mérindol, the president of Strasbourg 1, Louis Pasteur, publicly announced it. For a history of the merger, see Musselin and Maël Dif-Pradalier (2014).

19   Three universités: Panthéon Assas, specializing in Law and Economics, Paris Sorbonne, specializing in Humanities and Pierre et Marie Curie, specializing in Sciences, Engineering and Medicine), one université de technologie (Université de Technologie de Compiègne), one museum (Muséum National d'Histoire Naturelle) and one private business school (INSEAD).

20   These are a legal instrument that enables greater flexibility to integrate institutions with different legal statutes.

21   See the EUA Autonomy Scorecard (https://www.university-autonomy.eu/).

22   As R. Birnbaum points out: "Rather than more world-class universities, what we really need in countries everywhere are more world-class technical institutes, world-class community colleges, world-class colleges of agriculture, world-class teachers colleges, and world-class regional state universities" (Birnbaum, 2007). The task is complex because, as A. Usher argues, "it may not be so easy to divorce stratification in research outcomes from social stratification of the student body" (Usher, 2019).

References

Birnbaum, R. (2007). No world-class university left behind. *International Higher Education, 47*, 7–9.

Bornmann, L., & Bauer, J. (2015). Which of the world's institutions employ the most highly cited researchers? An analysis of the data from highlycited.com. *Journal of the Association for Information Science and Technology, 66*(10), 2146–2148.

Carli, A., & Ammon, U. (2007). *Linguistic inequality in scientific communication today.* John Benjamins Publishing Company.

Franzoni, C., Scellato, G., & Stephan, P. (2015). International mobility of research scientists: Lessons from GlobSci. In A. Geuna (Ed.), *Global mobility of research scientists* (pp. 35–65). Academic Press.

Harfi, M., & Mathieu, C. (2006). Classement de Shanghai et image internationale des universités: quels enjeux pour la France? *Horizons stratégiques, 2*(2), 100–115.

Janger, J., & Nowotny, K. (2013). *Career choices in academia.* Working Papers in Economics, No. 36.

Musselin, C., & Dif-Pradalier, M. (2014). Quand la fusion s'impose: la (re) naissance de l'université de Strasbourg. *Revue française de sociologie, 55*(2).

SIRIS Academic. (2019). *French research performance in context.* Retrieved May 12, 2020, from http://www.curif.org/wp-content/uploads/2020/02/French-Research-Performance-in-Context.-SIRIS-2019_compressed.pdf

Usher, U. (2019, May 1). Breadth of quality vs. concentrations of excellence. *Inside Higher Ed.* Retrieved May 12, 2020, from https://www.insidehighered.com/blogs/world-view/breadth-quality-vs-concentrations-excellence